Fostering Global Citizenship Through Faculty-Led International Programs

Fostering Global Citizenship Through Faculty-Led International Programs

Jo Beth Mullens
Keene State College

Pru Cuper
Keene State College

INFORMATION AGE PUBLISHING, INC.
Charlotte, NC • www.infoagepub.com

Library of Congress Cataloging-in-Publication Data

Mullens, Jo Beth.
 Fostering global citizenship through faculty-led international programs /
Jo Beth Mullens, Prudence Cuper.
     p. cm.
Includes bibliographical references.
 ISBN 978-1-61735-831-9 (pbk.) – ISBN 978-1-61735-832-6 (hardcover) –
ISBN 978-1-61735-833-3 (ebook) 1. Foreign study. 2. International
education. 3. College students–Travel. 4. College teachers–Travel. I.
Cuper, Prudence H. II. Title.
 LB2375.M85 2012
 370.117–dc23

                                                          2012011508

Printed in the United States of America

Dedication

We dedicate this book to our parents, Jody and J. L. Mullens and Fran and Bill Hobbie who gave us a great start; and also to all of the students who have joined us on our learning ventures abroad.

Contents

PART **II**

International Program Organization: Undertaking the Tasks   *69*

PART **III**

*The Learning: Realizing the Potential of Faculty-Led
International Programs* *143*

Preface

With awareness of both the opportunities and challenges presented by globalization, there is a growing trend among colleges and universities across the country to commit resources to the goal of internationalizing their campuses. This can occur in a number of different ways, but a common thread involves exploring the concept of global citizenship and finding ways to embed this concept in undergraduate curricula. For faculty, this may call for moving beyond the comfort zone of the campus classroom into determining new approaches to teaching a generation of students who will live and work in a complex global environment. A method for accomplishing this work that is growing in popularity involves offering short-term faculty-led field courses to international settings. More students in higher education today participate in short-term study-abroad opportunities than more traditional semester and/or year-long program models.

Faculty and administrators who want to capitalize on short-term international programs as a means for internationalizing their campuses need practical resources to help them realize this challenging but important goal. They not only need support in developing the course curricula and logistics, but also in constructing authentic means for assessing the multifaceted learning that occurs. As professional educators with deep experience in curriculum development, assessment, and the design and implementation of international programs, we created this text to provide our colleagues with such resources and support. In fact, this is the very text we wish we could have read prior to teaching our first international course.

Fostering Global Citizenship Through Faculty-Led International Programs, pages xi–xiii
Copyright © 2012 by Information Age Publishing

Based on our respective educational histories and areas of expertise, the text includes information and resources that will guide faculty new to the international teaching arena—from initial course consideration through program assessment. We have included real-world travel tales at the opening of each chapter (taken from our own travel experiences, both rewarding and extremely challenging), practical checklists, grading rubrics, discussion starters, and a comprehensive literature review spanning the onset of study abroad through the practices and beliefs that prevail today. Our text also features in-depth review of the historic and contemporary discourse on engaged learning practices and the commitment to develop global citizenship among undergraduates. We discuss not only *why* faculty-led international programs are critical to institutes of higher education today, but also *how* faculty can go about designing and delivering successful programs.

Certainly there are other resources available for faculty stepping into the international teaching arena, both online and in hard copy, but few are written by faculty for faculty. With information ranging from the most detailed travel particulars to the most overarching, conceptual considerations, the audience for this book is primarily academic, with specific focus on current and prospective faculty leading international field courses. We designed the text to be an invaluable multidisciplinary resource for those leading programs to a range of international locations. While the primary audience for this text focuses on higher education, the book is also suitable for secondary educators (and related personnel) engaged in international study with students. Administrators and/or staff charged with supporting international faculty-led programs may also find this text helpful. A final audience includes NGOs, third-party providers, and other organizations that facilitate and work with academic faculty-led international study programs.

Specifically, we believe faculty from the following departments will use this text both in the classroom and in the field: geography, sociology, anthropology, education, history, biology, political science, art and art history, international studies, women's studies, and modern languages. Additionally, honors programs are showing increased interest and commitment to study-away experiences; therefore, faculty teaching in these programs will also appreciate the text. For all potential audiences, the book includes resources such as cross-disciplinary journal prompts and discussion starters for use in field settings as well as a range of related assessment instruments.

Ultimately, we created and offer this text as a resource for those involved with the development, execution, and assessment of faculty-led international programs. We believe that such courses, when carefully planned and executed, engage the participants (both students and faculty) in unique learning experiences that can involve service, research, and critical analysis of what it truly means to be a global citizen. Additionally, we believe that such work helps define the somewhat nebulous but worthy goals of furthering global citizenship and internationalizing college and university campuses.

Acknowledgements

$\mathbf{A}$s we put the finishing touches on our text, we thought of the many people who have supported us in our efforts to develop and lead international programs over the years. Accordingly, we would like to thank our colleagues Skye Stephenson, Steven Spiegel, and Marche Brown from the Keene State College Global Education office. We also owe a debt of gratitude to Keene State College Honors Program directors, Margaret Walsh and Helen Frink, who afforded us the opportunity to pioneer two of the first *Global Engagement* Honors courses. These courses unquestionably provided the impetus as well as much of the material for our text.

In addition, we would like to thank colleagues Brian Green, Al Rydant, and Christopher Cusack, who have co-taught international courses with us over the years—in each case, bringing unique talents and perspectives to the endeavor.

Most of all, we would like to thank the students from the international courses we have led as it is their growth that truly inspired us to write this text. A special thanks goes to the following students who participated in the first two Honors *Global Engagement* courses to Peru and Belize: Ella Brockelman, Erica Burke, Kaitlyn Carter, Michelle Devine, Nicole Ferri, Brigitte Gray, Thomas Green, Krist Hausken, Katherine Henthorne, Adam Hogue, Michael La Crosse, Kimberly Layman, Janine Lescrinier, Kevin Malicki, Liselle Milazzo, Elizabeth Mitchell, Alicia Morrison, Kelly Payeur, Rebecca Pine, Emma Rivers, Kyle Skov, Nicole Turgeon, and Kirsten Whyte. These students generously allowed us to use their words and experiences to make our text all the richer.

Fostering Global Citizenship Through Faculty-Led International Programs, page xv
Copyright © 2012 by Information Age Publishing

Introduction

A hero ventures forth from the world of common day into a region
of supernatural wonder: fabulous forces are there encountered and a
decisive victory is won: the hero comes back from this mysterious adventure
with the power to bestow boons on his fellow man.

—Joseph Campbell

INTRODUCTORY TRAVEL TALE: Our Call

In the fall of 2008, two professors from a small, liberal arts college in New England experienced a call to adventure in the finest sense of Joseph Campbell's words. In this text we share that adventure with you—detailing when the call came, how we responded, and subsequently, what we learned about traveling, teaching, and life as we ventured forth with our students. Our adventure began, as many adventures do, as a result of leadership change. In our case, the change involved a near-complete turnover in our college's administration.

Over a 5-year period and in the hands of a new administration, our college began moving in exciting new directions—adding programs and redefining its goals and mission statement to reflect some of the latest and most rousing trends in higher education. High on the list of new initiatives was a commitment to fostering a sense of global citizenship among all members of the college community. A second high-visibility initiative was the creation of an interdisciplinary Honors program. A key requirement for students in this new program was participation in a short-term,

Fostering Global Citizenship Through Faculty-Led International Programs, pages xvii–xxi
Copyright © 2012 by Information Age Publishing
All rights of reproduction in any form reserved.

faculty-led international field course. The goal, in this case, was to forward the students' growth by immersing them in a location and culture different from their own, even if only for a short time. This Honors program goal intentionally dovetailed with the college's newly crafted mission of developing global citizens by increasing students' understanding (and hence appreciation) of the wider world.

In the midst of this college-wide change, our call to adventure—our chance to encounter "fabulous forces" and, hopefully, to "bestow boons on our fellow men"—came to us from the new Honors program. As faculty members within this small campus group, we agreed to develop and co-teach one of the first Honors travel courses—a trip that would take us deep into the Andes Mountains of Peru.

We began by calculating what we had going for us as a teaching team—a geography professor with field-course experience and an education professor with no international teaching experience. The geography professor, coming from a discipline committed to international learning, had taught in such locations as Eastern Europe and Central and South America. But while the travel/teaching experience was familiar territory, she had historically paid more attention to logistics and background preparation than to curriculum design. While less experienced with international field courses, the education professor brought a deep understanding of curriculum design and assessment. Developing learning objectives and means for realizing and assessing those objectives came very naturally to her. As we examined what we had, we took heart. Our combined skill and experience set wasn't bad.

But even with our pooled knowledge and expertise, the task of leading an engaging and purposeful Honors field course presented us with certain challenges. The first of these challenges was home based and human. From the outset there were many people who wanted a say in our endeavor. From administrators, to parents, to the student travelers themselves, each stakeholder had his or her own expectations, worries, and goals related to the program.

A closely related second challenge involved the multidisciplinary nature of our student travelers. Given the disparate content interests of the group, we pondered how to create a course that would foster academic growth related to each student's disciplinary focus. We wanted to develop robust learning opportunities that would have meaning for all of the student travelers and simultaneously meet the mission and goals of the Honors program and the College.

A final (and very weighty) consideration was the short-term nature of the experience in light of lofty new institutional expectations. We wondered how we could possibly meet the college goals in such a restricted time frame. In approximately two and a half weeks, how could we actually forward global awareness and cultural responsibility within our students? Essentially, how could we create a course that would have long-term impact despite its short-term duration?

And from prior experience, the seasoned traveler of our faculty team knew that these challenges were just the beginning. Once we were en route, she knew we would encounter in-field challenges as well—unanticipated "forces" that would call upon us to adapt or even abandon our initial plans and more fully join our students in the adventure. There was much work ahead, but we were excited and determined to maximize the potential of this unique, albeit short, learning opportunity.

We began by laying out a structure for the course and dividing tasks according to each of our areas of expertise. Multidisciplinary learning objectives served as the basis for designing all aspects of the course—from assignments to assessments. The ultimate goal was to help our students forward their academic growth while simultaneously exploring their roles as global citizens. To this end, we selected readings on Peruvian history and culture as well as on the broader concepts of cultural awareness and global connectedness. We designed multiple and meaningful discussion starters, journal prompts, and research opportunities. But most importantly of all, we left room for the priceless spontaneous learning that was sure to occur in the field. After a year of planning and a semester of preparing our students for the journey, the time finally came to leave campus and venture forth on a 17-day service-focused field course into the Sacred Valley of Peru.

The Peruvian experience lived up to all expectations, featuring both hoped-for episodes as well as moments of stressful uncertainty. Continuous journaling and in-field discussion helped us capture the richness of our day-to-day events. And when we returned, we joined our students in reflecting upon what we had experienced and how we had *all* grown. Through careful, candid, and deep reflection, we realized that, although short-term in duration, the course was definitely not short-term in impact.

As the faculty team who lived this story (and subsequent travel stories), we hope that our text may provide guidance and support for others engaged in short-term faculty-led international programs. Whether you are an instructor, administrator, or staff member, we present a unique portrait of the changing nature of international study in U.S. higher education. We also offer ways to help ensure success for those designing and delivering short-term, international field courses. Ultimately, our text is designed to shed light on the practical challenges as well as the distinctive rewards involved in this rapidly evolving and increasingly prevalent opportunity for learning.

....

Structure of the Text

After preliminary consideration, we decided to create the very text that would have proved invaluable to us when we first received our call to adventure. This text is therefore designed to provide you with practical as well as motivational information. Whether you are considering offering an international field course for the first time and need guidance, are a veteran field-course leader who would like to take your work to the next level, or are an administrator or staff person attempting to encourage and provide needed support for faculty-led international programs, we believe this book will prove useful to you.

We present the text in three overarching sections, each composed of four to five chapters. A unique feature is the inclusion of a brief *Travel Tale* at the opening of each chapter. The tales involve particularly salient experiences (some funny, some perplexing, some heartwarming) from our own faculty-led international courses. We included these experiences to give the related chapter material a real-world context and a human face.

Part I, *Faculty-Led International Programs: Examining the Value*, explores the *why* of faculty-led field-course development. In this section, we offer five chapters exploring ideas and research behind the delivery of meaningful short-term international programs. Chapter 1 examines current trends in international study and discusses the benefits and challenges to staff, faculty, and students who become involved. Chapter 2 reviews international field study in light of current and past theories of experiential learning and student engagement. Chapter 3 explores the effects of international field study on students' personal and academic development, with emphasis on forwarding critical thinking skills and reflective practice. Chapter 4 examines the somewhat nebulous concept of global citizenship and how it can be fostered during short-term international programs. Chapter 5 provides frank discussion of what participating faculty may expect from their involvement in international programs—from positives, such as international research opportunities and expansion of their pedagogy, to the more challenging reality of the time commitment and responsibilities involved.

Part II, *International Program Organization: Undertaking the Tasks*, moves from answering the question *why* into discussing *how* to go about developing and delivering a faculty-led field course. The four chapters in this section are therefore very practical in nature, focusing on the logistical planning that must precede departure. Chapter 6 provides information on selecting the field-course location. From reconnaisance visits to language considerations and selection of service providers, this chapter is particularly useful for those who have never led an international program; however, we believe it can also serve as a handy guide for those who have. Chapter 7 offers further details on setting up a field course. Building on the broader discussion provided in Chapter 6, this chapter examines the many decisions to be made and carried out. From developing a program timeline to setting up in-country homestays, Chapter 7 details the essential tasks to be completed. Chapter 8 focuses on legal considerations related to international field programs, such as insurance, health and safety issues, liability, and crisis management. Chapter 9, the closing chapter in Part 2, discusses today's student participants, from group dynamics to the many life lenses (age, gender, race, religion, background) that each will bring.

Part III, *The Learning: Realizing the Potential of Faculty-Led International Programs*, also presents a good deal of practical information. The four chapters that compose this section focus on curriculum and pedagogy best-suited to short-term international field study. Chapter 10 discusses learning goals, objectives, and assessments in a general sense before targeting international programs. Chapters 11, 12, and 13 then detail what is needed during each phase of the program. Chapter 11 centers on pre-departure preparation that will maximize in-field learning and growth. Chapter 12 explores best teaching practices while abroad. Chapter 13 focuses on return, reentry, culminating assessments, and determining means for sustaining and sharing the experience.

The conclusion of our text revisits our initial travel tale and Campbell's discussion of what can be gained from a hero's journey. Having taken up a call to adventure and returned safely and a little wiser for the experience, we examine what the elixir may include for each of the participants and stakeholders involved. Realizing how vitally important international study experiences can be in developing tomorrow's global citizens and leaders, we offer our thoughts not only on the need to create meaningful study-abroad experiences, but also on why we must make such experiences accessible to all.

PART I

Faculty-Led International Programs: Examining the Value

When a student, faculty member, department, or institution considers committing to a faculty-led, often short-term, international program, what is the expected value of such an endeavor? Without doubt, considerable resources will be required of all involved, from the institution to the individual student and certainly to the faculty. Given this, it is important to ask what the payoff may include. To answer such a question, it is helpful to have some understanding of the history of study abroad in the United States, including the motivational forces that have surfaced over time which have propelled it to the foreground for many institutions and for other stakeholders as well. And then there are questions surrounding how faculty-led programs fit into the overall study-abroad arena, in terms of both demand and worth.

Before getting into the design or "how-to" of a faculty-led international program, Part I of this text is designed to examine the "why" behind such a venture. Why would an institution seek to promote such opportunities when traditional study-abroad programs continue to be offered and appreciated by many? And what can a well-designed and implemented faculty-led program offer to students who opt for this type of international experience? Rather than looking at this model as a shortened and therefore less beneficial version of semester or year-long study abroad, what is the unique pedagogical strength of short-term faculty-led programs? Why have they

Fostering Global Citizenship Through Faculty-Led International Programs, pages 1–2
Copyright © 2012 by Information Age Publishing
All rights of reproduction in any form reserved.

been described as high-impact learning experiences for students and faculty as well? Along with these questions, there is the business of developing global citizenship to consider. Across its many definitions and dimensions, is this increasingly esteemed concept something that can be developed during shorter-term study abroad? If so, how might a faculty-led curriculum set the stage for such development?

Finally, there are questions related to the impact on faculty who decide to design and offer international programs. They will certainly be facing an exciting but also sometimes daunting array of challenges. On top of regular teaching, research, and service activities on their home campuses, what would compel them to pursue such a risky adventure?

Before offering guidance for designing and carrying out a faculty-led international program (the subject matter of Parts II and III), we first address the many questions regarding *why* these opportunities would be deemed worthy of the substantial resources they inevitably demand.

1

Trends That Drive the Need for Change

What, then, is the true meaning of preparation in the educational scheme?
In the first place, it means that a person, young or old, gets out of his present
experience all that there is in it for him at the time in which he has it . . . it is then the
business of the educator to see in what direction an experience is heading.

—John Dewey

TRAVEL TALE 1: After the Excitement

A s Dewey so aptly stated close to 100 years ago, it certainly is the "business of the educator" during course preparation to examine the direction an educational experience may take. When the educator accomplishes this task thoughtfully and realistically, all involved are likely to enjoy a valuable learning experience. While we wholeheartedly agree with Dewey's point (and therefore selected this quote to anchor our first chapter), we quickly realized that determining the direction of an international course is an atypical exercise. The problem, when we move the experience to an international setting, is the substantial number of variables

Fostering Global Citizenship Through Faculty-Led International Programs, pages 3–12
Copyright © 2012 by Information Age Publishing
All rights of reproduction in any form reserved.

involved—variables related to language, culture, health, student nervousness, faculty apprehension, parental concerns, and the list goes on. Such variables are not only nearly impossible to control, they are equally difficult to anticipate. As we began to consider these (and many other) factors, we felt our initial excitement gradually decelerating. The reality of the task that lay ahead hit us.

We had committed to teaching one of the first international travel courses for our college's new, high visibility Honors program. We now had to sit down and carefully determine what the course might actually entail—in Dewey's words, what direction it might take. One of us had prior experience with international service-learning and knew how valuable this could be. We determined to include some form of it in our course. Our Honors Council and college administration expected emphasis on global citizenship. While we weren't exactly sure of our entry point into this concept, we were determined to include it in our curriculum. And there were many other items to address as well—goals and objectives, a location, field partners, assessment tools. Taken together, it felt overwhelming.

As the time approached to actually begin teaching the course, we did what most academics do when they face a challenge—after losing a little sleep to anxiety, we began reading and reading and reading some more. We not only wanted to establish what direction our course might take, we also needed to find out what was going on in the field of faculty-led international study—where it had come from, where it was heading, what had worked for others, what hadn't, and why.

· · · · · · · · · · · · · · · · · · · ·

A Little History

Before examining current trends in international study, it is helpful to briefly review how this facet of U.S. higher education has evolved over time. Historically, U.S. study abroad, which is traced back to the 1920s, was limited in scope and availability. The practice emerged from the somewhat elitist European idea of the "grand tour," in which privileged students, almost exclusively White males, were encouraged to travel to Western European destinations to expand their knowledge of European arts and humanities (Hoffa, 2007). The result, whether intended or not, was to reinforce this groups' status as the intellectual and cultural elite.

The focus of international study shifted in the mid-20th century in response to global events such as World Wars I and II and, in the second half of the century, the stalemate of the Cold War. These events pointed out both the country's connectedness *to* other nations as well as its potential vulnerability *from* them. Accordingly, it became evident that the grand tour model for international study was no longer appropriate or even viable. Our country's youth, by certain measures its most valuable resource, needed a more robust and encompassing means for learning about the world and for eventually becoming contributing members of the global discourse community.

The Fulbright Program, established in 1946 in direct response to the events of WWII, presents a dynamic example of how international study in the United States responded to world events. It was hoped that the Fulbright exchange, an educational program designed to foster mutual understanding among the world's citizens, would lead to greater international goodwill and would thus help to reduce conflict among nations. The early success of this program, initiated by Senator J. William Fulbright of Arkansas, led to the creation of other international programs. In response, the international education community began to more fully appreciate the need for an expansion of its study-abroad goals and its accessibility to more (and more diverse) participants. Colleges and universities joined in this effort as International Education offices emerged across the country with the intent of increasing and facilitating study-abroad opportunities.

Today, we are experiencing change in the international study arena once again. Not surprisingly, the current change is also attributable, in part, to international conflict. While World Wars I and II as well as the Cold War presented higher education with reasons to emphasize global education, it was not until the events of September 11, 2001, (the first foreign attack on American soil since 1941) and the subsequent U.S.-led wars in Afghanistan and Iraq, that the shift in international educational goals could be described as seismic. Although triggered by tragic events, interest in understanding the values and motivations of different societies and cultures has accelerated considerably over the last decade and has been driven by more than just a reaction to conflict. We now find ourselves living and teaching in a more globally connected, post-9/11 era—a time of economic, social, and political connectivity unlike any other in recorded history. Marked by both the opportunities and challenges of globalization, it is an era in which higher education is being called upon to rethink its international study priorities and to embrace the concept of internationalization.

A quick search of college and university mission statements reflects the current commitment to internationalization, broadly defined as "the process of integrating an international, intercultural, or global dimension into the purpose, functions or delivery of postsecondary education" (Knight, 2008, p. 21). Meeting the goal of internationalization has resulted in expansion of international study opportunities for students from a broad range of disciplines. It has also spurred institutions related to the academic world to closely examine the value of international education. Joining colleges and universities, the Association of American Colleges and Universities' (AAC&U) Council for Liberal Education and America's Promise (LEAP) and Shared Futures initiatives also emphasize the need for institutes of higher education to foster the internationalization of campuses across the country (AAC&U, 2010; Hovland, 2006; Olson & Green, 2006). These broad-ranging initiatives are appropriately multidisciplinary in focus, encouraging international study as a critical component of higher education for all majors.

College, university, and related government organizations' emerging efforts to internationalize their collective work have been further encouraged by governmental interests. The result has been a number of proposed goals and initiatives, such as the Lincoln Commission Report, which articulated a national goal of having one million U.S. students studying abroad by 2016–2017 (Commission on the Abraham Lincoln Study Abroad Fellowship Program, 2005). This marks a significant increase over the approximate quarter million students currently studying abroad. To this end, the Lincoln Commission Report recommended national legislation (the Senator Paul Simon Study Abroad Foundation Act), with the intent of fostering greater participation in international study. The primary goals of this proposed legislation are creation of a more globally educated citizenry and the promotion of international study as a cornerstone of all U.S. higher education.

Just as the establishment and missions of the Land Grant universities in the 20th century met the changing needs of the American population at that time, today, government, business, and education are coming together again to meet an identified need within the country. But this time the need is being driven in part by concern over national and economic security within an evermore uncertain global marketplace. It also encompasses reinvigorated dedication to developing a sense of responsible global citizenship and ethical global leadership within our youth at a time when such a mindset is not an option but a necessity.

Descriptors such as *revolutionary* are being applied to current changes in study abroad (Lewin, 2009) as U.S. colleges and universities are being championed as the most active and innovative in providing worldwide programming (Altbach & Knight, 2007). Our educational institutions are now putting forth the message that overseas study can no longer be viewed as an optional and peripheral activity. Just as upwardly mobile professionals of the late 20th century were expected to cross the country for job advancement, professionals of the 21st century will be required to cross the globe for jobs in the new, increasingly borderless global economy. To this end, college and university mission statements are highlighting the need for international exposure as an essential part of the undergraduate experience, appreciating that such experience is crucial in preparing graduates who will work and live in a world that is irreversibly interconnected in as-of-yet undetermined ways.

There is a concurrent expectation of the international education community to expand target destinations beyond the traditionally selected countries of Western Europe. Destinations such as China, India, and Brazil, which are experiencing rapid economic growth and global influence, must be included. The benefits of having U.S. students travel to and interact with others in countries whose religious and cultural beliefs are new to them is another critical consideration; again, China and India would be targeted, as would countries in the Middle East.

And so what began as a small component of higher education that was available primarily to students with financial means is increasingly becoming a goal, if not a requirement, of the general undergraduate college experience. Certainly, it is a timely and necessary goal, one that reflects a real commitment within higher education to produce citizens who are mindful not only of their U.S. responsibilities but of their global responsibilities as well. Unfortunately, the challenge that higher education faces, particularly in times of such severe financial restraint, is determining how to realize this goal. An examination of current research offers a mixed picture of what is occurring in the United States in the field of international study.

Current Trends in Study Abroad

When examining present interests, trends, and initiatives in study abroad, it is initially encouraging to note that more students than ever before are electing to participate in an international study experience. But this increase in numbers is misleading; the *percentage* of college students engaged in international study has grown by only a negligible amount. There are simply many more students enrolled in college today than there were as little as 20 years ago. A study by the American Council on Education (2008) found that 55% of college-bound high school students expressed an interest in studying abroad as part of their college experience. It is unfortunate that this increase in interest is generally not realized, with fewer than 10% of U.S. college students today actually completing an international study experience (IIE, 2011); further, in any given year only 1.5% of students study abroad (Williamson, 2010).

In addition to the large gap between those who express interest and those who eventually travel, the demographic of student participants is even more constrained. At a time when the diversity of our nation is expanding rapidly, a very small percentage of U.S. minority students ever study in an international setting. In the 2008–2009 academic year, 80.5% of U.S. students studying abroad were White. Diversity of majors has also remained stagnant until quite recently. Social science majors have dominated study abroad, with business and management majors increasing their participation over the past decade (Hoffa, 2007). Science, technology, engineering, mathematics (STEM), and education majors continue to lag behind in study-abroad participation; in many cases this is due to core graduation requirements that make it difficult to schedule the traditional semester or year-long study-abroad experience.

Historically, and still today, Western Europe serves as the top target for U.S. studies abroad; however, there has been a notable increase in locations outside of this region recently. In 2008–2010, of the top 25 countries selected, 15 were outside of Western Europe, including South Africa as well as China and countries in South and Central America (IIE, 2011). Infrastructure to facilitate study abroad in these newer locations is emerging but is not yet fully realized. Over time, studying in countries outside of Western Europe should become more feasible and will thereby expand the reach and scope of the internationalization effort afoot on many U.S. campuses.

As U.S. colleges and universities aim toward having more students gain international experience, they must realize that this goal is not necessarily easy to accomplish, particularly from the student perspective. Serious barriers for students may range from financial constraints and inflexible degree requirements to personal and family concerns, including trepidation about "soloing" abroad for a full academic semester or year without faculty support, along with related unease around the safety of international travel, particularly since 9/11.

A recent trend in international education that has helped to address the concerns and barriers mentioned is the implementation of programs that are shorter in duration, more guided and structured, and often led by faculty and/or staff from the home institution (Gutierez, Averbach, & Bhandari, 2009). While typically offered by only a select few departments in the past, such shorter-term, often faculty-led programs have been increasing in general popularity and demand. Over the last decade, a significant shift has occurred in terms of the length and type of study-abroad programs students are most frequently selecting. Out of the total number of students who do participate in a study-abroad experience, over half are now opting for shorter-term programs that differ significantly from the more traditional study-abroad models.

Historically, the typical U.S. student spent a full semester or academic year enrolled in a program at an institution abroad. However, since 2003–2004, more students have opted for short-term, largely faculty-led courses for their international study experiences (Chieffo & Griffiths, 2009). The nationwide Institute of International Education's *Open Doors Report* (2011) found that of the 270,604 U.S. students who studied abroad for academic credit in 2009–2010, approximately 56.6% selected shorter-term international study, while 35.8% opted for a semester-long study-abroad experience. Only 3.8% elected to study abroad for a full academic year. For those committed to advancing international education, this shift in student demand is considerable and bears close attention.

Rising Popularity of Faculty-Led International Courses

While the exact number of faculty-led study-abroad programs in the United States is unknown, it appears that these opportunities now make up a significant percentage of the shorter-term programs serving students. The positive results related to this shift in program type are many. Short-term faculty-led field courses have created greater and oftentimes more accessible and feasible opportunities for students to travel and study internationally and are proving to be particularly helpful when attempting to attract students who have not elected to study abroad in the past. Currently, the typical student who elects to participate in all study-abroad programs is White, female, and in her junior year of college; however, short-term faculty-led courses have begun attracting a good number of racial/cultural minorities, students with disabilities, and students from lower-income families (Forum on Education Abroad, 2009).

A second promising trend related to short-term faculty-led course offerings is the fact that faculty from disciplines not traditionally involved with international study are beginning to take part in this teaching and learning opportunity. For this reason, along with increasing administrative encouragement, a new and more diverse faculty contingent is adapting curriculum and path-to-graduation requirements and opening this opportunity within disciplines that did not have "space" for such courses previously.

These trends denote a marked change in how U.S. campuses, students, and faculty are approaching international education—a change that is occurring concurrent with the nationwide increase in both interest in and demand for international study opportunities. Given U.S. higher education's commitment to internationalization and the trend toward student selection of short-term faculty-led international programs, faculty are now, more than ever before, playing a critical role in international education. For those of us who decide to step into this new teaching arena, it is essential to do so with care, with open eyes, and with clear learning goals in mind. As with any new educational endeavor, there are both benefits and obstacles to be considered; we examine these in detail in the following chapters of our text. But let's begin with a quick snapshot of notable positives as well as challenging aspects of faculty-led international field courses.

Benefits for Learners

It is not surprising that faculty-led international field courses trigger high student engagement. Rather than learning course content at a distance, students (and faculty) get a chance to grapple with it firsthand as they experience direct contact with a place, people, and culture that is different from their own. Research has proven time and again that such engaged, experiential learning leads to greater retention of targeted content across the academic disciplines. Such learning also leads to the creation of new and deeper knowledge about cultural difference and varied perspectives on business models and scientific research as well. The ethnocentrism that is so natural to young people who have not experienced any culture other than their own can be gently uncovered in the international "classroom."

Needless to say, such student learning does not happen without the careful guidance of enthusiastic and well-prepared instructors. By default, these instructors also sit in the role of learners as they navigate the new terrain of teaching not only off-campus but also out of country. As instructors prepare to lead their students into this venture, setting aside time for both personal and communal reflection has proven to be extremely worthwhile—for the students and for the instructors as well, as they co-process their own norms and customs in light of the culture they are visiting.

Shared reflection leads to a second strong benefit of faculty-led international field instruction: the formation of a natural and supportive community of learners whose collective experiences can eventually benefit the home campus. Barriers between students and faculty (and among students at times too) that may occur on campus somewhat dissolve as a faculty-led cohort of learners moves into new and oftentimes unpredictable territory together. The exchange of insights, observations, and evolving perspectives tends to draw the group together. After short-term faculty-led international courses end, participants frequently bring home what they have gained, both in their actions and in their ways of looking at their roles as global citizens, thereby helping to ensure that campus goals involving internation-alization become more than just well-intended words.

And the Flip Side of the Coin

Along with the good news about faculty-led international study, there are certainly challenges and questions to be considered. At the forefront of this list are questions regarding the quality and value of these shorter-duration experiences, especially as they now surpass traditional semester and year-long programs in terms of student interest and enrollment.

The short time frame in the field is arguably the most critical consid-eration for faculty preparing to design and deliver a course of this nature. As faculty move into this arena, we must discover ways to ensure that our courses have moved beyond the educational tours of the past to the more valuable learning experiences that are needed today. Of particular concern is finding ways to replace the cultural immersion that occurred naturally in longer-term study-away experiences with meaningful opportunities for stu-dents to have in-depth interactions with a culture different from their own. The shared reflection within student cohorts mentioned earlier is essential, but determining what the students will be doing on a day-to-day basis (the grounds for their reflection) must come first.

Another consideration involves the very act of teaching a short-term in-ternational course. It is an invigorating yet demanding personal and profes-sional undertaking, with many variables and detailed planning to carry out. Faculty must select a viable setting and hopefully visit that setting before teaching the course. We must determine purposeful activities—pre-, dur-ing-, and posttravel. We must find a way to finance these trips and to make adjustments to our teaching loads to cover our regular courses as well as bal-ance our personal lives while we are away. We must recruit a broad range of students and hope they have the wherewithal to see the experience through. We must find someone, preferably a co-instructor, to accompany us.

But despite what faculty need to undertake, more and more are opting for the experience. This may be likely due in large part to the perceived gains experienced in carrying out an international program. On a most promising note, the National Survey for Student Engagement (2007) iden-tified study abroad as one of the high-impact college experiences that led to significant personal and intellectual growth. Further, the survey found that "the amount of time one is abroad is not as important as whether a student has had such an experience" (p. 17). While designing and deliver-ing an effective short-term international field course is a major responsibility, one that requires significant time and energy, such teaching is proving to be a rich and rewarding experience for both students and faculty who are getting involved.

Return of the Excitement

We offered a travel tale at the opening of this chapter that focused on how we felt as we began planning our first co-taught faculty-led field course. As we digested the material we have presented in this chapter, we found ourselves regaining the initial excitement we'd felt upon agreeing to teach the course. Certainly there was much to consider and much work to do to ensure an optimal learning experience—the kind of carefully directed experience that Dewey (1938) described; but we felt enthusiastic and ready to join (one of us for the first time) the ranks of those opting to teach in the short-term international study arena. In the following chapters, we offer a detailed portrait of our experiences and of the many things to be considered by those who have, or are considering, joining these ranks.

2

Experiential Learning and Student Engagement

*Disequilibria alone can force the subject to go beyond
his current state and strike out in new directions.*

—Jean Piaget

TRAVEL TALE 2: Who's Helping Whom?

We were on campus when the course started, meeting once a week in preparation for a 17-day journey into the Sacred Valley of Peru. It was a particularly snowy New England winter; we came to class each week bundled in down jackets, commiserating about drafty dorms, slippery sidewalks, and days that grew dark by 4:30 p.m. But despite the seasonal discomforts, we were starting to get excited about what lay ahead as we read about Peru's history and culture, perused Peruvian newspapers, listened to guest speakers familiar with the country, even took a few Spanish lessons so we could manage basic communication with our

Fostering Global Citizenship Through Faculty-Led International Programs, pages 13–26
Copyright © 2012 by Information Age Publishing
13

host families. We read about the Andes Mountains and the indigenous villages where extended families lived together in one or two-room dirt-floored homes. We learned about the service-learning project we would complete under the guidance of our service provider, whose staff would facilitate the project and communicate in Quechua, the language of the village where we would be working. We were to build mud stoves in village homes. The stoves would feature ventilation pipes—brick and mud-mortared structures that would vent through the roofs thereby abating respiratory problems for the dwellings' inhabitants and reducing the buildup of creosote on the walls and ceilings. The stoves would also burn more efficiently and help to conserve the short supply of wood in the Andes region. It sounded like such important work! We were anxious to get started.

We had been in Peru 5 days when we finally made our way into the village where we were scheduled to build stoves. Our students were feeling tired, sweaty, and a little cranky. They had spent over an hour on a crowded and dusty bus and were still getting adjusted to new foods, a different language, and an elevation that left them feeling either breathless or nauseous. When we disembarked, they asked where the bathrooms were. Our guide pointed to a nearby field.

When the group reassembled, we made our way into a half dozen village homes where our students worked in pairs—mixing mud mortar laced with animal hair and in some cases animal feces, following the directions of our guide, a native of the area who spoke Quechua with the village residents, as he showed our students how to build the stoves. In most homes, multiple generations of family watched, shooing away the chickens and cuy (guinea pigs) that scurried about underfoot. Getting a new stove was a big event, but not something the villagers couldn't have constructed without us, we soon realized; they simply did not have all of the materials that our provider had supplied.

At first our students worked slowly and seemed uncomfortable with the task, but as the hours passed and we walked from one home to the next to monitor their progress, we observed a change taking place. Their t-shirts were covered in red mud; in many instances, their arms and faces were too. But we witnessed how they gradually began to take pride in their work, and began to laugh and interact with the families despite the language barrier. Slowly they became more focused on their work than on themselves. In one particularly small and dark home, one of our students, Adam, later told us that the grandmother cried when he finished the stove, then offered him an Inca cola, a neon yellow treat that was surely dear within this village where processed food of any sort was a rarity.

Later that night, when we were all back in our home-base community,

we met with our group. Despite being tired, enthusiasm was running high
and stories filled the air. They talked about what they had learned that day,
how clumsy they had felt at times, and how amazed they were to be in
a place where some residents had never ventured beyond the borders of
the village, where technology not only did not dominate, but wasn't even
present. Finally Adam, who had been given the cola, said, "We were supposed to be helping today, but the service was the other way around. They
opened their homes and let us in."

● ● ● ● ● ● ● ● ● ● ● ● ● ● ● ● ● ● ● ●

Engaged Learning Abroad

Over the years, a number of educational theorists have compared the benefits of "progressive" methods of teaching to more "traditional" models.
Frankly, we question the need for such a dichotomy. There is nothing
wrong, in our opinion, with what is oftentimes described as the traditional
pedagogy that takes place within the four walls of a campus classroom. Assigned readings, lectures, discussions, and follow-up exams can be effective teaching approaches for certain learners and in certain circumstances.
We view such models as part of the overall educational landscape that has
been in use in the United States and around the world for decades, even
centuries. While *experiential learning, student engagement, deep learning,* and
participatory learning are appreciated as the better (and more progressive)
pedagogical models today, they are in fact models that have been employed
in campus classrooms, to one degree or another, for many years.

In this chapter, we examine how the *opportunity* for such dynamic teaching approaches comes both easily and naturally in the international learning
environment—be it in an open-air classroom such as the mud-floored homes
we described in Travel Tale 2 or knee-deep in the trash-removal project we
describe in Travel Tale 6. Ultimately, no matter how distant or stimulating the
field setting may be, what takes place lies in the hands of the teacher—in his
or her ability to make best use of the learning opportunities an international
"classroom" inherently affords. The interaction between educational theory
and practice during international study is therefore our focus in Chapter 2.

Theories That Underlie Good Practices

We presented many reasons for promoting short-term faculty-led study
abroad in Chapter 1. One of the most notable reasons is what such pro-

grams provide in the way of profound and long-remembered learning experiences for students. When considering why these courses are often noted as so powerful, even transformative, during the college years, it is useful to explore the ways in which students learn and grow academically and personally. Given that international field-courses take place, for the most part, in a location that is both unfamiliar and unpredictable, the student growth that occurs is firmly grounded in the concept of experiential learning. As Montrose (2002) points out in her discussion of the academic context of international study, students are sent out "... into a world that is complex and interconnected, challenging their prevailing world view and their ability to take responsibility for their own learning" (p. 2). According to Montrose, appreciating and applying experiential pedagogy is the basis for successful short-term faculty-led international field courses. So beyond the obvious explanation—humans learn best by doing—what is experiential learning all about?

Classic Contributions

To begin answering this question, the first person who comes to mind is American philosopher and educational reformer John Dewey, who saw learning as a process whereby students construct new knowledge, skills, and philosophic understandings by directly engaging with the phenomena they are studying. In the international arena, for example, instead of reading about a culture different from their own, students live in that culture for a period of time, taking in the values, language, traditions, beliefs, and conduct expectations firsthand and through all of their sensory channels. They have the opportunity to listen, observe, taste, smell, and feel the new environment as they figure out ways to communicate with the people living there, oftentimes despite stark differences in language and culture.

Learning in such a multimodal way is very powerful, as it elicits complete learner engagement; in some ways, it even begs the question of how a teacher could add anything to what the students are able to gain on their own. According to Dewey (1938), the teacher's role (in whatever the learning environment may be) is not to transfer information to students through lectures but rather to facilitate opportunities for rich and authentic knowledge construction (faculty-led field study being a perfect example) and to then process students' observations and responses with them as they make sense of the phenomena they have encountered. The length of the course is not as critical as the presence of the teacher as an observer, questioner, and guide for the students as they sort through what they are experiencing.

This is why the short-term faculty-led model can be a very effective method for student learning during study abroad.

In direct line with Dewey's philosophy, Engle and Engle's (2003) classification of international program types notes that the primary goal of study abroad is to guide and challenge students with authentic cultural encounters that engage them both intellectually and emotionally. Experiential learning, therefore, would not be simply a matter of setting students free in a strikingly new environment and hoping they might grow from the experience. Of course there would be some amount of growth in such a circumstance, but the growth becomes long-lasting and valuable when the teacher works with his or her students to analyze and appreciate what they have felt and observed in light of what they already know and believe about the world they inhabit.

Another basic tenet of Dewey's experiential theory that aligns well with international education is what he termed *collateral learning*. Dewey (1938) described this as the learning that occurs when new experiences blend with existing experiences in a way that helps students better understand what they have encountered. According to Dewey, an extended web of knowledge is constructed by learners as they come to recognize how their many life experiences, both existing and incoming, are interconnected. Such understanding enhances learners' confidence in their ability to grasp new information and ideas, resulting in intrinsic motivation to extend the web— to learn more.

The fact that each student's web of constructed knowledge will vary according to his or her own cultural history and life experiences adds individualized value to the concept of collateral learning. Zamistil-Vondrova's (2005) analysis of the value of short-term study-abroad programs reflects Dewey's (1938) discussion of collateral learning. In analyzing the benefits of such field study for students, a major theme she identifies is the personalized nature of what each student gains; further, how the construction of new knowledge is substantial in each case, but varies greatly from student to student. Each is able to absorb and adapt to the cultural nuances of the unfamiliar field environment in his or her own way and in his or her own time under the careful tutelage of the instructor.

Development psychologist Jean Piaget's work also relies on the concept of constructivism as the basis of learning, with experiential opportunities being an essential element of the process. In direct line with Dewey's (1938) philosophy, Piaget believed that knowledge must be built from within rather than transferred from the teacher's brain to the student's. Piaget (1975) explained that each learner's mind holds basic knowledge that has been gained over the years through significant personal experiences. This base of knowledge signals to them how things should happen in the world around them. Piaget called this knowledge base the learner's schema. As the learner's world expands through life experiences, the schema must take in new information and devise ways for it to make sense in light of what the learner already believes to be true based on prior experiences. In some cases, when the new information is distinctly different and/or broader than what the learner believed to be true, the learner experiences a sense of disequilibrium—"This doesn't fit!" It is easy to see how this might happen in the international setting, particularly in developing countries, non-English-speaking locations (unless the student travelers are multilingual), and if there are rich, but possibly challenging, experiential learning opportunities (such as service-learning projects) involved.

Piaget's (1975) theory goes on to explain how learners naturally begin establishing mechanisms to cope when feeling disequilibrium. Piaget explained this internal work as the process of adaptation. The learner first assimilates or *fits* the new phenomenon into existing schema to the extent possible. If this isn't sufficient and the learner still feels uncertain, he or she accommodates what is occurring by changing existing schema to bring in the new phenomenon. *Adaptation* is the overarching term Piaget gave to the process of moving from feelings of disequilibrium to those of equilibration by assimilating and/or accommodating new information. The process occurs within the learner's mind but can be helped along with careful and caring teacher guidance.

Brazilian educator Paolo Friere, known for his contributions to critical theory and pedagogy, was also a proponent of constructivist teaching. His work agrees with Dewey (1938) and Piaget's (1975) arguments regarding the ineffectiveness of static teaching methods. Friere (1970) referred to this as a "banking concept of education," in which teachers believe it is possible to deposit their knowledge directly into the minds of their students who then, miraculously, own the new material—transfer complete, with no student inquiry or input involved. Dewey, Piaget, Friere, and many other enlightened educators over the years appreciated that learning simply does not often happen this way. Students' brains are not empty receptacles needing to be filled by their teachers. Instead, learners need to be directly in touch with what they are studying.

When lessons are carefully crafted, significant learning can certainly take place in a college classroom. But opportunities for rich and meaningful learning are far more prevalent and easier to realize during faculty-led international study. When the learner is invited to construct new knowledge by the very "classroom"—a classroom that is unfamiliar, perhaps even quite unsettling (as is often the case during study abroad)—the learner's ability to move from a state of disequilibrium to equilibration marks some of the most engaged, substantial, and enduring learning of all.

Contemporary Influences

Today, there are a number of resources that can be helpful to faculty who are planning to employ experiential learning models in their international programs. The best of these reflect the educational theories of Dewey (1938), Piaget (1975), Friere (1970), and their progressive counterparts. One of the most widely known is Kolb's (1984) *Experiential Learning Cycle*. Based on the earlier work of German social psychologist Lewin (1952), Kolb's model (portrayed below), reflects many of the classic theories of experiential pedagogy, honoring the fact that the most active role in the learning process must belong to the learner. Kolb explained experiential learning as "the process whereby knowledge is created through the transformation of experience" (p. 38). His 4-stage learning cycle explores how learners move from concrete experiences into having the ability, confidence, and motivation to apply what they have experienced in new situations (Figure 2.1).

Dewey's (1938) concept of collateral learning is clearly evident in Kolb's (1984) model, which demonstrates the interplay between experi-

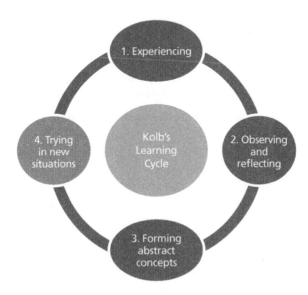

Figure 2.1   Kolb's Experiential Learning Cycle.

ences, personal reflection on the experiences, conceptualization of how the experiences relate to the learner's general perceptions of life, to experimentation with what has been learned in other situations. One way to look at the model is to examine how the learner progresses from an internal focus—"my" experiences and "my" analysis of those experiences—to an external focus, that is, a generalized ability to formulate useful theories regarding what has been learned so they can be applied in new situations. For faculty planning curriculum for an international program, the model offers a means for helping students process and grow from the experiences they are having abroad. Some of these experiences may cause distinct feelings of disequilibrium at the time they are occurring, but they can prove to be very powerful following thoughtful reflection (with fellow travelers) and the opportunity for real-world application.

Kuh's (2008) work with the Association of American Colleges and Universities' (AAC&U) Liberal Education and America's Promise (LEAP) project sheds further light on experiential learning and student engagement. In his role as a member of the LEAP National Leadership Council, Kuh interviewed faculty, administrators, student-affairs staff, and trustees from institutions across the country, asking what could be done to increase student engagement and success on campus. The result was a list of high-impact educational practices that clearly spell out why some educational activities are, in fact, more powerful and long-lasting than others. The list focuses primarily on student engagement and demonstrates the value of the experiential theories and practices that are inherent in faculty-led international field study.

While Kuh's data involves more than the following list, we present the gist of his findings as a means for seeing the cross-walk between high-impact practices and international study. High-impact educational practices

1. Demand that students devote considerable time and effort to purposeful tasks.
2. Put students in circumstances that [require them] to interact with faculty and peers about substantial matters.
3. Increase the likelihood that students will experience diversity with people who are different from themselves.
4. Include opportunities for frequent feedback [not to be confused with grading] about their performance.
5. Give a chance to test what they are learning in unfamiliar situations.
6. Deepen learning and bring one's values and beliefs into awareness.
7. Help students take the measure of events and actions and put them into perspective. (Kuh, 2008, pp. 14–17)

When examining these points, it is not surprising to see why study abroad was singled out as one of the most high-impact activities students can engage in during college. Of course, not all items hold true for all international programs. Faculty designing a program will identify with various items depending upon factors ranging from disciplinary focus to course location. For example, the travel tale offered at the opening of this chapter demonstrates how a number of Kuh's high-impact educational practices can occur very naturally in an international course featuring a service-learning component. In the 2 years since the Peru course ended and in the months since Adam (the student quoted in the travel tale) graduated, we have had a number of chances to interact with him. Adam is now an ESL teacher in Seoul, South Korea. He has told us on several occasions how much the service-learning project in Peru made a difference not only in his thinking but also in his eventual life choices.

Experiential Models in International Settings

Over time, the concept of experiential education has triggered various pedagogical approaches that have been used regularly in international settings. The most common of these include: (a) service-learning, in which students are direct participants in meaningful community service projects; (b) problem-based service-learning, in which students are challenged to understand and collaboratively work toward the resolution of complex, real-world problems, and; (c) research-based learning, in which students undertake investigative learning under the tutelage of faculty. By engaging in these experiential models, students have the opportunity to construct new knowledge as they also develop a valuable skillset that will serve them in their postgraduate years. Skills such as creative and independent thinking, problem solving and collaboration, self-regulation, and critical decision making are called upon as students engage in service-learning, problem-based service-learning, and research-based learning. The difference between these models is worth noting for faculty who intend to include one or more of them in an international program.

We Can Make a Difference: Learning Through Service

Civic engagement, in one form of another, has a long history within U.S. higher education. As early as the 19th century, faith-based campus groups and later Greek fraternities and sororities emphasized service as vital to a thorough college education. In the 1960s, the Civil Rights Movement, the Peace Corps, and Volunteers in Service to America (VISTA) presented broader opportunities for college-aged students to engage with their communities and with the world. However, while such compelling opportunities were available, the number of students who actually participated in them did not increase concurrent with the rise in students attending U.S. colleges and universities each year. Instead, research conducted in the 1990s suggests that college students felt increasingly detached from the communities beyond their campuses, reporting feelings of being lamentably self-focused, living and studying without impacting others in a positive way (Putnam, 1995). The concept of an Ivory Tower existence, which had long been applied to college and university faculty, was apparently trickling down to the student body as well.

In reaction to the research and the parallel lethargic student interest in service opportunities, institutes of higher education across the country began taking a more active role in providing and encouraging service-learning as part of the undergraduate experience. Their mission statements reflected this commitment as many created service-learning offices and developed new opportunities for students to connect to their home communities, other U.S. communities, and host communities abroad. The resulting range of service-learning opportunities in the 1990s was extensive and interdisciplinary in nature—from constructing houses (Habitat for Humanity), to working in soup kitchens, tutoring ESL students, conducting river assessments and clean-ups, to developing and staffing adult literacy programs, to name a few. Service-learning opportunities have expanded even further over the past decade. A concomitant rise in student interest and participation is heartening.

Despite the rapid expansion in both opportunities and student interest, longitudinal, quantitative studies of service-learning's longer-term impact on students' lives are limited (Bernacki & Bernt, 2007); however, qualitative studies have registered consistent themes regarding some of the more immediate benefits. These include increase in empathy (Wideman, 2005); growth in self-reflection and self-understanding (Raman & Pashupati, 2002), reduction of prejudice (Erickson & O'Connor, 2000), and enhanced critical thinking ability and academic motivation (Bringle, Phillips, & Hudson, 2004). Such promising results demonstrate the value of including service-learning projects within both U.S. coursework and international study; in fact, including service-learning in international programs is becoming so prevalent that it is referred to simply as ISL.

Many of the service-learning opportunities listed above as well as countless other location-specific examples work particularly well in short-term faculty-led international programs. For most projects, a 2–3 week residency is ample. With faculty present to arrange, guide, and encourage students to reflect on their work, the benefits of the service experience can be maximized. Most important of all, student involvement in ISL projects promotes a sense of in-country purpose. Such work moves them beyond a tourist position to being a visitor who is willing to support some aspect of host country life. Through in-country ISL projects, students are able to take in the environs in a more purposeful way. As Steinberg (2002) states, the students' service placement provides them with "a window on a host society" (p. 212). It also provides the host society a clearer window on the student as a representative of the United States. This is a concept that merits careful dialogue with would-be student travelers. Not only are you observing your hosts, they are also observing you.

One of the most promising outcomes of faculty-led ISL programs is their potential to integrate higher education's prevailing focus on civic engagement with its concurrent focus on internationalization. As Battistoni (2002) noted, service-learning is not only about *learning to serve*, it is also about *serving to learn*. When taken into the international setting, this type of engaged, civic learning invites students to work both *in* and *with* the host community (Plater, Jones, Bringle, & Clayton, 2009) and thereby offers a richer and deeper perspective of the host community's customs, priorities, and needs. As students engage in ISL, ongoing reflection on the privilege involved in conducting such work as well the impact their actions and reactions can have on the host community is understandably critical.

And so we again return to the travel tale we used to open the chapter. While the stove ventilation project offered our students a rare window into learning about the lives of a small Peruvian community, it was the community's willingness to open their homes to a group of American students, as Adam pointed out, that made the learning opportunity possible. The degree to which such a personalized scenario will apply varies according to the projects undertaken, but it is important to keep in mind (and to remind students) of the reciprocal nature of service-learning.

We Can Figure This Out: Problem-Based Service-Learning

Problem-based service-learning (PBSL) is similar to service-learning in some ways, but quite different in others. Rather than stepping in to offer help with an identified community need, students involved in PBSL are presented with a real-world, community-based problem and asked to determine and implement the best possible solution. All of the good effects of service-learning are still in place, but the opportunity to determine how to actually help solve a community problem and to then go about enacting the solution adds a high-stakes, analytic component to the cooperative, hands-on value of service-learning.

The approach, when first designed in the 1960s as a hypothetical exercise rather than a real-world experience, sought complex problems with multiple solutions, the best being debatable and/or not immediately clear. The point was to encourage deep and critical thinking on the part of students from a variety of disciplines (the more interdisciplinary the problem, the better) and to build intercommunity respect as students shared possible solutions with each other, building upon the knowledge base of various group members as they jointly determined the best path to take. Although the approach began with hypothetical situations, the problem-based learning method was never a closed-classroom situation. Instead, faculty regularly invited professionals from the field under study to participate; sometimes helping evaluate student work, other times discussing the viability of various student-generated solutions.

It is easy to see how this experiential model would be particularly valuable in a faculty-led field course and why some of the most successful international initiatives fall within STEM disciplines. Students involved in Engineers Without Borders, for example, join with faculty in response to calls from developing countries seeking affordable and sustainable technical advice for engineering projects. Another successful program, Living Routes, involves students in the building of "eco-villages," sustainable living communities dedicated to environmental activism (Hovey & Weinberg, 2009). When engaged in such PBSL work, students determine ways to address host-country engineering challenges as they work with local residents and experienced faculty to put their solutions into practice.

Taking the model into a real-world setting in this way ups the immediacy of finding viable solutions and asks the student problem-solvers to take into account such contextual factors as the cost of the various solutions, the involvement and buy-in of the community being "served," the sustainability of the solutions, and the availability of resources. In this way, what was originally an interesting classroom exercise can grow into a learning experience with lasting effects on real people's lives.

We Can Add to the Knowledge: Student-Faculty Research

A third experiential model that is growing in popularity within faculty-led international programs is undergraduate student-faculty research. This coincides with, and is probably prompted by, the growth in such research on campuses across the United States (Hovey & Weinberg, 2009; Katkin, 2003) that followed the publication of the Boyer Commission Report (1998), *Reinventing Undergraduate Education: A Blueprint for America's Research Universities.* Boyer's report clearly encouraged colleges and universities to develop ways for undergraduate students to become involved in research projects with faculty mentors in much the same way their graduate counterparts had over the years. While a commendable suggestion, a major challenge has involved finding the time for such work to happen—from both the perspective of the faculty (the number of students seeking a mentor) as well as the students (depending upon the major, fitting research classes into already full path-to-graduation schedules). Despite such challenges, the potential for expanding undergraduate skills and encouraging independent inquiry has fueled the growth of this experiential model, particularly in faculty-led international settings in which students are focusing on one course versus the three- to four-course traditional academic semester. An obvious added bonus is having the faculty mentor in residence.

In order for faculty and students to realize purposeful research projects in the relatively short time available to them, there is a certain amount of pre-travel work involved. This includes (a) researching and identifying a worthy project appropriate to both the course destination and the student's field of study; (b) providing coursework on research methodologies; (c) developing and sharing the proposed research agenda with in-country contacts to be sure it is viable; and (d) working with the Institutional Review Board, as needed.

While there are obstacles to overcome, encouraging students to become involved in academic inquiry within an international setting is a most worthy educational endeavor. In the words of Streitwieser and Sobania (2008), "study abroad research presents an ideal opportunity to learn about academic inquiry and to engage in the exhilarating search for answers in an independent, self-driven way as nascent scholars" (p. 6). Keeping in mind that undergraduates are nascent scholars, helping them determine a reasonable research project can encourage a deeper understanding and appreciation of aspects of the host-country people, traditions, and culture than they might have experienced without such a project. And when given the opportunity to process and share their findings with their traveling peers and co-leaders, everyone's learning is strengthened.

Live Learning

Students can certainly learn about settings very different from their own through reading, watching videos, and listening to a faculty leader and guest speakers who are either native to or well-traveled within the location.

But no matter how carefully a teacher crafts such learning opportunities, there is a level of detachment when students read or simply hear about a place, its people, and their traditions from a distance. While such input can offer a solid introduction, nothing can replace the full/sensory experience of living and studying in another country or setting. When this happens, students learn firsthand what the place is about through observation, reflection, and interactions with the people who call it home.

During short-term faculty-led international study, particularly those programs that use Kolb's Learning Cycle (1984) as a curriculum guide, students are continuously observing, engaging, and comparing their experiences abroad with their previously known world. In fact, according to Che, Spearman, and Manizade (2009), the less familiar the destination, the greater the "potential for student development, social good, and for increasing cultural awareness and global mindedness" (p. 104). Adam's realization, mentioned in the opening travel tale, illustrates this point; the grandmother in the village household had been the true contributor by willingly sharing her home with him. Such nuanced learning occurs best in unfamiliar settings, in places, and through experiences that leave learners feeling disturbingly off balance; experiences that cause them to reflect long and hard on their own understanding of the way life works and what they can do, as Piaget's opening quote suggests, to strike out in new directions.

3

Sense of Self and Reflective Growth

One of the most effective ways to learn about oneself
is by taking seriously the culture of others.

—Edward Hall

TRAVEL TALE 3: Why Doesn't This Feel Sacred?

One of the highlights of the Peruvian field course was, admittedly, a highlight for most travelers to the country—visiting Machu Picchu, named one of the Seven Wonders of the World when the legendary list was updated in 2007. We were finished with the service-learning projects, feeling tired but satisfied with our work, and ready for an adventure into the renowned and sacred Incan site. Our service providers had warned us that Machu Picchu was likely to be crowded in late May. They therefore booked us a hotel near the entrance to the national sanctuary the night before our visit.

After having dinner with the local woman who was going to guide our tour, we spent a little time talking with the students about how they were feeling now that we were finally so close to our destination. They were very excited! We were too. We'd read about Machu Picchu together, seen dozens of photos of the misty mountains and terraced landscape, and heard about the site from the awed perspective of past visitors. The Sun Temple, the Royal Tomb, the House of Chosen Women—we were about to walk this ancient ground. Our students admitted that their feelings could probably be best described as reverent, with a little trepidation thrown in as well.

We got up very early the next morning—4 a.m. in fact. Not only did we want to climb the grassy hills of Machu Picchu, we also wanted to be among the 400 visitors allowed each day to climb Wayna Picchu, the mountain overlooking Machu Picchu. When we got to the tour buses that would take us to the entrance of the sanctuary, we were amazed to see, in the semidarkness, how long the lines were. There were couples and families and tour groups and student groups. There were people with cameras, hikers with backpacks, people with megaphones directing traffic, people speaking English, German, Japanese, and Spanish, along with other languages and dialects we not only could not understand but also could not recognize.

The sun came up. The day got hot. We piled out of the buses and stood in long lines to purchase tickets. We scrambled behind our guide who knew a shortcut that would get us to the entrance of Wayna Picchu quickly in the hope that we might be in the third group of 100 allowed to make the climb; (we made it, just barely). We climbed Wayna Picchu in a long line of other visitors—clutching mountainside steel ladders, stopping for water breaks, letting people pass us, passing others. When we got to the rocky summit, there was barely room for our group to stand together and take in Machu Picchu stretched below. But we did, briefly, before clambering back down the hill so that the next group of 100 could begin their ascent.

The rest of our visit ran along the same lines. Yes, we were walking the grounds of Machu Picchu. And yes, it was extremely beautiful, and yes, there was a certain overlay of mystery, despite the crowds. We took the perfunctory pictures that would show that we really had been there. We sat on a wall of stone and gazed down at the sacred landscape together. But we also noticed that, while our students were taking in the experience on some level, there was a feeling of disillusionment in the air. We had so wanted this to be a life-long memory, but the tourist overlay was definitely affecting the experience.

After some gentle gnashing of teeth, we decided to take action. No, we hadn't planned it this way, but we needed to offer a means for grappling with what we were all feeling. That evening, when we gathered to process the day, we broke with the usual open-discussion format and gave the students a writing prompt instead, explaining that we would share responses afterwards. "What do you think Peru has both gained and lost from the world's discovery of Machu Picchu?" There were a few moments of quiet puzzlement before pens began to fly. The ensuing conversation was rich and thought-provoking; and while it did not dispel the disillusionment we'd felt, it gave us a means for processing and better understanding it.

·····················

Making Sense of the World

When questioning the link between cognitive engagement (the subject of Chapter 2) and the reflection and self-awareness that enhances engaged, experiential learning opportunities, it is helpful to consider three points made by Caine and Caine (1997) in their brain and learning research. First, they note that the brain is complex and adaptive. Second, the brain is social; and third, the brain's search for meaning is innate. While these points may sound like nothing more than common sense, we believe it is important to remind ourselves that they are also scientifically based. As such, they can prove useful as we determine goals for our programs and design learning opportunities for our students.

If, for example, we consider Caine and Caine's (1997) points in light of the Machu Picchu travel tale, we can see how their research findings apply to an experiential-learning setting. At first, the students were puzzled by their response to the much-anticipated experience. While they tried to be enthusiastic and to legitimately feel the sense of awe described by others, they knew this was not *all* of what they were feeling (the complex brain). Taking the time to reflect upon and process their responses, both internally and with each other (the social brain), helped them better understand their initial feelings. Examining Machu Picchu from a critical perspective, considering both the advantages and disadvantages the site affords Peruvians, gave our students a means to move beyond dichotomous thinking and to thus make clearer sense of their responses (the adaptive brain and the brain's search for meaning).

With knowledge of how to deconstruct an international learning experience such as our Machu Picchu example, faculty preparing to lead an international program must focus next on developing the learning outcomes and skills most commonly identified as critical higher education targets in the 21st century. We identify four of these outcomes and skills to be not only applicable but also essential to successful international coursework: reflection, critical thinking, self-awareness, and self-efficacy. These, of course, are not mutually exclusive skills; in fact there is a good deal of overlap among them. Additionally, successful growth in one seems often to lead quite naturally to successful growth in the next.

Stop and Think About It: The Value of Reflection

As Kolb's (1984) experiential learning model demonstrates, the value of an experience largely rests in a person's ability to stop and make sense of his or her response to it. In effect, it is a person's ability to reflect on the questions, "Why am I feeling this way about what I am experiencing?" and "What am I bringing from my own background that is influencing my response?" that can help give the experience both meaning and enduring value. Without taking time for such thinking and questioning, unique opportunities for learning and growth (which are inherent in international study) can easily be underplayed or even missed altogether.

In Stone's (2006) discussion of the core components of intercultural education—emotional intelligence, knowledge, motivation, openness, resilience, ability to reflect, and sensitivity—the ability to reflect is singled out as particularly important. As Stone explains, "systematic reflection on one's own ways of thinking, feeling and doing can enhance the self-awareness that allows major progress in relating to people of other cultures" (p. 348). We appreciate how Stone's words suggest that productive reflection results in action; in this case, the ability to relate to people of other cultures. In keeping with this observation, a clear grasp of the reflective process along with understanding of what can be done to encourage students to be more intentionally reflective can be invaluable to faculty as they design and lead international programs.

Once again, the work of Dewey offers a logical starting point. An early proponent of reflective practice, Dewey (1933) described it as, "the active, persistent and careful consideration of any belief or supposed form of knowledge in light of the grounds that support it and the further conclusions to which it leads" (p. 9). Dewey contended that reflective practice can be developed in students when they are encouraged to question and thereby deepen understanding of their lived experiences. As reflective practice has drawn increased attention over time, Dewey's early work has given rise to various models describing the stages involved in the reflective process. We find the work of Moon (1999) as well as Williams and Wessel (2004) to be particularly useful within the international education arena. Fortunately, while 5 years separate their studies, their findings correspond regarding the steps involved in reflective practice, and they agree that the final step must involve changes in attitude and behavior. Both models start with in-depth and careful description of an event or experience. If there is emotion or a problem involved, which is oftentimes the case, the next step is analysis of what happened along with clarification of whatever issues may have been present and how those issues might be addressed. Final review of the careful processing that has occurred "verifies" the learning and indicates both a purpose and a means for changing future behavior.

To put this in a real-world context, consider the case of a U.S. student with limited ability to communicate in Spanish sitting down to dinner with her Latin American homestay family who have equally limited ability to communicate in English. The meal that has been carefully prepared in her honor includes a main dish she does not eat regularly for personal or religious reasons (so starts the experience). How does she explain this to her family without offending anyone? And what about the obvious cost involved in providing such a meal? As the student ponders what she should do in this situation (analysis of the issues involved), she is presented with a chance to consider how it might have been avoided and what she needs to do in the future to ensure that such a scene does not happen again (thereby determining a means for changing future behavior).

Issue-laden experiences such as this, as well as others with even more serious consequences, are not uncommon during international study programs. Sometimes they can be predicted in advance, but many times they spring up unexpectedly. Keeping dynamic models of reflective practice in mind can help faculty make use of such experiences rather than fervently hoping they won't happen. In their study of the value of short-term study abroad programs, Spencer, Murray, and Tuma (2005) state, "the best short-term programs balance the experience itself with processing of the experience" (p. 376). They further point out that it is natural for students to focus on what they are seeing and doing rather than on what they are learning; so it is up to faculty leaders to ensure that reflection and thus appreciation of the new learning actually happens. It is also up to faculty to ensure that the deeper understanding that has (hopefully) been gained will eventually translate, in one form or another, into responsible future actions.

According to Whom? Thinking Critically

If reflection involves taking the time to process life experiences, critical thinking can be thought of as what occurs during reflection, particularly the unpeeling of prior assumptions in order to closely examine the many "texts" or human stories that we encounter throughout our lives. As early as 1999, Tsui described critical thinking skills as "essential to safeguarding a democratic society . . . in an increasingly complex world" (p. 185). Not surprisingly, critical thinking also falls within the Intellectual and Practical Skills category of the essential learning outcomes identified by AAC&U's LEAP initiative (Kuh, 2008). So, with growing appreciation of its importance, what does critical thinking actually involve?

To begin with, we find Paul and Elder's (2008) definition of critical thinking particularly clear and accessible, explaining that it is "the art of analyzing and evaluating thinking with a view to improving it" (p. 2). Beyond this, they note universal intellectual standards and essential intellectual traits that mark the critical thinker: integrity, humility, confidence in reason, perseverance, fair-mindedness, courage, empathy, and autonomy. How wonderful it would be if such intellectual traits could be universally realized. Paul and Elder argue that this is possible, but that intellectual standards and traits must be explicitly taught in order for them to "become infused in the thinking of students, forming part of their inner voice and guiding them to reason better" (p. 8).

Such teaching begins by pushing against the natural tendency toward egocentrism, considering instead the needs of others and reconsidering long-held but possibly inaccurate assumptions. This asks the learner to question her/his own personal reference points and potential biases and begin to realize that there are many truths and perspectives that need to be taken into account throughout life. The need to think critically (and empathically) becomes even more pressing during international travel as students encounter belief systems and ways of living, or life texts, that may be altogether new to them. As they engage in reflective examination of what they are feeling, and consider the question, "Why am I feeling this way?" they need to be taught how to realize what these new texts are grounded in—principally the perspectives and experiences of the people who created them.

While research on the pedagogical approaches that encourage critical thinking has not been applied directly to faculty-led field study, strategies commonly used in this arena do involve the basic tenets of critical thinking. Courses that promote critical thinking are marked by emphasis on problem solving and search for meaning through reading (also described as inquiry-based learning), writing, active participation, instructor encouragement, and peer-to-peer interaction (Gibson, 1985; Kaplan & Kies, 1994). Add to this the need to question the texts (both written and lived) and the perspectives of the authors creating them, and it is easy to see how all of these approaches are a natural fit for faculty-led study abroad programs.

With thoughtful faculty guidance, forwarding the intellectual traits that mark critical thinking and infusing the related strategies into international study can help realize Freire's (1974) worthy educational goal of conscientization or *conscientização*—self-reflective awareness of difference and privilege. While such a goal might hold particular relevance for U.S. students traveling in developing countries, we believe that considering its applicability within their own country is also critical. But before such consciousness can happen, students need to take the time to apply their critical thinking skills to their own lives and to their developing individual identities.

The Many Faces of Me: Self-Awareness

Viewing self-awareness as nested within the broader (and more broadly researched) business of identity formation offers a way to examine the two concepts concurrently. We find such work to be particularly important as self-awareness and consideration of one's cultural identity have become frequently targeted learning outcomes of study-abroad programs.

Identity formation is commonly viewed as an ongoing process that starts, as Erikson (1959) described, with the adolescent drive toward creating a sense of self marked by both unity and purpose while attempting to integrate the various aspects of the self. More recently, the *study of lives* or narrative tradition discusses identity in a somewhat different light, viewing identity as being multiple rather than a singular aspect of self that can be consistently integrated or unified (Raggatt, 2002). While not negating earlier views of identity formation, the narrative tradition suggests that viewing identity in this way, even accepting that some identities (or life stories) are likely to be in conflict with each other, can help people come to terms with the many positions they are required to take within their lives. As Raggatt explains, "In some places the view is clear, and your life makes sense to you. In other places, perhaps, stories make no sense at all" (p. 291). We have found that appreciating the natural drive to unify one's identity while simultaneously accepting its multiplicity offers faculty members a healthy platform for addressing issues related to self-awareness and cultural identity norms with their students during study abroad.

There are a number of instances in life that cause us to pause and consider ourselves in light of what is happening around us—times that make us aware of our identities within a given situation. Oftentimes such instances are triggered by feelings of uncertainty and heightened emotion, by a change in the people we are interacting with and/or the ground (both figuratively and literally) we are standing on. This is certainly the case during international study, but it can also occur at many other life junctures.

Perhaps we have moved to a new town or left home to attend summer camp for a few weeks. More monumentally, perhaps we have gone to college in another part of the country and won't be returning home for months on end. At these times, it is natural to fall back on what we have learned over the years, the identities we have carried with us from our family culture and history, from our home and community upbringing as well as from our personal store of known responses. It is easy to understand how international field study can fall within the category of such starkly new experiences and would thereby be a time ripe not only for heightened self-awareness but also ripe for growth in this area—for considering the multiple identities or "stories" that we embody simultaneously.

With this thought in mind, Dolby (2004) argues that study abroad offers an unparalleled opportunity for students to not only encounter the world but also to encounter themselves. This is particularly the case, Dolby adds, when they consider their own national identity—what it means to be a citizen of the United States (the state) as well as a citizen of America (the nation)—realizing, perhaps, that these identities are perceived somewhat differently. There is the United States as a global political entity and America as a democratic dream. Such examination of what it means to be an American when studying overseas can result in students questioning previously held assumptions and may result in new formulations of "self." Along this line, Bile and Lindley (2009) build on the work of Petras (2000), arguing that study-abroad programs should be designed to "allow students to challenge official views of people and places, develop more nuanced and critical understanding, and gain an appreciation of a plurality of views and interests" (p. 152). This might include closely examining multiple views of their own country for the first time as well as considering their roles not only within the United States (their national identities) but also their roles beyond U.S. borders (their global identities).

Research into self-awareness, cultural identity, and study abroad offers an interesting portrait of what U.S. students bring into the experience as well as what they may bring out of it, if carefully guided along the way. As Zamastil-Vondrova (2005) discovered through her study of short-term faculty-led field programs, when students are invited to reflect upon what it means to be an American, they tend to feel that Americans lack linguistic and cross-cultural skills, are materialistic, and are too demonstrative about America's status in the world. On a more hopeful note, she also states that short-term faculty-led programs encourage students to examine their own individual strengths and weaknesses and can help them build confidence regarding what it means to become better global citizens. Lewin (2009), too, calls for the need to encourage civic engagement and a sense of wider (global) citizenship within U.S. students, whose primary expectations for travel are oftentimes "adventure and general pleasure seeking" (p. 9). Such a self-involved initial mindset is understandable and not to be held against students. Instead, we believe it offers a realistic starting point upon which faculty can build program curriculum and learning opportunities.

To move students forward in terms of both self-awareness and commitment to civic engagement as citizens of the world, there are a number of useful intercultural frameworks that detail the steps involved in the process. One of the first and most widely used frameworks is the Developmental Model of Intercultural Sensitivity (DMIS) created by Bennett in 1986. The 6-staged DMIS rests on the supposition that understanding of cultural difference is a developmental process that becomes more advanced through direct experience with cultures other than one's own. The overarching concept of *ethnocentrism*, the view that one's own culture is central to all reality, marks the first three stages of the DMIS: denial, defense, and minimization (the belief that there is no real difference in cultures—"we're all human"). *Ethnorelativism*, or the appreciation of one's own culture in the context of many other cultures, marks the final three DMIS stages: acceptance, adaptation, and integration (the ability to move nimbly among different cultural worldviews). Taking time to review their own development through these stages—before departure, while in the field, and upon returning home—can offer students and faculty a firm and nonjudgmental basis for examining their own growth.

Another productive means for examining cultural identity formation and self-awareness is the global perspective model originally developed by Chickering and Reisser (1993) and further contextualized by Chickering and Braskamp (2009). Grounded in psychosocial development theory, this model identifies four vectors involved in developing and internalizing a global perspective among traditional college-aged students. The vectors include moving through autonomy toward interdependence, establishing identity, developing purpose, and managing emotions. In this case, the vectors are not necessarily linear with one building upon the next. Instead, they are reflexive, involving ongoing development between and among the categories. Consider, for example, the need to manage emotions as identities are considered, adapted, and eventually reestablished in a more encompassing way during study abroad.

In his discussion of teaching for citizenship in a global world, Banks (2004) offers faculty yet another means for exploring cultural identity formation with students participating in faculty-led study abroad. Banks explains that developing a global identity comes after attempting to deeply understand one's own identity. "Citizenship education should help students to develop thoughtful and clarified identifications with their cultural communities, nation-states, and the global community" (p. 296). Banks offers a cultural identity typology that, like Bennett's, includes six stages. Banks' typology begins with *cultural psychological captivity*, in which an individual is caught-up in negative beliefs about his or her own cultural group, and culminates with *globalism and global competency*, which Banks describes as "individuals who have the ability to function effectively in their own culture and in other cultures," and when they reach this stage, they "have a commitment to all human beings in the world community" (p. 297). As with the Bennett model, the goal is to attain a level of ease and comfort moving within and across a variety of cultures. This is essential to what might be described as the development of a global identity: the realization that one's identity can be far larger than what it was originally perceived it to be.

Ultimately, it may prove useful to consider the process of global identity formation in what Antal and Friedman (2008) describe as "negotiating reality"; from reflection to critical analysis to self-awareness, it is a process that "frames intercultural competence in terms of an active, reflective social construction of reality" (p. 364). We would add that it might also be marked by reflective appreciation of one's multiple roles within the world.

I Can Make a Difference: Self-Efficacy

The growth that students experience when they successfully take on the internal work of reflection, critical thinking, and self-awareness during international field study has been sometimes described as "transformative." But what does such transformation produce in the long run? Is it simply that students better understand themselves and their roles within the world? Certainly, this is important. But equally important is how (and if) they feel empowered to act differently, to contribute differently, and in a more informed manner based on this "transformative" learning. These are among the core principles underlying the concept of self-efficacy put forth by Bandura (1986): "self-efficacy does not refer to one's actual capabilities, but to one's belief in one's capabilities" (p. 3). When a sense of self-efficacy is awakened, students begin to take on tasks that can change existing social conditions for the better. Bandura uses the concept of human agency to describe what is occurring—that people who believe they can make a difference will act upon this belief, even in the face of weighty obstacles. Others, who may have more actual power to make a difference will do less if their sense of self-efficacy has not been realized.

Fortunately, the many challenges students face and must understand and overcome during international field study lead to internal growth and subsequent self-efficacy (Adler, 1987; Milstein, 2005). As Adler explains in his discussion of culture shock, ultimately it is "an experience of self-understanding and change" (1987, p. 29) that occurs; an experience that leads to greater intercultural appreciation and greater personal appreciation too. As students successfully negotiate their new and sometimes challenging international surroundings, their sense of internal empowerment and capability grows. It is easy to see how Banks' (2004) definition of citizenship education during international study encompasses self-efficacy: "It also should enable them to acquire the knowledge, attitudes, and skills needed to act to make the nation and the world more democratic and just" (p. 296). When this occurs—when students take newfound appreciation of their roles in the world into responsible actions—the international study experience can in fact become transformative.

Appreciating the Change

Faculty-led international study offers students a unique opportunity to become more reflective, to think critically, and to become more aware of themselves as global citizens who have both the ability and the responsibility to contribute to the greater common good. The extent to which such goals are realized certainly rests with students; but it also rests with faculty who must make best use of the learning opportunities international study affords. To this end, we believe it is vital to encourage reflection as often as possible, whether it comes naturally to students or not, and to talk with them about what stopping to process their experiences can do for them. It is important to set aside ample time for this work; to provide prompts that encourage deep and critical examination of international experiences, particularly those that prove challenging and involve emotional responses. Keeping in mind Caine and Caine's (1997) point that the brain is social, it is imperative to let them do this work together in an environment of non-judgmental acceptance.

Beyond this, faculty must encourage students to examine their histories and cultural identities through an appreciative but also critical lens—to understand how their own identities have been formed thus far and how those identities have become more expansive based on reflective practice when encountering other cultures. And finally, faculty must put the business of self-efficacy squarely on the table by asking students directly how they are feeling about their own potential to make a difference in the world around them. What will they do to put such feelings into actions? What might their personal legacy involve?

The potential for far-reaching academic and personal growth during faculty-led international field study is substantial. With support and ongoing guidance from dedicated faculty, the words of Özturgut (2007) can certainly apply:

> Students who participate in study abroad programs come back as different people with different perspectives and most importantly with a greater empathy toward other nations. There is a significant change in their commitment to peace by living in and observing other cultures. (p. 43)

4

Promoting Global Citizenship

I am not a citizen of Athens, or Greece, but of the World.
—Socrates

TRAVEL TALE 4: Kim's Journey
• •

From the outset, one of our primary goals for the Global Engagement course to Belize was clear—our students would develop a sense of global citizenship. We were feeling enthusiastic about the journey ahead and particularly about realizing this important course goal. But when we first met with the interdisciplinary group of Honors students enrolled in the course, there were quite a few who were feeling a good bit less enthusiastic than we were. Some looked at the course as yet another Honors' requirement and not necessarily pertinent to their particular discipline; others were concerned about the costs involved. Kim, a biology major and a leader within the group, was markedly less than thrilled about what lay ahead. When we finally arrived on Caye Caulker and realized the extremely primitive level of accommodations we would be sharing with

---

Fostering Global Citizenship Through Faculty-Led International Programs, pages 39–54
Copyright © 2012 by Information Age Publishing
All rights of reproduction in any form reserved.

39

our students (and a rich mix of vagabond/travelers) for 8 days and nights, Kim (along with others in our group) was even less keen on the venture. Quite honestly, we had our doubts at this point as well. In fact, maintaining positive attitudes seemed a more likely goal than global citizenship.

We had read and talked about intercultural competence and culture shock and global citizenship and the many related scales, descriptors, reviews, and ratings of the international experience. We had prepared our students, to the extent faculty can accomplish such a task, for what they were likely to feel as they moved into the new, and possibly uncomfortable and challenging, international environment of Caye Caulker. This was not going to be a tourist experience; we understood that in advance. But where we were staying, a hostel that was even more basic than we had anticipated (with alligators creeping onshore each night, shared toilets that rarely worked, cold saltwater showers, bedding that was disturbingly alive, and no locks on anything, anywhere) reinforced the initial reluctance of Kim and many of the other students as well.

It wasn't until we met our in-country environmental educator Ms. Ellen, a 60-something ex-patriot who had been living on Caye Caulker with her Belizean husband and grown sons for over 20 years, that Kim (and all of us) began to look beyond our physical discomfort to the function and purpose of the course. We were there to help preserve a marine reserve; to clean buoys around the coral reef; to learn directly from Belizeans (residents both by birth and by choice) about the environmental, human-generated threats to island and the reef. Viewing Ms. Ellen's impassioned slideshows of the delicate and varied marine inhabitants of the coral reef and the many threats they were facing began to register deeply with Kim, and with all of us. Subsequently, it was Kim who felt most outraged when we witnessed the careless treatment of the fragile reef during our snorkeling tour—the story we share in Travel Tale 6. It was Kim who rallied her classmates to respond to the situation. As a leader within our group, Kim's growing consciousness of her potential impact on our host country, her ensuing journal writings, in-field actions, and eventual final course project helped to engender a sense of global responsibility within the entire cohort.

No, it was not global citizenship fully realized; it was one young person's first steps into the continuing process.

•••••••••••••••••••••

Emerging Global Citizens

Socrates spoke to his youthful followers about citizenship 2,000 (plus) years ago. His point, that citizens must extend their sense of allegiance and care beyond the confines of their home communities to encompass the needs of humankind, underlies the concept of global citizenship that many institutes of higher education are actively pursuing today. Study abroad has been targeted as one means to promote such citizenship. In fact, as we explained in Chapter 1, study abroad continues to be regarded as one of the most effective diplomatic tools for our country—a means to create citizens who are willing and able to begin addressing environmental, social, and economic challenges present in the world. As such, it is a priority of the collective and something that institutes of higher education cannot view as an optional goal but must view instead as a necessity. As we have explained, short-term faculty-led programs are one of the most feasible means for moving toward this goal.

We do not pretend that, after participating in a faculty-led international course, students will be able to proclaim that they have achieved global citizenship and can now move on to their next goal. We *do* argue that faculty-led study-abroad programs, when intentionally designed and delivered, provide a critical opportunity for students to begin exploring their roles in the world—an important first step that may lead to others. Even more so, we argue that faculty-led study-abroad programs may be one of the best entry points for student development in this arena. Through carefully selected and structured readings, discussions, and activities, faculty can lead their students into frank internal and external dialogue about what it means to be a global citizen and what form it may take for each of them. To begin such work, it helps to consider the multidisciplinary, multicultural nature of the concept and how it has developed over time.

Any review of the concept of global citizenship quickly reveals both its complexity and the variety of definitions that have been applied to it. We therefore begin this chapter by exploring the contemporary theoretical discourse on global citizenship before moving on to examine how it can be furthered in faculty-led study-abroad programs. The intent of this chapter is not to provide an exhaustive analysis of the robust discourse surrounding global citizenship, but rather to highlight key ideas, concepts, and models that should be considered by faculty who hope to further global citizenship within their study-abroad programs.

Global Citzenship: A Fundamental but Nebulous Concept

As we have noted, the concept of global citizenship is not new. In fact, the general notion of it emerged early and often, in both intellectual and political arenas, and has experienced waves of escalated attention over the years. Dating back to ancient Greece, the term *cosmopolitan* first captured the general philosophy of what we describe as global citizenship today. Early advocates of *cosmopolitanism,* including Socrates and Diogenes, called for all people to extend their sense of ethical responsibility past their limited local jurisdictions outward—to the universe and to all of humanity (Appiah, 2006). Beginning with these early philosophers and moving forward to the writings of Thomas Paine, Immanuel Kant, and such current theorists as Martha Nussbaum, prominent thinkers have argued for practicing what we currently describe as global citizenship. Not surprisingly, fateful world events have oftentimes triggered such arguments.

The most recent call for cosmopolitanism or global citizenship began in the early 1990s as the world witnessed the tearing down of the Berlin Wall, the consequent opening of the Eastern Bloc countries, and the dissolution of the Soviet Union (Schattle, 2009). In the two decades that followed, a series of events brought further attention to the concept. These included (but were not limited to) 9/11 and increased worldwide focus on the threat of terrorism, greater global economic interdependence, and advancements in technologies that connected the world's populace in unprecedented ways. As the world's citizenry witnessed and experienced such trends and events, the need to develop a more "cosmopolitan" human bearing became increasingly evident and was subsequently targeted by institutes of higher education as a critical goal.

Contemporary versions of the term *global citizenship,* while wide-ranging, most often involve extending an individual's civic awareness of, responsibility to, and engagement in the global arena. However, review of the discourse reveals no consensus on defining the concept or on the approach needed to support individuals in becoming global citizens. There *is* consensus that today's citizens are living in a diverse and globally interconnected world (economically, socially, environmentally, politically), and that it is therefore imperative for institutes of higher education to move decisively forward with plans to design a curriculum that supports students in succeeding in this globalized environment.

In large part, this explains higher education's growing commitment to internationalization and to fostering global citizens among its graduates. To this end, Collins (2009) highlights three worldwide phenomena today's students will face that reinforce the need for colleges and universities to emphasize internationalization and global citizenship in their curricula. First, our students will have continuous and numerous encounters among and between cultures. Second, cultural interrelationships are complex, with impacts that are both positive and negative. Third, as we have moved beyond being predominantly an industrial economy, the cognitive skills required of today's graduates will include methical approaches to inquiry, understanding, and expression—skills needed in our current, information-based economy. So, how does the quest for global citizenship fit with and address the demands, perspectives, and skills Collins highlights? Specifically, how can relatively short-term faculty-led international programs move our students forward as global citizens? Consideration of the current discourse on global citizenship offers an initial means for answering these questions.

Upon review, it is readily evident that global citizenship has great appeal as a concept. It is acknowledged and sought after by institutions in the United States and around the world, but it is also exceptionally nebulous to define, practice, and/or apply. Unfortunately, more questions than definitive answers surface when attempting to demarcate what global citizenship actually looks like. For example, what distinguishes someone as a global citizen? Is there a specific set of beliefs and values that are embodied by such a person? Must individuals have direct and continuing international experiences to be deemed global citizens, or are we all global citizens by our very existence? Does this concept only refer to conscientious global stewards? What attitudes and actions count as indicators of global citizenship? And finally, is the concept of global citizenship too broad or vague to be useful in 21st-century efforts to foster a greater/global common good? To respond to this second set of questions, it is helpful to analyze current definitions of the concept of global citizenship while keeping in mind Stromquist's (2009) cautionary point that conceptualizing global citizenship as an extension of one's national citizenship to a transnational level is just too simple. In truth, Stromquist adds, when you look more deeply at this concept, it will lead you to a "complex, multidimensional world, with varying definitions and many interests at cross-purposes" (p. 6).

A frequently referenced definition of global citizenship from the Association of American Colleges and Universities (AAC&U) stresses knowledge and understanding of global places, cultures, and issues. The AAC&U definition calls for helping students to develop a more sophisticated understanding of the increasingly interconnected and interdependent world, including its complexities, inequalities, and conflicts both at home and abroad (AAC&U, 2002). In emphasizing acquisition of knowledge and awareness, the AAC&U definition focuses on the overall goals of global education: investigating issues and problems that are not bounded by state borders and forwarding the conviction that it is important to know, understand, and appreciate our global neighbors and their cultures. Such knowledge and appreciation, the AAC&U definition adds, must include the struggles and perspectives we share with our global neighbors as well as those that set us apart. Representing values steadfast within U.S. higher education, the AAC&U definition rests on knowledge acquisition, arguing that in order for our students to meet the challenges and opportunities they are sure to face, they must first understand the world, its people, and its complexities.

The nongovernmental organization (NGO) Oxfam International (2006), known for its enduring promotion of global citizenship, organizes their definition of the concept around the development of knowledge, attitudes, and skills—the categories educators frequently use as a basis for assessment. For Oxfam, growth in *knowledge* targets global interdependence and social injustice. Growth in *attitudes* and *values* focuses on empathy for others and respect for diversity. Development of *skills* concentrates on critical thinking and conflict resolution. The Oxfam definition goes on to discuss global citizens as those having an awareness of the wider world, how it operates, and a sense of their own role within it. Oxfam further states that a global citizen is one who respects and values the multitude of cultures in the world, is opposed (in action and thought) to social injustice, and is willing to act to counter inequity. As an international organization committed to reducing poverty and injustice, it is not surprising that Oxfam's emphasis centers on human rights and the elements that must be fostered to secure greater social justice in the world. Oxfam is not alone in this emphasis; the theme of human rights, egalitarian ideals, and promoting the general welfare of others is a strong component of a number of attempts to define global citizenship (Ladson-Billings, 2005).

A related entry point into the discussion and defining of global citizenship involves awareness of self and awareness of others. McIntosh (2005), for example, notes global citizenship as the ability to see oneself in relation to one's role in the wider world. She highlights the need to balance awareness of one's own realities with the realities of those outside of the perceived self. This individual dimension, which focuses on gaining a reflective understanding and empathy for others, McIntosh argues, is a starting point for becoming a global citizen. Others join McIntosh in her assertions. Emphasis on perception of self in light of perceptions of others is a theme running through many definitions of global citizenship.

Another theme within global citizenship discourse centers on the need for a sense of shared membership and shared global values. From this perspective, it is our shared common fate on the planet that should, and at times *does*, pull us together. Arneil (2007) cautions that the problem with anchoring global citizenship in shared values is that the chosen values are likely to be those articulated by dominant Western cultures. Arneil explains that this can lead to further erosion of global cultural diversity and could even be considered a form of imperialism—as the West imposing its own values on non-Western peoples. Still, shared global values and fate, despite concerns around identifying whose values and whose fate, have shaped a number of definitions of global citizenship.

Joining the discussion from another angle, Lagos (2002) notes that because global citizenship does not impart a legal status, it is best understood and expressed associatively, in a distinctly different manner from expressions of state citizenship. He explains that "global citizenship remains the purview of individuals to live, work and play within trans-national norms that defy national boundaries and sovereignty" (p. 4). Thus, his definition brings us back to focus on the individual dimension of the term. Reinforcing the importance of the individual dimension, Stromquist (2009) also highlights the grassroots or bottom-up movement associated with the concept of global citizenship. Without legal political status or recognition—or for that matter, cultural, ethnic, religious or linguistics commonalities— one's efforts to become a global citizen are voluntary and thus based on fluctuating and subjective criteria.

A number of the remaining definitions focus more on individuals' personal involvement and highlight the various roles that individuals assume in the international arena. Falk (1994), for example, puts forth five distinct types of global citizenship based on the position or role an individual may play in the world. These include global reformers who attempt to move us toward "one world"; elite global business people who seek to move their economic ventures around the globe without global civic responsibility; global environmental managers who attempt to forge international problem-solving collaborations to tackle large global concerns; politically conscious regionalists who seek a new political community; and finally, transnational activists who take up global causes such as human rights and environmental protection. Unfortunately, focusing only on such roles raises the question of whether this contemporary interpretation of global citizenship is confined to the economically privileged. If global participation is required, then we must remind ourselves that the world is full of those who are not able to embrace direct participation in global discourse and action because they live in poverty and are struggling simply to survive. Thus, the focus on participation alone comes at the exclusion of a great many of the world's people.

Global Citizenship: A Framework for Faculty-Led International Programs

While noting that numerous individuals and organizations have proposed dynamic definitions of global citizenship, we feel that Schattle (2008) offers a useful starting point for not only understanding contemporary meanings of the concept but also addressing how it can be enacted through a faculty-led international program. In his text *The Practices of Global Citizenship*, Schattle proposes conceptual categories that integrate current definitions of global citizenship. These categories emerged from his interviews with over 150 self-identified global citizens and advocates of global citizenship from a variety of fields. Schattle states that the three primary conceptual categories within global citizenship are *awareness, responsibility*, and *participation*. In expanding upon *awareness*, he highlights the importance of both self-awareness and awareness of the larger world, noting that the former can be considered a foundational step for developing the latter. Awareness, in turn, can lead to realizing one's *responsibilities* and moral obligations to humanity beyond one's immediate known sphere. Eventually, this awareness-based sense of responsibility may well result in *participation*—civic engagement that promotes the global common good.

Schattle's 3-pronged framework (2008) offers a structured way to approach global citizenship that is very useful for operationalizing the term within faculty-led international programs. As we examined Schattle's primary categories and considered what we know to be true, both from our own experiences and the experiences of others, we quickly realized that *awareness* is the most realistic and attainable category to target during short-term programs. The other categories, *responsibility* and *participation*, are certainly equally (if not more) important, but the process of realizing global citizenship, to whatever degree and in whatever form, is developmental—beginning and ultimately resting upon increased awareness.

Awareness

Fully actualized global citizenship implies having a personal identity that transcends national boundaries and borders and is committed to the common good. As noted earlier, Stromquist (2009) found such a broad definition to be admirable but overly simplistic. We would add that, as Maslow (1954) discussed decades ago, actualization is not a constant state—something to be attained and then comfortably enjoyed. Instead, it is a developmental process that requires both internal and external work marked by ongoing reflection on how that "work" is actually working. This would include the need to understand and accommodate inevitable slips from the idealized state of being a global citizen (by whatever definition)—to be fully *aware*, instead, of the progress one is making toward such a goal and the areas in need of further development. Productive awareness, then, is the more attainable goal in the study-abroad arena. Such an awareness must be both candid and forgiving, resting on the ability to be keenly mindful of the motivations, needs, and history of the self, and equally mindful of the possible differences in motivations, needs, and history of the Other, thus encouraging an elemental human connection that crosses societally constructed differences.

Awareness of Self

As discussed in Chapter 3, before developing awareness of and knowledge about different peoples and places, it is critical for students to develop awareness and knowledge of themselves; specifically, how family, cultural history, and societal customs have contributed to their thinking, beliefs, and commitments. Such awareness is part of the larger work of identity formation, a natural human process that occurs, in one form or another, throughout our lives. According to Erikson (1959), the process begins in earnest and is most intense during adolescence (approximately ages 12–25), encompassing the age range of many of our undergraduate travelers and therefore a promising time for promoting enhanced self-awareness through international study. As students naturally explore facets of their evolving personal identities, faculty can invite them to simultaneously consider these identities in both national and international contexts. Indeed, Dolby (2004) argues that study abroad offers an unparalleled opportunity for students to encounter the world and to at the same time encounter themselves.

Encouraging awareness of self as a precursor to international study invites students to critically examine not only their personal identities but also what it means to be an American and to acknowledge (and in some cases work against) a U.S.-centered view of the world. Examining the concept of ethnocentrism as well as the biases and worldviews that are embedded in every culture can be a productive pre-travel experience that can lead to heightened awareness of self in the broader/global context. A study by Zamastil-Vondrova (2005), in which students reflected on what it means to be an American after completing a short-term study-abroad experience, found that short-term faculty-led programs help students examine their own individual strengths and weaknesses as they simultaneously build self-confidence and reflect on what it means to be better global citizens.

Banks' (2008) discussion of citizenship education adds to this argument as he calls for faculty to "help students to develop thoughtful and clarified identifications with their cultural communities, nation-states, and the global community" (p. 296). Banks goes on to posit that reflective examination of one's cultural identity and national identity can lead to the ability to appreciate one's global identity. Such work is essential to what might be described as the development of a global *citizen* identity, an identity that questions, "Who am I, who are others, and how do I responsibly relate and interact?" Because there are no global political structures that outline criteria for membership or *grant* this form of citizenship—global citizenship—to a large part, may be perceived as a constructed identity, one that people must intentionally seek out and define for themselves.

Awareness of Other

There is little dispute that global citizenship involves individuals' extended awareness, from their immediate *known* world to the wider *unknown* world, which holds cultures, perspectives, values, and ways of being different from their own. Fundamentally, global citizenship requires a basic knowledge about and understanding of this wider world. However, despite the indisputable increase in global connectedness and consequent agreement of the need for awareness of the wider world, we hear regularly and repeatedly that very few U.S. students have either basic global awareness *or* much in the way of background knowledge of locations beyond U.S. borders. A 2006 National Geographic Education Foundation and Roper Public Affairs Report released a sad story regarding geographic literacy and young Americans ages 18–24. This study found that the majority of young Americans are culturally illiterate, having little to no understanding of places, religions, and peoples outside of the United States (and in some cases, within the U.S. as well). The study also uncovered limited skills such as map reading that would help students improve their geographic knowledge. It seems ironic that at a time when young Americans can read a *tweet* from individuals in Afghanistan and *friend* someone in Indonesia, they may still not know where those counties lie or the general cultural and physical landscapes found in them.

The more recent Nation's Report Card for Geography, conducted as part of the National Assessment of Education Program, offers equally concerning findings. The geography assessment tested 4th-, 8th-, and 12th-grade students' knowledge in three content areas: Space and Place; Environment and Society; and Spatial Dynamics and Connections. For each of the grades tested, only 22% of students were considered proficient in knowing, understanding, and applying geographical knowledge (NEAP, 2011). Thus we can assume that a relatively high percentage of incoming college students will have a weak knowledge of global places and cultures, posing a real challenge for faculty planning to take students into international field study with an objective of developing global citizenship. Perhaps the most realistic first step in this circumstance is acknowledging the problem. From there, determining a means for addressing it must be a collective and interdisciplinary effort that would likely fall under the institutional heading of global education.

One of the most common institutional goals for global education is for students to gain an awareness of other cultures and countries. In fact, Carlsson-Paige and Lantieri (2005) assert that global awareness is *required* in order to claim to be a citizen of the world. Clearly, the findings discussed above indicate that our college students for the most part lack such awareness. Acknowledging this, the faculty-led international experience can offer a natural means for widening students' cultural knowledge base and for fostering their awareness of others.

Our students are not the only ones who can be called to task regarding ongoing awareness of others. At times, we all need direct experiences, such as those offered by an international study program, to make our awareness of others, their cultures, and societal realities salient to us. An international program with a faculty member guiding what students are experiencing may be one of the best ways to begin to develop the awareness needed to form a global citizen identity for students as well as faculty. In their study of undergraduates' perceptions of their global citizen identity development, part of the Global Citizenship Program at Lehigh University, Hendershot and Sperandio (2009) reported that the majority of the students identified the experiences with other cultures and places gained through the faculty-led international travel program as having been the most impactful in their development of a global citizen identity. We would add that teaching international programs has refocused our attention on what global citizenship entails.

We do not propose that one must have an international experience to gain awareness of others. Nor, as previously mentioned, do we think that one international experience is enough to develop a wide-ranging global citizen identity. We do argue that faculty-led international programs, if intentionally structured to do so, provide the opportunities that nurture the knowledge, skills, and attitudes necessary for students to address their lack of awareness of others and foster their commitment to further global education opportunities. *This* can lead to their becoming more effective world citizens. Giving the students the opportunity to directly experience other peoples and places and providing an environment that allows them to process those experiences can be one of the most impactful ways for constructing positive views and knowledge around the awareness of others.

Findings from the GLOSSARI Project, a University of Georgia system-wide initiative to examine and document the effects of all types of study abroad (including faculty-led programs) on student learning outcomes, had a number of notable findings regarding awareness of others. The study compared various learning outcomes between students who had completed a study-abroad program and those who had not. Global educational outcomes such as functional knowledge of cultural practices (e.g., *knows how to compare and contrast cultures*); knowledge of intercultural accommodation (e.g., *knows the importance of patience in communicating with other people from other nations*); and knowledge of cultural context (e.g., *understands the significance of language and cultural differences*) were significantly higher among students who had completed a study-abroad program (Sutton & Rubin, 2010). An unfortunate finding of the GLOSSARI Project was that both groups experienced a decline in knowledge of world geography over time, and there was no significant difference between veterans of study abroad and their peers who stayed home. These findings suggest that we face an uphill battle in helping our students acquire and retain the key geographic knowledge that can help them gain lasting awareness of other peoples and places. It also suggests that those involved in international programs may need to put greater emphasis on enhancing students' basic geographic literacy skills. But despite this last finding, the overall results from this lengthy study, which took place between 1999 and 2010, clearly demonstrated significant positive "awareness of other" effects on participants of study abroad.

A starting point for awareness of others can often occur with realization of what we *don't* know and in some cases, what others *do* know. During study-abroad programs, students routinely note their own lack of knowledge and understanding of the places they are visiting. They also speak of being humbled by the discovery that people in their host country know quite a bit about U.S. culture and geography. Such an awareness of their own limited knowledge and simultaneous awareness that others know quite a bit more can be transformative for U.S. students as they register, perhaps for the first time, feelings of academic inferiority. In an international program led by faculty, guidance and structured reflective practice can help students make sense of feelings like this and maximize their learning potential.

In addition to helping students come to terms with what they don't know about others, faculty leading study-abroad programs have both an opportunity and a responsibility to help their students critically analyze the controversial topic of globalization. From an economic standpoint, globalization implies an increasingly unfettered global economy marked by free trade, free flows of capital, and access to cheaper labor abroad. From a social standpoint, it has also come to be thought of as an unfolding force that is creating more cultural integration and interdependence around the globe. In *The Power of Place*, geographer Harm de Blij (2009) points out that globalization defies brief definition and is often best understood with a qualifier such as economic globalization, cultural globalization, or political globalization. While an in-depth discussion of globalization is beyond the scope of this text, we maintain that today any discourse relating to global citizenship cannot sidestep at least a cursory exploration of this force within the context of awareness of others. Biles and Lindley (2009) argue that while globalization has been used to justify the importance of study abroad, its process ostensibly aims to eliminate differences and thus local culture; while the practice of overseas study and thus the promotion of global citizenship seeks to promote the appreciation of these differences. Thus study abroad and globalization may, wittingly or not, have opposite goals.

Globalization can be seen from many perspectives—some positive, some negative. Discussion of this concept in a faculty-led international course thus enters into the uncomfortable territory of exploring our own role in supporting forces that perpetuate and reinforce inequalities and environmental destruction around the world, both in our daily lives and in our overseas study. We believe that faculty leaders must join their students in considering that international programs are not always positive or even neutral activities, especially for the host communities. Our very ability to travel and study in remote locations with cultures of lower income, education, and mobility requires us to consider the social, political, and environmental implications involved—in effect, the global impact(s) of our coursework. These considerations, in turn, should be a topic critically considered by students who are privileged to be participating in an international program.

Responsibility

Awareness and knowledge acquisition of self and others are important starting points for a developing global citizen; however, we agree with Sperandio, Grudzinski-Hall, and Stewart-Gambino (2010), who argue that it is not enough to simply be aware of ourselves and the wider world. We must next begin to acknowledge our roles and *responsibilities* within this context. For example, after noting the negative impacts of globalization, what is our responsibility to those *others* of whom we now have more awareness? Directly related to this is consideration of what actually takes place within an international program. Hovey and Weinberg (2009) note that study abroad can be either an extractive enterprise, taking advantage of partners and communities overseas for our program's benefit, or reciprocal ventures in which both overseas partners and our programs gain. Whether programs are reciprocal endeavors and thus geared toward an acknowledgment of the responsibility to act as good global citizens, falls to the faculty leaders. Stephenson (2006) calls for faculty to adhere to a study-abroad model that features community enhancement, inclusiveness, alternative visions, sustainability, diversity, and peace promotion. And just as faculty must elevate their intentions and actions, so too must students be mindful of their responsibilities to the host country and its inhabitants.

After determining what needs to be done, faculty must then bring their goals to fruition. One approach for encouraging a sense of responsibility within student travelers is to engage their moral and civic values, challenging them to define and adopt a global ethic which recognizes that all people, around the globe, have shared responsibilities for each other. It is one thing to study overseas and afterwards profess a feeling of responsibility toward others, but it is quite another to begin to demonstrate this new ethic in daily practice. And what might such a new ethic look like anyway, given that it is more of an internal process than an external achievement?

Deardoff's (2006) Process Model of Intercultural Competence might be used as a means for opening discussion with student participants on the topic of developing global responsibility. Much like global citizenship, intercultural competence is a term that is frequently mentioned but not easily defined. The basic premise is that an individual who has intercultural competence displays the ability to interact appropriately and effectively with individuals from differing cultures (Deardorff, 2009). Deardorff explains how such an ability comes about through a process that flows from internal recognition and processing to external outcomes marked by the ability to be open, curious, and willing to suspend judgment regarding the beliefs, values, and behaviors of others. Essentially, it calls for students to accept that their way is not the only way, nor is it necessarily the best or the right way. So too does it call for students to commit to developing attitudes and building skills necessary for continuing their cross-cultural growth—arguably one way to demonstrate their growing sense of responsibility.

Involvement

Through awareness of self and others, students may come to recognize the importance of activism as a one of the responsibilities of a global citizen. It is up to faculty to help students move toward a sense of self-efficacy and empowerment in this area so that they may begin to willingly engage in practices that personify individuals who are both informed about, feel a sense of responsibility for, and finally are directly involved in positive global action. This is the part of global citizenship that begs the question, "What have we done for the world and its people lately?" Undeniably, it is global participation, not merely global knowledge, that has captured the excitement of students and faculty in higher education.

Paige, Fry, Stallman, Josic, and Jon (2009) explain that global engagement as conceptualized by the SAGE project in part involves civic commitments in domestic and international arenas. Furthermore, their research reports that alumni of study abroad note that the experience significantly influenced their continued civic involvement, philanthropic endeavors, social entrepreneurship, and commitment to living more sustainably (i.e., practicing voluntary simplicity). They also found no significant difference in reported global engagement between those students who participated in a short-term study-abroad experience and those who studied abroad for a longer period. Thus, again, short-duration international study does not mean short lasting impact.

As faculty-led international courses have been viewed as a gateway experience for students seeking out longer study-abroad experiences, they too can be considered a gateway experience for students seeking to become more engaged in the global community, an inarguable characteristic of global citizenship. Hovey and Weinberg (2009) state that "as students engage with communities abroad, notions of global citizenship provide powerful transformative opportunities to explore one's own identity, lifelong commitments and allegiances" (p. 43). Zamastil-Vondrova (2005), reporting on a short-term faculty-led program to Central Europe, noted that students felt the experience gave them a greater understanding of what it takes to "walk" in a global society, specifically, to stay informed of international issues. Additionally, McLaughlin, Tzafaras, and McCollough (2008), when assessing the results of short-term faculty-led international courses at Penn State found that "done right, short-term studying abroad puts students on the fast track to becoming thoughtful global citizens" (p. 66). Again, we do not hold that faculty-led courses abroad will automatically produce global citizens out of our students. But we do argue that these programs can serve as one of the earliest and most feasible paths toward valuing and even acting upon the best principles embedded in this term.

In fact, the AAC&U LEAP project identifies study abroad, particularly with a service-learning component, as one of the most effective educational activities in higher education for "helping students better understand themselves in relation to others and the larger world, and to acquire the intellectual tools and ethical grounding to act with confidence for the betterment of the human condition" (Kuh, 2008, p. 17). This quote captures Schattle's (2008) primary concepts that global citizens embody—awareness of self and others, ethical responsibility to others, and participation in positive global action.

Moving Beyond the Rhetoric

Fostering elements of global citizenship among students requires significant planning and the development of curriculum that will challenge them to critically analyze the biases, prejudices, and assumptions that they have learned within their own culture. In order to turn the experience abroad into one that helps them develop more globally minded perspectives about self and others, students must be encouraged to welcome their own responsibility for those others and start to take informed and responsible action to cultivate a greater global good.

In order to capture the lofty goals in the new mission statements and general rhetoric of institutions seeking to promote global education, engagement, and ultimately, citizenship, faculty-led international programs can be one of most effective and feasible approaches. While faculty leadership and guidance does not guarantee student maturation in the global arena, it can help to move such maturation forward in a purposeful way. Dedicated faculty can design and deliver curricula that provide entry points into awareness of self, awareness of others, and understanding of what it takes to become a responsible and contributing global citizen. In addition, involvement in international programs can afford faculty the opportunity to expand beyond the peripheries of their individual disciplines into an evolving community of global educators. Thus, students are not the only ones who can gain from such ventures; faculty leaders have much to gain as well.

5

Personal and Professional
Faculty Development

Don't go where the path may lead, go instead where there is no path and leave a trail.
—Ralph Waldo Emerson

TRAVEL TALE 5: Do I Really Want to Go There?

Jo Beth Mullens

During my first sabbatical, I applied and was selected as a Fulbright Senior Scholar teaching in Brno, Czech Republic. Early in my tenure as a faculty member and excited by the opportunity a Fulbright held for my burgeoning career, I dove in with enthusiasm and spent 6 very eventful months in Central Europe—far from my Vermont home. On my return flight to the United States, feeling tired but optimistic about all that I had gained, I determined to use my experiences and contacts to build a short-term faculty-led course for my students. However,

Fostering Global Citizenship Through Faculty-Led International Programs, pages 55–67
Copyright © 2012 by Information Age Publishing
All rights of reproduction in any form reserved.

once I returned to my campus office and all of the responsibilities of being both back home and back at work, I began to realize the time and effort it would take to pull together such a course.

As luck would have it, it was at this point that I met a new faculty member from my school's sociology department who also had experience in Central Europe and who held a similar desire to design a faculty-led field course. This was exactly what I needed! Together we worked through the numerous tasks required to set up a 17-day field course in the Czech and Slovak Republics and Poland. Coming from different departments but with a common background in environmental studies, we designed our course around the theme of the environmental transition that was underway in Central Europe at the time, as it moved from a communist to a democratic political and economic structure.

Certainly there were many demands involved in designing and carrying out this cross-disciplinary course, but the rewards for me were considerable. First, I established a good working relationship with a colleague who, in the years following, would continue to work with me on another field course as well as on numerous campus committees. Since that initial course, he not only became a strong colleague but also a good friend. As we learned and traveled together, we also found ourselves developing more in-depth relationships with our students than we had ever experienced in the traditional classroom setting. In fact, students from that first course we taught together continue to surface in our lives today, decades later.

Another benefit I experienced from designing and teaching this course related directly to the requirements of the Fulbright Scholars Program. Recipients are expected to enhance not only their own educational portfolios but also offer new learning opportunities for students. Beyond the obvious learning that occurred for the students involved in our faculty-led field course, I was also able to offer my newly acquired expertise and appreciation of Central Europe with the students and faculty in my department. It was a win–win situation. And when it came time for my promotion review, my efforts and successes in offering this (and subsequent) international courses received both appreciation and praise.

While teaching this initial course (and the many field courses that followed) was not without sacrifice, especially in terms of time and energy, I can unequivocally say that my involvement in this arena has greatly enriched both my professional portfolio and my personal life.

••••••••••••••••••••••

What Triggers Faculty Interest?

In the opening chapters, we presented what students are likely to gain from a faculty-led international study experience. But how about the other participants in this venture, the faculty leaders? Why are we doing this and what is in it for us, both professionally and personally? While there are sound pedagogical arguments for offering faculty-led international courses, it is important to carefully consider why *you*, the instructor, want to undertake this type of adventure and what it might mean for your professional as well as your personal life.

If you were fortunate enough to participate in international coursework as a student, your interest in teaching in these environs may stem from your own understanding and appreciation of what such courses can offer. You may have had a sabbatical or other travel/study experience that inspired you to make active use of the knowledge and contacts you gained by developing a course related to this work. Still others of you may have a nascent or long-standing international research project you would like to undertake with your students. It is also quite possible that you are responding to an institutional or departmental charge to develop an international field course, a task that may or may not hold real interest for you. Finally, you may have personal interest in a world region but no direct experience in that location. What better way to learn about it than to develop and teach a course there?

These are some of the many circumstances that have incented faculty to design and teach international field courses. As you join the ranks of those who have taken on this work, it is helpful to consider what you can expect to gain in light of the effort that will be required of you. This chapter therefore examines both the rewards and challenges that lie ahead. We open with the good news: information on the professional and personal benefits that come with developing and leading an international program. We conclude with candid discussion of the professional and personal expenditures involved: the trade-offs you will likely make and the challenges you may face in this venture.

Rewards: How Will This Experience Benefit Your Life?

As Childress (2009) points out, faculty engagement is the key to internationalizing a campus. The best of institutional intentions and rhetoric do not mitigate the need for professional educators to plan and carry out the coursework. It therefore behooves institutes of higher education to determine how to both incent and reward those willing to move into this line of professional work. Currently there are three ways in which institutions provide support for faculty-led international programs: (a) increased financial compensation and/or release time; (b) professional recognition related to career advancement; and/or (c) administrative support for establishing the logistics of the course (Chieffo & Griffiths, 2009). Such institutional support not only makes the work less burdensome but also demonstrates appreciation of faculty effort. Additionally, we have found that the rewards involved in international field work can move well beyond the realm of institutional support.

Rewards to Your Professional Life

In most cases, faculty members' professional lives are channeled into three review categories—teaching, scholarship, and service. The weight of these categories may vary depending upon the nature of the institution, but they are consistently the areas into which faculty time and efforts are divided. Designing and delivering a successful international field course can enhance the professional portfolio (and as needed, bolster efforts toward promotion and tenure) in all three of these critical areas.

Category I: Teaching

The international teaching arena, which can be both challenging and unpredictable to even the most seasoned instructors, offers a number of ways to improve and more fully enjoy your professional craft. Four ways readily come to mind. First, you will have the opportunity to teach in a dynamic, international "classroom." Second, you will develop new teaching pedagogy—by necessity. Third, whether you want to or not, you will be a co-learner with your students. And fourth, you will be "on the ground" with your students, enjoying the excitement of their learning on a more personal level.

Faculty have consistently cited their international field courses as some of their most worthwhile and invigorating teaching experiences (Bodycott & Walker, 2000). Reasons for this vary, but most note that teaching in an international setting, far from the security and predictability of the home campus, encourages students to connect directly with people/places/issues in a way that would be impossible to replicate in a traditional classroom setting. In fact, an international, "real-world" classroom epitomizes the concept of authentic learning. Whether it be a rainforest in South America, a city block in Asia, a museum in Central Europe, or a local village in Africa, the international classroom is highly motivating as it brings learning alive for students and for faculty as well.

While international teaching can be a rich and stimulating experience, it can also be unsettling at times for faculty as they encounter worldviews as well as teaching and research methodologies that may be very different from what they are accustomed to. For example, while you may have had no reason to employ inquiry-based or problem-based learning at home, you may find yourself needing to use such pedagogical approaches in an international setting; further, the need to use these approaches may crop up unexpectedly, possibly in response to an unanticipated incident. Considering how to deal with a challenging situation can suddenly become a reality rather than a case example or illustration used to spur class discussion. Depending upon how you handle it, such a situation can provide a growth opportunity—a reason as well as a platform for you to expand and develop new teaching techniques (O'Hara, 2009). This call for responsive teaching is something you can discuss with your students and eventually transfer into more adaptable classroom practice on your home campus as well. As Hulstrand (2009) notes, "Engaging faculty in study, teaching, and research abroad can infuse exciting new energy, knowledge, and a more global perspective into the [home] classroom" (p. 48).

As faculty respond to unanticipated factors in the international classroom, students can learn by example how to develop similar skills. As mentioned in Chapter 1, one of the most common reasons cited for dedicating resources toward faculty-led international courses is that they can significantly impact student growth despite their shorter-term nature (National Survey of Student Engagement, 2007). In part, this potential impact stems from students observing their teachers' engagement with an unfamiliar physical and cultural environment. Observing the teacher as a co-learner who does not have all of the answers but who is modeling how to critically analyze a learning situation and respond accordingly will often result in heightened student interest in the course as well as a stronger relationship between student and teacher.

When you stand in the role of co-learner and co-traveler with your students, you not only serve as a model, you also have a chance to get to know each other better. Professional and personal barriers that are more rigidly defined on campus are more naturally relaxed when you are traveling and living with your students—eating meals together, oftentimes sleeping under the same roof, collectively taking in and processing a new culture. Such circumstances present a unique opportunity to discover the "whole" student—the personal likes and dislikes, worries, family and friend connections, hopes and plans. As Noddings (2005) states, "Students are . . . not mere collections of attributes, some to be addressed in one place, others to be addressed elsewhere" (p. 9). Living and learning together in a setting that is, in many cases, almost as new to you as it is to them, offers you a chance to relate in a more deeply human way.

With perceptive planning and an equally perceptive ability to capitalize on spontaneous learning opportunities, teaching an international course may prove to be one of the most impactful and rewarding experiences of your career. And not surprisingly, we have found that student evaluations from international courses may be among the highest you will ever receive.

Category II: Service

Leadership of a study-abroad program can not only enhance your teaching, it can also be a service to the home campus and department. This is especially true if you are fulfilling a campus-wide initiative, servicing a campus-wide program, or developing an interdisciplinary course that involves faculty (and staff) from other departments. If your institution, like many today, has internationalization as part of its mission, you will be operationalizing this campus goal by designing and teaching an international course. As noted previously, faculty involvement is critical. In the words of Dooley & Rouse (2009), "If we want to internationalize the university, we need to internationalize the faculty" (p. 47). Through your efforts, you are demonstrating campus leadership in an area increasingly valued at institutions of higher education across the country.

Whether your program stems from institutional pressure to engage in campus internationalization efforts, or you are stepping in to meet the increasing demands/desires of students for short-term study-abroad opportunities, your efforts should be considered a service to your institution. As research suggests, you are offering an international experience to students who may have been unlikely to participate in the longer-term, traditional study-abroad model. If your program includes service-learning, you are also giving students a chance to serve another community as they learn firsthand the many benefits of this type of work and hopefully continue to participate in service initiatives after graduation, in the United States or possibly abroad.

Designing and implementing an international program also gives you a chance to serve your department by expanding course offerings and credit hours. An added benefit, if your course is open to students outside of your discipline, is the fact that such an experience can be an effective recruitment tool for majors, a key concern for some departments.

Clearly some departments, such as those in the foreign languages and many within the social sciences, have a long-standing commitment to study abroad. These departments, along with the limited number that require majors to complete a study-abroad experience, are most likely to reward faculty efforts to offer an international program during the promotion and tenure process. Fortunately, as the push toward campus internationalization increases across the country, more departments will join in formally recognizing the value of faculty involvement.

Internationalization and global engagement can take many forms on your campus. However, through your coursework and involvement in another country, you could be in a position to connect your home institution to institutions, organizations, and key individuals abroad. When carefully fostered, this could lead to future international collaborations for you and your home institution. Formalized and long-standing exchanges and collaboration between "sister" universities have often resulted from connections made first through short-term faculty-led international field courses (Özturgut, 2007).

Category III: Scholarship

A number of faculty lead field courses because they want to expand their research interests by adding an international dimension. Undertaking an international program certainly requires originality, resourcefulness, and the ability to embrace new ideas, people, and approaches, all of which can enhance an established (or burgeoning) research agenda. Stepping into such an experience with an open outlook has led to mutually beneficial collaborations and fruitful lines of research for many faculty. Guest speakers and contacts in the host community oftentimes become more than temporary collaborators as they move into the roles of research partners, grant co-investigators, or simply rich and willing data sources. In many instances, contacts made abroad provide data that would be difficult, if not impossible, to access independently. It is therefore not surprising that faculty who have developed and taught international courses are 3 to 5 times more likely to develop a research agenda that incorporates an international component or focus (Finkelstein, Walker, & Chen, 2009).

Collaborating with non-U.S. scholars on a research initiative can clearly propel your scholarship into new and exciting directions, but there are other benefits as well. With increased attention to internationalization, many grants today (governmental and corporate) are slanted toward funding proposals with international linkage. Additionally, many campuses have established internal funding opportunities (oftentimes competitive) to support faculty efforts toward internationalizing their curriculum and establishing an international program (Childress, 2009).

And for faculty wanting to broaden the impact of their coursework, incorporating faculty-led community-based research is a means to significantly enhance course outcomes (Lewis & Niessenbaum, 2005). This type of work can be a valuable addition for faculty in all disciplines, but is of particular value to STEM faculty who have been historically less likely to offer study-abroad experiences. If you are in a discipline not commonly involved with international education, you may find that others on your campus will seek out the expertise you have acquired and will want to connect their work with yours in new lines of cross-disciplinary research.

Most colleges and universities across the country today, regardless of being primarily teaching or research focused, place a high value on undergraduate research as one of the most impactful educational practices that can be offered to students (Kuh, 2008). Consequently, numerous international programs incorporate either student independent research or student involvement in faculty research to promote "deep learning" for the students. Such experiences can lead to professional presentations and/or publications, for them and for you. They can also strengthen applications to such international opportunities as the Fulbright Scholar Program, which can certainly bolster your curriculum vitae.

Rewards to Your Personal Life

In addition to the professional gains involved in international teaching, you will also appreciate certain personal gains. From the time you leave the comfort of campus, you will be called upon to participate in activities with your students in an entirely new format—living, learning, and processing a life adventure in a way that does not occur when purely vacationing or traveling alone. While at times during the experience this may not feel like a reward, upon reflection after the course ends, shared and sometimes challenging learning and traveling circumstances may evolve into some of the richest moments of your life. Encountering your students' diverse perspectives and responses can be eye-opening and can give you a new appreciation of what it takes to move beyond the ethnocentric, provincial thinking that is quite natural for those with very little international travel experience.

Participating in an international program requires a certain level of maturity from students, but it requires an even greater level of maturity, endurance, and patience from faculty leaders. In the international learning environment (whatever form it may take), faculty need to cultivate their adaptability and tolerance for moving outside of a planned curriculum in order to best capture the *teachable moments* that are likely to happen. As Havighurst (1952) explained, when the timing is right, the best possible learning will occur—not *can* occur, but *will* occur. Faculty must thus remain keenly aware of the learning possibilities, that is, the capacity to develop true cultural appreciation in the open-air international classroom.

As with your students, international study can certainly help you become a more culturally aware and globally minded citizen (Dooley & Rouse, 2009). Teachable moments are not only for your students but also for you, and they will often extend beyond your academic discipline. If you are open to them and able to see yourself as a co-learner, they can expand your worldview as an academic and as a global citizen as well.

Challenges: How Will This Experience Test You?

Clearly, undertaking international instruction is not for every faculty member. Designing and delivering field courses requires extra work, creativity, flexibility, and a willingness to relinquish most of the control faculty members are accustomed to having. The experience is markedly different in almost every way from teaching in the more proscribed and traditional classroom environment. While many benefits can be realized, this instructional arena can also pose numerous professional and personal challenges.

Challenges to Your Professional Life

First and foremost for many professionals looking to expand into a new area of responsibility is the consideration of time. Developing and carrying out an international program will definitely take time away from other professional activities. The time required just for accomplishing logistical details such as securing contacts, tickets, and accommodations is likely to be time taken away from your latest research project or manuscript. Further, no matter how many hours you spend on planning and preparation, there are still some inherent risks involved. For example, are you certain you will be able to fill the roster? Certain locations and/or topics may necessitate extreme effort to secure adequate student interest and commitment. More than enough students may jump at the chance to travel to Italy to study art history, but how about an international course in Rwanda to study tropical forest ecology? Will you get enough students to make the course viable?

While many faculty are in departments and schools that support faculty-led international field courses, other departments may require you to "sell" your international course; not only to your students but possibly to your colleagues as well. No matter how supportive your campus may seem to be, it is still likely there will be those at your institution, and possibly in your department, who will not be as supportive. They may think you are getting paid for taking a vacation with students, or they may argue that scarce resources should be directed toward more traditional classroom needs or initiatives.

Depending upon the collegiality of your department, your course may also be questioned in terms of the legitimacy of the student learning outcomes. This is especially the case for faculty or departments that have been resistant to involvement in global education and do not fully appreciate the nature of the learning involved. Such a scenario can pose a problem during annual reviews. Fortunately, many faculty review processes allow for an additional faculty member from outside the department to participate. If this is the model at your institution, and you are concerned that your department may not fully appreciate the difficult endeavor you have carried out, it would be wise to invite a faculty member with short-term international teaching experience to join your review committee as she or he will be in a good position to articulate the value of your accomplishment.

Another way to reinforce the scholarly importance of your work is to reference such resources as the report Boyer (1990) produced for the Carnegie Foundation, *Scholarship Reconsidered: Priorities of the Professoriate*. Boyer (1990, 1996) argues for the need to redefine scholarship, to broaden its scope beyond classroom teaching and traditional research into a deeper and more encompassing range of faculty activities that include discovery, integration of knowledge, teaching, and service. Certainly, faculty work in the design and delivery of international field programs calls for application and integration of knowledge; it also features discovery of new modes of teaching and in many cases, infusing service into the process. As such, Boyer's work could be used as a strong argument for the scholarly value of developing and delivering an international field course.

Finally, there is the matter of funding. No matter how careful, thrifty, and creative you may be, your international program will need institutional and departmental resources, whether for travel funding, release time, overload compensation, or administrative assistance. While very few take on teaching a field course for the financial compensation, your institution should offer some form of reward for the significant amount of time and energy required. Compensation for leading a program varies from institution to institution and from department to department. It is therefore possible that you will be able to negotiate your compensation. Do you want your course to be part of your normal teaching load or an overload that is subject to additional financial compensation? Some institutions require student fees to cover the salary, while others depend upon department, school division, independent donors, or even study-abroad offices. If financial compensation is not available, release time might be negotiated. Bottom line, you should be compensated for your course, as it will offer students much and require much of you.

Where Does Your Institution Stand?

As noted, organizing and implementing a successful international program requires faculty to commit a significant amount of time and energy. If you are a new or mid-career faculty member still climbing the promotion and tenure ladder, it will be important to consider how developing a course abroad will impact your process. As international education has been elevated on many U.S. campuses over the past decade, designing and offering such a course will most likely bolster your curriculum vitae, whether you hope to advance your career at one institution or plan to seek opportunities elsewhere (Brustein, 2007). However, it is important for you to consider this in the context of your department, campus, and future career goals before getting deeply involved.

Begin by determining how your campus (both your department and the campus-wide evaluation committee) views faculty-led international course work. Do your colleagues consider time spent pursuing this venture as a valuable department/institutional contribution or a detraction from your teaching, service, and/or scholarship responsibilities? While over time fewer and fewer institutions and departments discount the academic value of global experiences (for both students and faculty), there are still those who fail in this acknowledgement (Siaya & Hayward, 2003). Obviously, if this is the case in your department or institution, you will need to think carefully about how to proceed.

While considering your home institution's response, you may also want to reflect on how this work might change the trajectory of your academic career. If your school does not encourage this line of work, but the work continues to hold keen interest for you, you may want to look into teaching at another institution, working for an international research office, or possibly joining the growing ranks of international service providers, either in the United States or abroad. As the field expands, the options for talented and interested personnel are becoming more varied and more viable too.

Challenges to Your Personal Life

Designing and carrying out an international program, while very rewarding, is also extremely hard work that can be personally taxing. Preparing for any new course is labor intensive, but preparing to conduct a course overseas can quickly become overwhelming because of the myriad details involved. In the initial stage you will determine your course location and the reconnaissance trip(s) that may be required to establish your program. If you are meeting students for pre-trip learning and travel planning (as we recommend), you will also need to spend time, possibly on top of your academic load, preparing and delivering pre-course material. In a related vein, it is also important to note that an increasing number of institutions are requiring faculty to go through training and to submit formal course proposals that will need approval before any funding will be released or travel authorized.

Then there is the international experience itself—the fatigue from traveling with and being in charge of students; the sometimes less-than-ideal accommodations; and the inevitable logistic and situational complexities that arise. These may range anywhere from problematic student/group dynamics to last minute changes regarding everything from student participation to customs regulations. Such challenging (and oftentimes emotional) situations will require you to move forward with authority while keeping everyone's confidence and spirits elevated, including your own.

When returning from abroad, you will need to spend time on assessment, quite possibly evaluating final projects from the course and determining campus expectations around sharing the experience. You will most likely want (and be asked) to contribute to campus internationalization efforts through campus presentations. One can quickly see that this type of course is significantly more work than a traditional classroom course. While it is certainly one of the most impactful learning experiences you and your students can have, it will also require you to consider your own personal energy as well as your home (family and community) commitments. When your personal life is in a high-demand phase (aging parents, teenaged children heading to college, health issues), you may want to postpone your entry into international teaching.

Related to family commitments is your decision regarding involving them in the experience. While many faculty members have included family in a study-abroad program, we recommend you approach this cautiously. Your course requirements and students should receive your full attention. This may be compromised when/if family needs emerge overseas (and may therefore be prohibited or discouraged by your institution). You will have more than enough to consider in leading your program without the potential additional demands that might arise with significant others and/or children in tow.

So, Do You Get Involved or Not?

Assuming that your institution is on board, we believe that the rewards of this endeavor far outweigh the challenges. Yes, taking on the leadership of an international program will cause you to feel uncertain and uncomfortable on occasion. It will ask you to stretch and accommodate, to admit when you've made a misjudgment, and to learn and grow right alongside your students. The difference is that you will need to appear confident and in charge, even when you may not be feeling that way.

The nebulous but worthy "transformative experience" that students and faculty talk about after international field study does not just happen without a faculty member's careful planning, extensive on-the-ground work, and from time to time, willingness to stand firmly in a position of complete uncertainty. By moving through an international learning experience with students, remaining open to what may occur outside of and beyond planned activities, you can garner some the richest rewards of all—those that create unanticipated human connections and spur life-long memories.

PART II

International Program Organization:
Undertaking the Tasks

After careful deliberation, you have decided that the intrinsic and extrinsic motivational factors are greater than the inevitable challenges you will face; you are ready to design and deliver an international program. While your initial excitement about such an endeavor may incent you to want to offer the field course tomorrow, you will probably need close to a year to plan for this experience. Before you board a plane with a group of excited students, there are hundreds, and we mean hundreds, of decisions to be made.

The first decisions will center on your destination(s) and simultaneously, the academic focus of your course. You will need to determine and articulate realistic and purposeful course goals and objectives as you consider destinations and related logistics. We often grapple with the question of which comes first, the course focus or the location. In the ideal case, they develop together.

Historically, faculty members would "do it all" with little to no input from anyone else in their institutions—from deciding to offer an international course to setting up the logistics and the academic components to recruiting students and collecting program fees to finally leading the program abroad. But this has changed over time. Today many campuses have implemented a formal process of review and approval for faculty-led

Fostering Global Citizenship Through Faculty-Led International Programs, pages 69–70
Copyright © 2012 by Information Age Publishing
69

international programs. If your campus has such a review and approval process, you will need to allow ample time to attend to all of the details required in the proposal as well as time for the review process itself. And after you have secured institutional approval, there are decisions to be made regarding your students. How many and who will you take? How will you adequately prepare them to make the most of this educational and personal opportunity? How will you handle wide-ranging issues, from safety to shifting group dynamics?

We designed Part II to help you consider the questions you will need to answer and the steps you will need to take as you select and organize your overseas program. We also present useful information regarding key policies and logistics to take into account as you plan your course—timelines, family stays, crisis management, and group dynamics, to name a few.

All faculty-led programs will face a certain number of trials and tribulations; some of these you will be able to anticipate, others will appear most unexpectedly. Fortunately, there are ways to reduce the number and magnitude of such problems. In a nutshell, you will need to conduct lengthy and thorough planning; the type of planning that considers not only the obvious issues, but some of the not so readily apparent possibilities as well. After that, you will need to simply welcome what comes your way with genuine enthusiasm.

6

The World is Your Classroom

Selecting the Country and the Setting

How hard it is to escape from places. However carefully one goes they hold you . . .
you leave little bits of yourself fluttering on the fences . . . like rags
and shreds of your very life.
—Katherine Mansfield

TRAVEL TALE 6: A Day on the Reef
....

O n the eighth day of our field course entitled *Ecotourism and Global Citizenship*, which largely took place on Caye Caulker in Belize, we scheduled a semi-free day for our students, asking them to select the day's activity from a short list of island possibilities. The class agreed upon a sailing and snorkeling adventure that would allow us to explore parts of the world's second-largest barrier reef. During the previous week, our class had spent hours with a very impassioned environmentalist, learning about reef protection and environmental threats. She had also engaged our group in service-learning projects that included

Fostering Global Citizenship Through Faculty-Led International Programs, pages 71–88
Copyright © 2012 by Information Age Publishing
All rights of reproduction in any form reserved.

conducting conch transects, planting mangrove saplings, and removing 40 years worth of cruise-generated trash from a local forest reserve. We were ready to take a little break from our work as we scheduled a day-long reef tour with a local company that had been recommended to us. We were all looking forward to a day of snorkeling and sailing and seeing more of the natural wonders in the aqua blue waters of the Caribbean.

After setting sail in the early morning, our first stop was an area frequented by large stingrays. We anchored the boat, immediately spotted rays swimming toward our vessel, and quickly realized why this was happening. Our boat guides were tossing food out to the rays to lure them in, as were several other tour boats around us. We exchanged troubled glances with our students as we began to question whether this tour was such a good idea given what we had learned the week before. We soon had an answer to that question. As we pulled up to the next designated snorkel stop, our guides once again anchored the boat. But this time they threw the anchor directly onto a section of fragile coral reef. In addition, one of the guides jumped into the water and grabbed a small shark to hold up for us to see. The final verdict was rendered when we were out snorkeling. One of our students noticed an oil sheen on the water after another of our local guides released tainted water from the bottom of the boat. At this point, our students were shaking their heads in frustration, quietly planning ways to confront the tour company.

In the evening, we brought the class together to reflect on what had occurred that day. We all agreed that we were responsible for paying money for an excursion that was contributing to the destruction of the reef that we were supposedly there to protect. After owning our own part in the problem, the students were still outraged that the local tour guides were engaging in practices that could have been easily avoided. And when we multiplied the damage we had witnessed during our tour by the number of tours conducted each week, the experience became that much more disturbing. The concept of a *teachable moment* was certainly alive in this instance. We had planned carefully and supplied some wonderful learning opportunities for our students, but despite all of that, we found ourselves standing firmly in the role of co-learners in that moment—shoulder to shoulder with our students.

• • • • • • • • • • • • • • • • • •

Oh, the Places You Can Go!

Many come to this adventure because of prior experience or knowledge about a particular place and what it has to offer students. In fact, some may have already developed a specific itinerary for a course. Others may have narrowed the list of possibilities but not yet determined the exact location. Still others have no idea where they might want to teach but are convinced they would like to teach a course abroad. For everyone, especially those not already locked into a destination, now is the time to take serious stock of the options.

There is no question that the location of your program will be critical to the course's academic focus and related learning goals and objectives. It is ideal when your course goals, objectives, and the geographic location emerge at the same time. However, it is not uncommon for one to come before the others. You may know you want to do a course on ecotourism but are not wedded to a particular location. Or perhaps you lived in Ghana for 6 months as a Fulbright Fellow and would now like to offer a short-term course for students there. But what should your academic focus be—women's rights, labor laws? You envision a number of sound possibilities, and they all align with your own experiences, interests, and research. Such initial questioning, while it may leave you feeling a little anxious at times, is a very important part of the overall decision-making process. With patience, careful planning, and some ingenuity, the course and the location are very likely to evolve into a good match.

We delve into specific aspects of curriculum development and assessment in Part III of our text; however, selection of the host location(s), close attention to logistic details within that location, and consideration of academic possibilities must come first. We therefore ask you to keep the following overarching questions in mind as you read this chapter and determine the place(s) you will go.

- How does this location fit with your academic interests and the mission of your institution?
- What does the location offer in terms of guest speakers, guides, interpreters, cultural or physical excursions, and accommodations?
- What safety and transportation issues exist in your location?
- Will this location give your students opportunities to interact with individuals in the community and/or with the physical environment?
- Will this location appeal to students?

The remainder of Chapter 6 offers an in-depth look at these and other, related questions, moving from major considerations you will face in selecting a site to discussion of those who may help and work with you (at home and abroad) to discussion of critical time factors in both the planning and delivery of your course.

The Big 10: Major Considerations When Selecting the Location

The list of items to consider when selecting your location could fill a text on its own. But there are a critical number that dominate the list; in fact, there are 10 such items that we have found to be nonnegotiable if you want the planning process and the eventual course to run as smoothly as possible.

1. Faculty Knowledge, Experience, and Contacts

It goes without saying that the better you know a location, the better you can judge its suitability for your program. This having been said, a superb opportunity may present itself to offer a course in a country in which you have limited knowledge and/or experience. If you find yourself in this situation, doing some focused research is likely to help you decide on the feasibility of the location. The best research, in this case, does not necessarily involve reading numerous journal articles or surfing the Web. You need human contacts, perhaps a colleague with experience in the location or a person or group who currently lives and works there. If you have trouble identifying contacts in the target location(s), your study-abroad office is another excellent resource. They oftentimes have partnerships or relationships with universities in various countries, governmental or nongovernment organizations, and third-party providers, all of whom can help you with program development.

Host country contacts, whether they spring from your own experience or the experience of others, are essential to solid program development. From finding affordable and safe lodging to engaging local English-speaking experts (as needed), these are the people in the best position to facilitate and provide meaningful experiences and opportunities for learning for your students and your course. Hulstrand (2008) notes that, "Setting up administrative support in the host country and seeking advice from colleagues who are experienced in teaching abroad are two of the best strategies faculty can use to create successful programs, and prevent as many problems as possible" (p. 76).

2. Student Interest

In order to fill your roster (the topic of Chapter 9), you will need to consider the level of student interest in the course itself and even more importantly, the location of the course. While you may find a little-known destination to be the ideal location for your course, unless a population of students is required by their major to enroll, you may be facing only a small number of students willing to shell out the program fee and make time in their busy schedules to participate. With work, you can probably sell most international sites, but certain destinations clearly hold more appeal for students than others. So if you have set your sights on a location that is not well-known to the students, you may need to do some preliminary salesmanship. Perhaps you could offer an engaging overview of the course on your campus Web site or an evening information session for students who once upon a time signaled an interest in international coursework but haven't as yet participated.

3. Vulnerability: Your Students and You

Although many of us who have sojourned extensively around the world might take a cavalier attitude toward words of warning when we travel, it quickly becomes a different affair when we are responsible for the health and safety of our students. A health and safety risk assessment will need to be factored in before you commit to specific countries, communities, sites, or excursions. While peril can be found in any location, some international sites may be just too risky in terms of crime, civil unrest, or ongoing health-related issues and other physical challenges.

Chapter 8 provides detailed information on this topic, but it is best if you begin to consider vulnerability early in the planning process in order to avoid likely health or safety red flags and subsequent program denial from your institution. For quick general information on health and safety issues in countries around the world, you can check with the Federal Centers for Disease Control and Prevention and the U.S. State Department Web sites. Both government agencies offer information specifically for travelers, however, they may be too broad or vague to accurately apply to your potential destinations. If you feel there may be more to the picture than what these Web resources can offer, you will need to research further. Again, your study-abroad office should be able to help you assess such critical issues before you commit to a particular location.

4. Vulnerability: The Host Country

When selecting specific location(s), we are ethically bound to consider the overall impact of our programs on the host communities. This is an area that has not been considered carefully enough. Some argue that short-term courses that enroll larger groups of students, often the case in short-term faculty-led field courses, are more likely to have negative impacts on the host communities than the more traditional model in which one or a small group of students spend a semester or more at a foreign educational institution (Schroeder, Wood, Galiardi, & Koehn, 2009).

The type of community that is being visited is a significant consideration in terms of vulnerability as well; small communities within developing nations are far more likely to be impacted than large communities within developed countries. The Forum on Education Abroad (2009) recognized the unique nature of short-term, often faculty-led study-abroad programs and offer guidelines for study-abroad best practices in the *Standards of Good Practice for Short-Term Education Abroad Programs.* This document calls for short-term programs to minimize the "harmful individual and program-related environmental and social-cultural impacts" (p. 3).

This serves as a reminder that, while having students travel to remote destinations in developing countries may be desirable from a teaching perspective, if not carefully conducted, it can lead to unintended negative consequences for the host community. In short, we need to fully consider what our programs might do to the "vulnerable places" in the world. Some of the key concerns regarding our impact include possible detrimental effects on the environment and resources of the host community, possible lack of respect for the beliefs and behaviors within the host society, and financial impact of the field course and how it might exacerbate economic problems such as income inequalities (Schroeder et al., 2009).

The Travel Tale we offered at the being of this chapter relates directly to discussion of host country vulnerability and related faculty responsibility. Yes, we were naïve, but we were also undeniably complacent about the potential impacts of the tour we decided to take. While we clearly did not intend to damage the very environmental resource we had attempted to protect, we failed to ask ourselves about the possible negative impact of our snorkeling adventure. As faculty members planning international courses, we must ask ourselves whether our presence is overtaxing the host community's key resources, both cultural and environmental. And the degree of detail in this area of planning is critical. For example, we must even take into account a host country's ability to handle the waste and pollution that we unwittingly generate during our stay. While sanitation structures may be taken for granted in the United States, many developing nations do not share this advantage.

Schroeder et al. (2009) offer sound recommendations for faculty to consider when developing their short-term study-abroad programs. These include making sure that you are aware of and understand the vulnerabilities of your field location and, with this in mind, taking steps to mitigate your program's negative impacts. If your impact appears unavoidable and beyond what the host country can handle due to student numbers or any other factor, the answer is simple: **Do not go there!** Additionally, this research reminds us to help our students become invested in the host communities and to alter or eliminate behaviors that damage the environment or culture.

5. The Ease, Cost, and Safety of In-Country Transportation

Given the often shorter-term length of many faculty-led programs, the availability of public and/or private transportation options will be another important factor to consider. This is especially the case if you plan on an itinerary that involves a significant amount of travel within the host country. Transportation availability (or lack thereof) may constrain even the best of plans. Even when readily available, the cost of in-country transportation can be prohibitive in some locations (think Western Europe) and can greatly inflate your overall program fee. In other locations (such as small communities in developing countries), transportation may be limited and will call upon you to make careful arrangements, with the knowledge that, despite your forethought and planning, you may not be able to move about in the way you had hoped. In other cases, the costs are low and the providers are plentiful, but safety is an issue; driver qualifications or poor vehicle conditions may give you serious pause.

So, again, there will be trade-offs regarding your program location. While you may wish to locate your month-long course in a remote village in a developing country, this may limit the excursions you will be able to make. Whether using public or private transportation, you will need to determine early how you will shuttle your students from one place to the next in a way that is both safe and relatively inexpensive.

6. Cost of the Program

For the majority of faculty-led shorter-term international courses, the direct cost of the program is borne by the participating students. For some programs, faculty can secure institutional funds or endowments to subsidize student costs. If your goal is to increase accessibility to all students, keeping the cost low will be key. Program costs will, in turn, be likely to influence where you decide to go. While you would love to offer a month-long course in Iceland, the cost in food alone might price this above what many of your students can afford. Based upon the profile of students attending your institution, we suggest that you realistically evaluate their ability to finance a shorter-term course.

Fortunately, the selection of sites from around the world has been facilitated by the increased availability of programs and accommodations for student travelers. But these are not the only factors to be brought forward as you select your field location. Certainly your students need to be able to afford the program, but you also need to select a site that aligns with what you want your students to experience and learn.

7. Gaining Buy-In From Your Institution

Some institutions closely regulate where faculty may offer courses, giving ready support to those willing to travel to locations where the administration and/or international education office has recent or long-standing affiliations. If you are firm on the host country you would like to visit, you may want to contact staff in your international education office to determine the likelihood of institutional support. If you have not yet decided on the host country, those involved in ongoing international education efforts on your campus might be able to help you identify countries that your institution would eagerly endorse for a faculty-led program. When possible, using affiliations that are already in place can make your planning much easier, as you will not only have instant in-country contacts but also people on your home campus to offer sound counsel.

8. Physical and Psychological Demands of the Location

Traveling and teaching abroad places higher than normal physical and psychological demands on most of us. Leading students through a full day and often evening of learning and traveling activities may require you to be on the go for days (even weeks) at a time with little down time. You will also be living in and moving through a cultural and physical environment that is likely to be very different from what you are accustomed to. Whatever your destination, you will be experiencing constant close contact with strangers for a large part of the course. This can prove overstimulating and taxing for your students and for you as well. It is safe to say that your sensory system is likely to be on overload much of the time that you are abroad with your students. It is therefore wise to consider this aspect of travel when you are selecting your site, and if you are planning on a residential program, these considerations apply to your home base as well.

Beyond the sensory/emotional impact of your trip, there is the physiological side of what lies ahead to consider. If your setting requires a moderate to high level of physical fitness, such as a program involving high elevation and extensive trekking, you will need to be honest about which students you can take and how you (and other faculty involved) will hold up physically. Health and physical fortitude are important factors that must be taken into account in the planning stage.

9. Language Considerations

Unless your course takes place in an English-speaking country or one where English is commonly used, you (and your students) will need to be prepared to navigate potential language barriers when enlisting guest speakers, during intercultural interactions, and when simply living, even for a short time, in the country. Depending upon the goals of your program, giving your students the humbling experience of navigating a non-English speaking program location can enhance student outcomes, particularly if they involve developing a greater awareness of Americans' monolingual tendency.

Laubscher (1994) points out that when U.S. students are traveling to non-English-speaking locations, their linguistic awareness is heightened, quite possibly for the first time. Zamastil-Vondrova (2005) found that students are initially confused and frustrated by a foreign language, but then learn coping mechanisms to navigate the language barrier. Ideally, you hope that they become more patient with individuals speaking in languages they do not readily understand. Some even return home vowing to learn a second language.

On the other hand, you may want to select a country in which English is the official language or is commonly spoken. This is particularly important if your course intent is to promote independent student research involving verbal communication with host community members or extensive literature reviews. In this instance, language could prove to be a significant impediment to your learning goals.

10. Viability of Continuing Connections With the Host Country

Biles and Lindley (2009) encourage faculty to select locations for faculty-led programs where they and the host community can make a long-term commitment to working together. Such *geographic continuity* has obvious benefits for all involved.

Making a long-term commitment to a location can certainly facilitate research efforts that, in many cases, involve finding ways to contribute to the host community. Geographic continuity can also lead to the development of regional expertise. This can prove advantageous to the home campus in numerous ways, with heightened awareness of the institutions' international focus and related recruitment opportunities (both student and faculty) being high on the list.

As you plan your program, it can be fruitful to consider what form future connections might take and what the focus of such connections might be; from scientific research to enhanced cultural appreciation, the possibilities are vast. For example, depending upon the learning goals of your course, the degree of exposure to the host culture can vary. A biology instructor who has been taking students to Costa Rica for the last decade stated that his program focuses on the physical—the flora and fauna—and he is therefore not as mindful of the cultural elements of the location. While we may argue the interrelated nature of the two, the reality is that we generally develop field courses that focus on topics critical to our individual disciplines and research interests. In the best-case scenario, you will select a location with potential future research connections that are beneficial to you, future student groups, your institution, as well as contacts within the host country.

The Reconnaissance Mission

Whether you have traveled to your proposed course location before or lack any prior experience in the targeted country or region, we join NAFSA and the Institute of International Education (IIE) in recommending that you undertake at least a limited reconnaissance mission to the proposed host area to develop firsthand knowledge of the place and its resources, and to make initial contacts there. Even if you have determined you will be enlisting a third-party provider to establish your host-site logistics, there is really no substitute for directly experiencing your international course setting. Through a reconnaissance journey, you can set up reputable travel excursions, determine accommodation options, connect with potential guest speakers, and even develop a comfort level with safety issues and on-the-ground logistics that you will eventually navigate with students in tow.

Having said this, there are times when funding or other constraints preclude you from spending time in the location of your proposed field course. If that is the case, we again recommend that you seek out those who have direct experience or contacts there. You may also decide that you need to enlist a co-leader for your course who has prior experience and/or knowledge of your destination and can thereby mitigate your limited experience.

Your Helpers at Home and Abroad

Once you have decided upon your location, it is time to firmly establish who your program helpers will be. While going it alone may have been part of the American value system years ago, in the international teaching arena today, that approach simply does not make sense. While you are the one ultimately responsible for ensuring positive outcomes, you will need layers of assistance along the way, both on your home campus and in the field.

Co-Leaders

It is best if two or more faculty team up to offer an international program. While pairing up for an on-campus course may present challenges over work and teaching styles, it offers overwhelming advantages when taking students abroad. For starters, it offers two or more presentation styles and perspectives for your students. You and your co-teacher may also bring different strengths to the table that will greatly enhance the course. In our case, for example, one teacher had strong background in travel-related content and the other had more practical experience in curriculum development.

Given that you will be responsible for students 24/7 while abroad, sharing responsibilities with another individual can preserve your energy and generally make for a more enjoyable and productive course. Team teaching allows you to divide and tackle whatever problems may arise while you are out of the country with your students. Medical issues present the most common scenario that faculty must handle (we offer a vivid example of this in Travel Tale 8). Whether it is a student or a faculty member experiencing difficulty, back-up during a medical crisis is essential.

Whomever you select to work with, developing a strong co-teacher relationship is critical before drafting the course and certainly before boarding the plane. You will need to have frank discussions around certain issues, such as general expectations for the course, how you will share responsibilities, your teaching and leading styles, policies for student behavior, and how each of you deal with uncertainty and changes in plans. As faculty, we are accustomed to being in complete charge of our courses and classrooms. When co-teaching, you share the lead. Therefore when entering into an agreement to co-lead an international course, it is particularly important to be honest with yourself and your teaching partner. Do you have difficulty allowing someone else to lead when it involves working with students?

Are you somewhat insecure in new situations and therefore need to prove yourself to others? Or are you more likely to sit back and let someone else do the work and take the lead without pitching in your share? While these questions may seem harsh, by exploring them with a potential co-teacher, you may be able to avoid difficulties when you are abroad.

Another consideration when selecting a co-leader is the individual's disciplinary focus. While it may be comfortable to select someone from your home discipline, we find that selecting someone from another discipline offers the advantage of a different perspective and entry point into course topics. Two or more disciplines can complement each other and enrich the learning for everyone. And when you return to campus, cross-disciplinary presentations are likely to appeal to a wider audience and generate more campus-wide interest.

Offices of International Education

One of your greatest champions throughout the planning and implementation of your course will be the director and staff of your international education or study-abroad office (assuming that your campus has one). As noted, they may be able to assist you with country and site selection and contacts in your host destination. They may also be in a position to connect you with other individuals who have offered international courses in the location(s) you are considering. Essentially, if you have an office with directors and/or staff, they can be invaluable to you when narrowing down your course destination(s). They may also be willing to visit your class prior to departure to supplement and reinforce what you offer in the way of logistical and safety reminders. Some offices will even be in a position to lead pre-departure intercultural training sessions for your program. In sum, it is in your best interest to seek assistance from and work with staff from your campus' international education office.

Host Country Contacts and Partnerships

If you have had the opportunity to live and work abroad in your intended course location, you may already have numerous contacts to help you plan. Those who have served as Fulbright Scholars are also likely to have numerous contacts, in this case, from the universities where they were based. Such contacts may be used to plan for guest lectures, reservation of classroom space, or special academic activities. Some of your contacts may even be willing to help you with other logistics that are best accomplished on-site. Even if you personally lack contacts in your selected country, again, your international education office may be helpful in connecting you with individuals and institutions that can assist in planning and even executing your study-away course.

If you have little prior experience and/or support from your home campus, doing some careful online research and subsequent, informed "cold calls" can result in working relationships with local community leaders, educational institutions, and in-country faculty. If this is your situation, be sure to carefully consider both what you need and what you can offer so the future relationship may be mutually beneficial.

Third-Party Providers

When your knowledge of and contacts within a selected country are not substantial, you may wish to work with a program provider or with what has come to be known in international education as "The Middlemen of Study Abroad" (Redden, 2007). While these providers have been around for decades, their numbers, locations, and scope have increased greatly of late. They also vary significantly in terms of what they can and will provide. While some providers simply help you set up in-country logistics such as travel accommodations, others offer an inclusive academic/travel program including ongoing service-learning opportunities and/or research projects in which you and your students can participate. Such offerings work for some study-away programs, while other faculty leaders are looking for a provider to make a limited number of in-country arrangements. These hybrid providers supply a range of services, from helping secure in-country travel, residential logistics, interpreters, and guest speakers to offering service-learning in local community projects. After a faculty leader determines program needs, provider services and the fees for them are negotiated.

Given the enormous task of designing an effective faculty-led study-abroad program, offloading some of the burden to a third party can be extremely helpful. While you are in the middle of a busy academic term at your home institution, their staff can be interviewing families for homestays, securing language instruction for your students, and hiring guides for your travel excursions. This will be particularly helpful when establishing a course in small communities that are off the beaten tourist track. With their relationships and understanding of your host country and the local communities where you will stay, they can greatly expand your program's opportunities. For example, they may recommend little-known but truly valuable experiences that will expand on the renowned cultural sites you planned to visit with your students. In a word, if you lack local personal or professional contacts who can help you with the often complex task of planning and on-the-ground organizing, a provider can mean the difference in being able to offer a program or not.

Having said this, while many third-party providers have been established out of good intentions (such as service to local communities), they are ultimately organizations that hire staff and charge you program fees that, in turn, must be covered by your students. Some providers waive faculty program costs if you are bringing a specified number of students, but oftentimes faculty costs are actually wrapped into the per-student costs.

A key point to remember is that third-party providers are not all equal in terms of your program needs. We offer the following information in Table 6.1 to consider if you elect to use a third-party provider.

TABLE 6.1   A Guide to Third-Party Providers

Considerations	Suggestions
Reputation of the Provider	• Get references from other groups who have used the provider and contact them for direct feedback. • Contact your institution's International Education Office. Even if they have not connected directly with a given provider, they often attend conferences with other study-away staff who have. Ask them to inquire on your behalf. • Many providers offer services in a number of countries. While they may have a good reputation in one country, they may be less effective in another. Make sure they receive glowing recommendations in the country you have selected. • Determine how much experience the staff of the organization has with short-term faculty-led programs; also, the organizational philosophy regarding study abroad.
Cost of the Provider	• This can vary and needs to be locked in as early as possible. In some cases, a provider can lower the per-student program fee, but in others, it can unnecessarily raise fees, making the program too expensive for some students you may be attempting to take.
Range of Services and Flexibility	• While there are limits to the requests you can make of any group, be sure to determine if the provider meets your overall program needs. • Ask about their in-field flexibility. Are they locked into a rigid schedule or is there some leeway?

TABLE 6.1   A Guide to Third-Party Providers (continued)

Considerations	Suggestions
Range of Services and Flexibility *(continued)*	• Check to be sure the provider has a good network of contacts in your selected host area. • Determine how much pre-departure information they provide for you and for your students.
Contracts, Insurance, and Emergencies	• The provider should deliver a written contract early in the planning process, which spells out what they will and will not provide as well as their required payment method and dates. • Increasingly, providers offer their own insurance plans for your students. Check about this and about your institution's policy on student travel insurance. • Ask how they deal with emergencies and about in-country emergency services.
Communication During Program Development	• Ask about the provider's communication protocol, then check to be sure it is being followed before your departure. • Ask if they will assign you to a specific, responsible staff member who will be available to regularly negotiate program details and give you updates. • Develop and agree upon as many program details as possible early in the process. Be sure that a calendar and itinerary are part of the planning process.
Age of Staff and Turnover Rate	• When interviewing providers, ask about their staff turnover rate. Having your staff person resign at the last minute can be a real problem (and it does happen!). • Along with this issue, many providers' in-field staff is made up of energetic individuals who are straight out of college. While this can be quite beneficial to your program, make sure that there is also seasoned leadership available to assist you.

Time Considerations

After you have determined your location and set up your home and host-country support systems, you are ready to answer the final very important questions—when will we go and how long will we stay?

When Will You Go?

Just as faculty have time constraints, students have many competing obligations that impact their ability to participate in international field courses; for students, these include such things as work, family responsibilities, and the many course requirements for their majors. The dates of your international course must therefore be established early as this will significantly influence which students will be able to enroll. For example, while traveling during the fall or spring semesters may present too many conflicts for an education major involved in school-based methods courses, this same student might easily fit in a shorter-term study-abroad course during an official school break. Frankly, conflicts arise during the traditional fall and spring semesters for most majors. This is one of the reasons semester breaks have emerged as desirable dates for field courses. Winter break is particularly advantageous as it commonly offers multiple weeks, and falls between academic terms.

The climate of your host location is another key consideration when selecting travel dates. Monsoon season in South Asia or the height of the hurricane season in the northeast Caribbean might create too many potentially unfavorable conditions for operating your course. And how about the rainy season in Guatemala, which may make your excursions to key Mayan sites impossible due to impassable roads? Such factors may lower travel costs at certain times of the year, but the trade-off may not be worth it.

Climate considerations can put physical limitations on the scheduling of your course as can trying to avoid the tourist season! Many faculty attempt to plan their courses during their host country's non–tourist season in order to avoid higher costs and long lines. This issue becomes more of a concern when your destination is on the most heavily beaten path. Planning your course to Florence, Italy, during June or July will guarantee waiting to tour the Florence Accademia and standing in line at the Uffizi Gallery. If, on the other hand, you can travel during late April or even early May, you may be able to march your students right up to Michelangelo's David without any pressing crowds. But as you lock in those low-tourist dates, factor in national holidays in your host country. These may be times when key sites are less accessible, if not closed.

How Long Will You Be Away?

It would be wonderful to have free reign in determining the length of your course, but certain factors are likely to preclude your ability to do this. For starters, the time of year is sure to have an impact on your program length. If you have elected to travel during spring or fall break, your time in the host country may be limited to only 7–10 days. Additionally, while it may be desirable from a curriculum perspective to spend a month or more abroad, costs, student availability, and demands from your own professional and personal life may make this impractical or even impossible.

But each time-related issue you face oftentimes has a counterbalancing positive element. For example, while a shorter period spent abroad may not result in the level of cultural immersion you would like, it could allow a greater cross-section of students to participate. This would include not only a more diverse disciplinary focus, but also diversity in terms of prior travel experience. Students who are hesitant about traveling overseas for 2 weeks or more might be comfortable spending their 7-day spring break abroad, getting a taste of international living and learning while earning credit toward their degrees.

In a study of international field courses offered by American geography departments, Mullens, Bristow, and Cuper (2012) found that the most common length of time spent abroad was 2 weeks; however, 7-day field experiences are the norm during the shorter fall and spring academic breaks. January, referred to at some schools as the winter or J-term, can afford 2–4 week programs away from the home institution. And for faculty who really want to dive in and offer a longer study-abroad experience, the full summer break (3 months) or a semester, trimester, or quarter might be the best choice. But as you consider offering more time in the field, keep in mind that fiscal concerns and student availability may decrease demand for the more extensive programs.

In sum, there are a number of factors you will need to take into account as you decide upon the length of your course. If your host country is halfway around the world, or if your program involves multiple destinations that are a significant distance apart, consider offering a longer course to mitigate for such things as jet lag and required travel time. If the cost of a month-long program is too high for the majority of your students, consider a shorter program with more student travelers. Also, remember that fatigue can set in when you are living and traveling abroad for a lengthy period. This is especially true for faculty, who are in charge of the students and the program 24/7. It is wise to remember that when you are planning the length and itinerary a year or two in advance of the actual travel, you need to consider many things simultaneously, not the least of which is the personal impact of running a month-long course away from home.

You Are on Your Way

We hope the information in this chapter, from our own missteps highlighted in the opening travel tale to the scores of items you need to take into account as you select the location and dates of your field course, proves helpful to you rather than daunting. Yes, there is a great deal to consider, but by beginning early, establishing strong support systems, and pacing your efforts, you are on your way to developing a sound and successful international program.

$$7$$

Designing and Planning the Essentials

There are some things you learn best in calm, and some in storm.
—Willa Cather

TRAVEL TALE 7: Going Local
••

Jo Beth Mullens

One goal of my international courses is to challenge my students to become travelers, not merely tourists—essentially to "go local" and truly experience the host country instead of merely giving it a passing glance. This requires that I immerse my students in the native community and culture as much and as often as possible. With this in mind, I have tried to select accommodations and modes of travel that will put them into direct contact with citizens of the country as they go about their daily lives. I believe firmly that we as travelers should be a part *of* the place we are in as much as possible, not a part *from* that place. However, despite this, there are occasions when my beliefs and best intentions don't quite work as I had hoped. One such occasion occurred when

Fostering Global Citizenship Through Faculty-Led International Programs, pages 89–110
Copyright © 2012 by Information Age Publishing
All rights of reproduction in any form reserved.

I was working with a group of students in a Central American location known for its large tourist trade and even larger drug trade.

There were 18 of us in our group: 16 students, my co-teacher, and me. On the recommendation of our service provider, we had rented a local backpacker hostel for the week—a rambling old barn of a structure located on a dirt path one block from the main street of town and directly across from a questionable "boardinghouse" that featured a stream of comings and goings that we opted to overlook.

One evening close to our departure date, the hostel owner and her cook kindly decided to make a special dinner for our group. It was a Friday night and the town was starting to buzz in anticipation of the weekend ahead. About halfway into our event, a group of three local men and one woman who had clearly been enjoying a few too many *cervezas* wandered onto our compound. While they might have been harmless, I asked them to leave, and they immediately became angry with me, using a few expletives that I was sure my students had heard before, but not when they were so far from home. It was clear from our exchange that the four uninvited visitors perceived me to be an American excluding locals from their rightful place.

While I initially dismissed these comments and fell back to a position of justifying my actions based on the safety threat it might pose for my students, seeds of doubt crept in over time. In fact, it was one of my students who prompted these feelings. He was an outgoing, confident young man who wanted to extend our party to the local residents. His response, while not representative of the majority of our group, made me question whether I should have allowed them to stay or at least handled this situation in a more tactful way. Days, weeks, and even months later, I continue to consider this exchange. Was I right to ask them to leave or should I have welcomed them? Was I behaving as just one more American walling them out based on my power and privilege, or was there a real threat to my students' safety?

······················

So Much More to Plan For

Travel Tale 7 offers a glimpse into what can happen during faculty-led field travel that falls beyond what we can anticipate or plan for. There are times when even the best of plans come up short and decisions must be made spontaneously, sometimes having positive results and sometimes (as illustrated) leaving us with feelings of uncertainty, or in Willa Cather's terms, "in storm." This is simply a part of the overall undertaking; but our tale is not offered to suggest that solid planning is not beneficial. It certainly is! It is more than beneficial; in fact, it is downright necessary. This chapter therefore addresses the many tasks that must be completed to get your international program successfully off the ground.

As noted earlier in our text, there are many, many decisions to make and tasks to complete before you actually travel. The information covered in this chapter is meant to help you think through and organize some of the first tasks you will face. Based on the nature of your international program and the specific requirements of your institution, these decisions and tasks will vary somewhat. With that in mind, the topics covered below intentionally cross most campuses and disciplines, and are best dealt with early in the program planning process.

The Timeline for Program Logistics

Just as we oftentimes encourage our students to develop a timeline for a major undertaking, this exercise can be extremely helpful to you when you begin designing a study-abroad program. This holds particularly true of the many logistical tasks that must be accomplished before you head off with your students. As noted, most faculty-led international programs take at least a year of lead time to adequately develop. When establishing your timetable, it is useful to break down your tasks into monthly categories leading up to your departure date. But before starting such planning from scratch, check to see if your institution has a suggested timeline. If so, it should have all the major institutional requirements and due dates clearly established.

As we know, all courses will differ to some extent. For example, those that involve service-learning or student on-site research will need to include set-up requirements for these activities in the planning timeline. If you are working directly with a host-country organization and/or a third-party service provider, you will need to determine when to initiate the planning and correspondence process with them. The sample timeline below is not meant to be an exhaustive list of all the tasks you will need to accomplish nor are the tasks listed necessary for all faculty-led courses. We offer it, instead, as a baseline document to demonstrate how you might go about organizing the numerous tasks associated with offering an international program.

Pre-Trip Planning

13–18 Months Prior to Travel
- Gather information about possible course destinations.
- Select country, determine course length, and tentative travel dates.
- Make in-country contacts.
- Meet with international education office staff at home institution.
- Determine institutional policy and process for course approval.
- Make reconnaissance trip to international location(s) under consideration.

9–12 Months Prior to Travel
- Gather preliminary information on major course costs: transportation, accommodations, program fees (if using a provider), meals, excursions, other.
- Prepare tentative course budget.
- Submit formal program proposal (if required) for your institution's approval.
- Recruit and select students:
  - Post campus/department advertisement.
  - Offer formal student application (and possibly program fee deposits).
  - Review and select student participants.
  - Have students sign a financial commitment form.

6–8 Months Prior to Travel
- Secure contract for services and costs from service provider (as needed).
- Finalize program costs.
- Initiate student billing process.

4–5 Months Prior to Travel
- Start pre-trip meetings/classes with students.
- Finalize airfare and schedule transportation.
- Establish host-country accommodations/meals/excursions.

2–3 Months Prior to Travel
- Help participants complete forms required by your institution.
- Hold pre-trip meetings with students.
- Secure means for handling site costs while traveling.

---
1 Month Prior to Travel
- Conduct final meetings with students for final instructions.

Then, of course, there is the travel itself, which should run a little more smoothly if you have planned carefully and attended to the many details mentioned. But before we leave the topic of planning, there is one more item to add to the list; not a pre-trip activity per se, but something that is best determined before you leave.

1–4 Months After You Travel
- Determine your posttravel events (campus and/or conference presentations, assessments, etc.).

Institutional Policies for Course Approval

Not long ago (as noted in Chapter 6), faculty members who wished to offer a study-abroad course simply designed the course, got a verbal okay from their department head or dean, recruited students, and took off. Those days are long gone, as most colleges and universities today have adopted formal policies and procedures for approving faculty-led programs abroad. Institutional liability concerns around student risk and safety as well as the need to ensure quality academic programs have been a driving force in the development of these policies. And while such institutional requirements can seem excessive to a faculty member looking at all the daunting tasks involved in simply offering a course, the requirements can actually help us in structuring and carrying out a first-rate international academic opportunity for our students. In fact, many of the procedures now required ensure that we have thought through all the critical issues, thoroughly mapped out our courses, and made contingency plans for the unexpected.

An early step in the course planning process should therefore be determining your institution's policy and the requirements and protocols for course approval. In most cases, these guidelines will be accessible online from your institution. After reviewing the guidelines and policies, institutions now commonly require that faculty submit a formal proposal to a campus review board for approval, usually a year before the course takes place. Such policies, which require faculty to start early and plan thoroughly, generally ask for the following information:

- Course description, itinerary, and in some cases, syllabus
- Names and roles of all administering the program, both faculty and others enlisted in executing the program in an official capacity

- Timeline for planning and course implementation
- Budget
- Accommodations and meal arrangements
- Transportation
- Excursions
- Academic background of targeted participants and expected enrollment
- Academic objectives, learning outcomes, and proposed pedagogical methods

In addition to such formal program application requirements, some institutions also ask for a breakdown of the specific roles and responsibilities of faculty leaders, student participants, and campus offices of international education (or the equivalent). After all of this is completed, proposals are usually reviewed by an established committee or senior academic official.

Despite the fact that international program proposals require extra work on the part of faculty, the planning and thought required is time well spent. Such work demands you to determine logistics and support for your program, define all academic components, and consider how the selected location(s) and itinerary will support targeted learning outcomes. These are basic requirements for any effective course. Even if your institution has not yet established official policies and procedures for course approval, you may still want to examine the Web sites of other institutions that do. Such course approval steps are likely to help you outline and organize the tasks in front of you.

Creating the Budget

As noted in Chapter 6, cost is an obvious top consideration when planning your program. You will probably be asked to create a program budget months before you know how many students will travel and what the exact airfare prices will be, not to mention the cost of other activities you would like to include. Despite some financial uncertainties, the first question students are likely to ask when contemplating the course is, "How much will it cost?" This means that early in the course planning process, you will need to devote time to researching and calculating estimated student costs. Again, the policies and guidelines for the financial aspect of faculty-led international courses are handled differently from one institution to the next, so before you begin defining your budget, it is worth taking the time to check on your institution's requirements.

In order to provide more precise program cost estimates, you will need to establish the duration and likely program dates as early as possible. This information will greatly impact program costs in locations such as in Western Europe, but may have less of an impact in developing countries that tend to have lower housing, food, and in-country travel costs. Either way, the sooner you can determine the duration and dates, the easier it will be for students to determine if they will be able to afford the program; and if they can, begin making their own financial decisions and plans.

Another budget-related question is the number of students participating in your program. If you are using a program provider, for example, faculty expenses may be waived if a specified number of students (often 8–10) are enrolled. Also, the chance of securing lower group rates for everything from airfare to museum tickets will be impacted by the number of participants involved. With that said, the availability of group rates should not be the sole determinant of the number of participants in your program. There are other travel considerations, such as space in rental vehicles and tour buses, and availability of homestays (if used) or other accommodations to take into account. While it is ultimately up to you to decide the number of students you can work with effectively, student numbers *will* directly impact your overall budget as well as the total cost to students. We therefore suggest calculating a budget range that takes into account both scenarios: low student numbers and higher program costs (the high-end estimate) as well as higher student numbers and lower program costs (the low-end estimate).

Two other issues that will need resolution before you can draft your budget involve how you and other faculty leaders will be compensated for your work and how faculty travel costs will be covered. It is often the case that faculty are compensated for their work directly from the home institution, which in turn covers the salaries from student tuition dollars. If this is not the case at your institution, you will need to ask your administration how you and other faculty leaders will be compensated. If your program is run, for example, during the academic fall or spring semester, it may be that your salary and your students' tuition will already be covered by their inclusive semester fee. If, however, your course is run during the summer when your salary (and other instructional costs) are not covered by revenue generated during the normal academic year, a separate source of financial support will be needed. In some cases, the institution or an institutional donor covers the faculty travel costs. This situation is particularly advantageous as it lessens the financial burden for the students and demonstrates a commitment (from either the institution or a donor) to international travel.

Another issue occurs when a student wishes to participate but not enroll in your course. Your school will have an audit policy to guide you regarding such a student's fees or other requirements. It is also likely that your institution has a policy for when someone does not want to audit the course but wants to simply pay you a program fee to travel with your group. We strongly recommend that you not allow nonregistered students to participate solely in the program travel. In such a case, you and your institution could run into trouble from both liability and tax standpoints as you are not running a travel company. If an individual is committed enough to participate in your program, have him or her register to at least audit.

Although summer may be the ideal time to run your program, high "summer school" tuition in addition to your program fee, as stated above, may be cost prohibitive for some students. It is common for summer field courses to be significantly more expensive for students than those taking place within the fall or spring semesters. Some faculty leaders have skirted this scenario by having students take the pre-travel part of the course during the regular academic semester and scheduling the travel after the semester ends. For example, students traveling abroad during the break in January would enroll in the previous fall semester, or those traveling in summer would enroll for the preceding spring semester. To deal with possible grade submission deadlines related to this scenario, faculty can give a grade of either "In Progress" or "Incomplete" until students' final assessments are turned in. While this is not an ideal situation and may be frowned upon on some campuses, it represents the kind of collective "work around" that you and your institution may need to consider.

Faculty leaders usually try their hardest to hold costs to the lowest level possible in order to open the program to as many interested participants as they can and to ensure full enrollment. Providing a lower-cost study-abroad experience is a goal in and of itself when you are attempting to get students overseas regardless of their financial status. The cost of study abroad, whether a shorter faculty-led program or a longer semester or academic year experience, presents a significant barrier to many, but even more so for underrepresented ethnic, lower income, or first-generation college students. Martinez, Ranjeet, and Marx (2009) state that such students, who are not study-abroad participants historically, may not see the future and far-reaching benefits of such an experience but instead focus on the immediate and extra expense involved. But even faculty leaders wanting to provide students with a low-cost program, thus opening it up to a larger pool of participants, must be careful not to underestimate the costs. It is far harder to go back and ask students for more money than it is to refund unspent dollars.

For this reason, we suggest having a contingency fund that can be refunded to the students if not needed. You might want to add 5% to 10% to your estimated program fees to cover unexpected or higher costs. Additionally, each program will have unique associated costs that should be added into the budget. For example, if your program involves service-learning, you may be asked to contribute money or materials to the host community. Finally, keep in mind the issue of exchange rates and how they can change over time, severely impacting overall costs.

As you take into account all of the items mentioned, determine if your institution has a program approval process in place that will require you to submit a program budget in your proposal. Institutions that require a formal budget will most likely provide you with at least a budget planning sheet if not a standardized budget form. We offer Table 7.1 for early planning and/or for those whose institutions do not have a standardized budget process for travel. Online budget forms from other institutions can provide you with additional examples.

Travel Arrangements and Costs

One of the greatest potential costs of your study-abroad program will be the travel necessary to transport you and your students to the host country. For some locations, the costs associated with getting around while abroad will also be substantial. This is a very important consideration that needs to be addressed early, as transportation availability and feasibility in the host country may constrain the ability of your program to traverse the terrain as fully as you might have hoped.

Unless you have the ability to check all the possible "deals" for group airfare and in-country transportation, securing airfare and within-destination travel options might be a task best left to travel agents and, in the case of the ground travel required when there, host country establishments. Tour offices or service agents within your selected country may be needed if you plan on scheduling a significant amount of travel within the visited country and public transportation is limited or does not accommodate your needs. Your institution's international education office may also be able to help you explore transportation options or at least provide you with reputable individuals or agencies that can assist you with this task.

Airfare: Getting to Your Location

Unless you are planning a course that involves driving across a border, you will need to secure airfare for your students and yourself. Before you begin to undertake the task of securing airfare, check with your institution regarding policies for travel reservations, specifically the securing of air-

TABLE 7.1   Sample Budget: Travel and International Site Costs

Categories	Items	$ Amount
Student Costs	• Travel: Airfare and Airport Transfers	_____
	• Visas	_____
	• Airport Exit Taxes	_____
	• Travel In-Country	
	– Van Rentals	_____
	– Tour Buses	_____
	– Boats	_____
	– Trains	_____
	– Metro Tickets	_____
	• Accommodations	_____
	• Excursion Fees (itemize each)	_____
	• Third-Party Provider Fees	_____
	• International Student Identity Card (as needed)	_____
	• Program Insurance	_____
Faculty Costs	• Travel: Airfare and Airport Transfers	_____
	• Visas	_____
	• Airport Exit Taxes	_____
	• Travel In-Country	
	– Van Rentals	_____
	– Tour Buses	_____
	– Boats	_____
	– Trains	_____
	– Metro Tickets	_____
	• Accommodations	_____
	• Meals (per diem & group meals)	_____
	• Third-Party Provider Fees	_____
	• International Student Identity Card (as needed)	_____
	• Program Insurance	_____
Course Costs	• Student Program Tuition	_____
	• Faculty Stipend and/or Salary	_____
	• Books and Materials	_____
	• Guest Lecture Fees	_____
	• Translator Fees	_____
	• Classroom and/or Facility Rental Costs	_____
Other Costs	Any additional costs incurred in the program should be included. Other common expenses are those associated with publicity and marketing, cell phone rental when traveling, or an administrative fee charged by the institution's international office.	_____ _____ _____ _____ _____
	Total:	

fare and airport transfers. Your institution may have a contract with a local travel agency that you will need to honor. At some universities, faculty are required to use or at least establish quotes from contracted travel agents. Unfortunately, this can sometimes mean paying a small fee for each ticket issued, a cost that you may or may not be able to have waived for your group. Whether your institution contracts with specific travel companies or not, you should obtain quotes from other agencies, especially if your institutions' agency does not regularly make student-related travel arrangements. You may want to get quotes from national travel agencies that specialize in group or student fares. They may offer special rates for blocks of tickets.

While being careful with costs, keep in mind when reviewing different scheduling options that the cheapest flight might not be the cheapest in the long run, particularly if it involves inconvenient times or numerous stops along the way. Jet lag should be factored in when contemplating travel to countries in faraway time zones. When talking to travel agents, you will need to provide the group size and the likely departure and return dates. Flexibility around the travel dates might net you a cheaper rate. We also strongly suggest that you make sure to ask about policies regarding flight changes and delays and if there are any free tickets provided within group purchases. In some cases, airport transfers and/or a night in a hotel can be arranged in a group package. As this may result in a substantial saving for your group, it is definitely worth asking.

When an agency and flight have been selected, you will need to secure the booking with a deposit. If your students have already paid their program fee, this should not be a problem. However, if this date comes in advance of your student payments, you will need to determine how the deposit will be covered. Again, check with your institution to determine if policies allow for bridge funding prior to student fee collection.

To avoid dealing with the hassle of securing flights for all participants ahead of full program fee collection, some faculty elect to have students purchase their own airfare. While this can simplify the faculty job of booking everyone's flights, and students may be able to find good deals or leave from an airport closer to their homes, it can also create problems. One problem is that some of your students may not arrive by the time your course is slated to begin, as it is not uncommon for airlines to experience flight delays or changes. During one field course in which participants booked their own air travel, the pilots of a carrier used by a few of the students went on a last minute strike. This resulted in those students missing the beginning of the course; it also meant faculty were required to reroute the planned host-country travel schedule to accommodate the students who arrived late.

For these reasons and others, many faculty leaders elect to secure airfare for all participants.

In-Country Travel: Trains, Planes, and Rental Vans

In some countries, train travel becomes the cheapest, easiest, and sometimes the only way to go. In Europe, for example, train travel can take you to or close to most of the key locations on your planned itinerary. Also in Europe, train schedules, the costs, and the ability to book reservations are generally available online. Of course, a travel agent will also be able to secure reservations for you. If you do not book ahead of your arrival, be sure to at least check about the general availability for certain routes, especially during the tourist season. Frustration will mount if you attempt to buy your train ticket in-country only to find that all seats are sold out and you and your students must stand for the 6 hours it takes to get to your destination.

When traversing large distances in your host country or when moving through multiple countries, you may need to secure additional flight(s). Again, unless you are well-versed in booking group flights, this may be best left to your travel agent. Boats and public buses are another option for moving students around in some programs. As with trains, while it may be fine to wait and purchase your boat transport in-country, find out about the general availability ahead of time.

Another means of in-country transportation are rental vehicles. These are usually contracted in-country. In most international settings, we have found that it is best if faculty leaders leave the driving to local individuals employed by a reputable transportation or tour company. If something happens—a flat tire, accident, or blown transmission—they are responsible to fix the problem. Unless you want to deal with unfamiliar traffic laws, roads, and the general hassles surrounding driving in a foreign country, we recommend hiring a good company to handle this aspect of your program.

Where to Stay

In selecting where to stay during your course, there is yet another list of considerations that must be weighed. Is a primary goal of your program to have students interact with individuals in the host community? Do the constraints of your daily schedule require that your students be easily rounded up at a moment's notice? What about safety issues in your host community and/or your students' comfort level in living with strangers? These are important considerations. There is also the issue of your group's impact on the local host community and how your accommodations play into that impact, either negatively or positively. In some communities, there may be few choices for housing student groups, while in others the choices may be numerous.

For programs that emphasize cultural exchange or foreign language skills, it may be critical to select "authentic" housing options that represent the reality of the local host community. In such a case, the students' lodging experience may play an important role within the curriculum. For other programs, it may be more important to select housing that facilitates group movement in order to engage in research or service-learning projects.

When selecting the program lodging, faculty often need to strike a balance between the desire to keep costs low by selecting a more modest setting that is culturally appropriate, and the desire to be adequately comfortable given the living standards to which U.S. citizens are generally accustomed. While we want to avoid the "bubble effect" of keeping our students in tourist-quality lodgings, we also need to be mindful of the impact that poor accommodations can have on our program. As the Travel Tale at the beginning of this chapter illustrated, sometimes housing that is either too modest or too public can create problems for all involved. We ultimately agree with Stanitski and Fuellhart (2003), who state that unpleasant or dilapidated housing abroad "can greatly detract from the overall learning experience" (p. 212). It is good to remember that the very act of traveling and studying abroad may present unsettling experiences for both faculty leaders and students. At the end of the day, while we do not need to retire in luxury, it is often beneficial to have safe, clean, and adequately comfortable overnight facilities. Keep this in mind if the lodging is being arranged for your program by a program provider or in-country contacts. Be sure to clearly communicate with them about the quality of housing options. You do not want to arrive at your program site to find out the booked accommodations are in one way or another unsuitable.

Where the accommodations are located in your host country is likely to play a role in your selection. For shorter-term programs with a full itinerary, you will need to select lodging that can expedite student movement to scheduled educational sites. Having students housed in homes great distances from the daily programing sites will be problematic. So too must you consider the safety of various housing options. While parts of major cities will present cheaper hotels than others, check on safety in those lower-rent neighborhoods, particularly if you are planning to let your students step out on their own occasionally (which they are likely to want to do).

In summary, considerations that are vital to keep in mind include the need to: (a) carefully evaluate the available options, as some will be good and some will be very, very bad; (b) be sure that you clearly convey your needs and expectations if someone else is booking your accommodations; and (c) understand that your final selection will often come down to a compromise between costs and location.

With all of the precautions mentioned, there are a number of likely housing options you will encounter when setting up your program.

Homestays

A common goal for study abroad is to have your students interact with individuals from the host community. One of the best ways to facilitate more student involvement in the culture of the host country is through homestays. Homestays allow students to live with a family at night while participating in the faculty-led program during the day. For many homestays, the host family will provide meals, and students will essentially be added as a guest or even member of the family. Homestays are the preferable option for programs with a goal of having students experience a cultural exchange (Fusch, 2010).

As with other lodging options, there are good and bad homestays. Homestays are usually established and facilitated by a local organization or study-abroad provider. You will want to be sure that the homestays used by your program are adequately comfortable, afford a degree of privacy overnight, and are selected with the logistics of the program itinerary in mind. If you are considering this type of housing accommodation, it would be ideal if your provider could arrange a visit to a sample local homestay during your pre-program reconnaissance trip. This will allow you to make a more informed decision regarding how this option fits your student and program needs.

When using homestays, it is often a good idea to work with families who can accommodate more than one student. Pairing students can ease their apprehension around living with a family in a vastly different cultural setting. This is particularly the case for shorter-term programs in which there will be less time for the student to become comfortable in the homestay environment.

Hotels

Hotels often offer modern conveniences and are, in many cases, easier to secure from afar. The price of hotels may be prohibitive for programs of longer duration, but hotel owners may also be willing to negotiate the price if you have a large booking for one or more weeks. Many hotels abroad include breakfast, and they may have rooms that you can access and use for classroom space. Hotels may also be the best selection if your itinerary involves continuous travel and you need to secure housing close to targeted educational sites. However, Guerrero (2005) notes that the use of a hotel can also have drawbacks, stating, "Ironically, the very same things that make it so appealing, make it that much harder for students to engage in activities in which they can become immersed in the local culture" (p. 43). While hotels are often the best choice for some programs or portions of programs, as Guerrero points out, they can pose obstacles to your students' ability to truly absorb the local surroundings.

Hostels

Hostels are also available in many larger communities worldwide and are frequently less expensive than hotels. Hostels usually consist of multiple-bed larger rooms with a shared bath. They typically provide kitchen facilities for guest use. Like all other accommodations, hostels range significantly in quality, so it is best to assess them carefully. Unless you are able to book the entire hostel for your program, you will be sharing rooms with other guests. Concerns over securing valuables, student nervousness and/or safety may therefore make these facilities less desirable. However, they may also provide a wonderful way for your students to interact with other travelers in the host country.

University Housing

If you or someone from your institution has established contacts with a university in the host community, you may be able to secure dormitory rooms, especially if your program takes place during a university break period. In cities within Europe, these accommodations can be helpful in keeping costs substantially lower than you would face if using a hotel or even a hostel. This housing option also gives your students a chance to see and even experience what campus life is like for students in the host country.

Other Lodging Options

Your program may have the option of being housed at another type of facility altogether, such as a dormitory owned and operated by a nonprofit organization, a local school, or a research station affiliated with a university.

Some programs, most notably those with a science or natural resources focus, have boarded their students in campgrounds or within more primitive natural park areas.

Again, because the accommodations selected for your course can have a significant impact on student and faculty morale, it is important that you select carefully. Once in the host location, it may be difficult or even impossible to change lodging if you find your selection turns out to be unsanitary, unsafe, or fails to meet other basic needs. If you have students with physical disabilities or health concerns, you must also carefully consider their needs when making lodging arrangements.

After all accommodations have been secured, be sure to fully inform students of the conditions in which they will be staying. It is likely that at least a few of your students will be anxious about the lodging but may be reticent to ask. Offering them information about their home base will provide them with reassurance and allow them to mentally prepare for their adventure.

Program Fee

One of the trickiest aspects to navigate with students is the program fee. As previously noted, the program fee will be one of the first concerns of most students and will determine, to a large extent, whether some will be able to participate. Having said this, it is very important to clearly convey from the first conversations and information meetings several aspects of the cost of your program. You will need to give prospective students a good faith estimate of the total cost of the program, how and when they will pay, the program expenses covered and not covered by the fee, and the amount that will be nonrefundable if they withdraw prior to travel.

Defining Program Costs for Students

If you initially estimate the student fee to be $2,500, it is better to give the students a range rather than a solid figure (e.g., $2,200 to $2,800), unless of course you are able to guarantee a solid figure. For many students, especially those who work to put themselves through school, the extra costs for your course will call for cautious budgeting. To you, and some students, adding an extra $500 dollars to the estimated $2,500 does not seem to be a big deal. But to other students, this can be the difference between participating and not participating. Again, we advise giving the students an estimated range, then waiting until about 80% to 90% of the costs are solidly known before giving the final amount.

Equally important is conveying clearly what the program fee does *not* cover. If your students will need to purchase meals (even only a few meals), be sure to tell them about this when you give them the overall fee range. Also, inform students that they will be responsible for securing their passports. In some cases, additional medical or travelers insurance will be needed. Tell them about the International Student Identity Card (ISIC), if you require this, which will provide them with travel discounts and basic sickness and accident travel insurance. Other program-related costs that your students will need to assume separately include required books or class materials, inoculations, and travel spending money.

Some of your students might be receiving financial aid and will need to file for this prior to the fee collection dates. Make sure they have sufficient information on the program costs to move forward with your institution's financial aid office. They may be required to submit a detailed list of program costs when submitting their application for aid. A limited number of campuses across the country also have specific study-abroad scholarships that are open to students hoping to participate in a faculty-led program. Bring this to the attention of your students if this is the case on your campus.

Refunds for Students Who Withdraw

Before students sign on to participate, they must be clearly informed of the refund policy for the program if they are not able to participate for whatever reason. It is common for students to change their minds, get sick, have unexpected emergencies, or family issues that result in their withdrawal from the program prior to travel. If your institution's international education office has not already established a refund policy that covers faculty-led international programs, you will need to develop such a policy for your course and be sure that students share this information with their families (as appropriate).

Depending upon deposits for such things as accommodations or purchases of airline tickets, you may want to increase the amount that is nonrefundable over time. Students who have paid initial program fees might be able to withdraw and receive a total refund if you have not committed them to deposits or tickets. As you move closer to your travel date and incur more expenses on their behalf, you will need to retain more of their program fee. A month before travel, you may need to make the program fee nonrefundable in all but the most extreme cases.

End-of-Program Refunds

Because you will need to set student program fees 5% to 10% higher than your estimated costs, you are likely to have money left over when your program ends. While some institutions have policies for dealing with refunds on study-abroad programs, others do not. If your institution does not, you will need to decide how to handle this situation. You may determine that the unused money will be refunded to the students, or you may establish a policy of retaining the money to support future programs. Other options include using the money to have a reunion when returning to the home institution to share pictures, stories, and to stay in touch. As with many faculty-led programs, your choice may depend upon the amount of money in question. If the amount is very, very small, you may decide to use it for a participant reunion or retain it for supporting future programs. If a larger amount is left over, say over $100 per student, you may find it more judicious and fair to refund the excess dollars. Whatever you (or your institution) decide, convey this clearly and equitably to your student participants.

Program Commitment Form

When students sign on for the course, have them sign a program fee commitment form. This form should outline the total amount due, the required payment due date (or dates, if the fee can be paid in installments), and the refund policy. Your international education office may already have a form that can be used, or at least modified for use within your program. Have the students sign this form, explaining that it will function as a contract. Requiring this early will help ensure that those who sign up are truly serious about program participation. This form can help protect you when you are required to pay for the arrangements that you have booked. You will be glad you did this, especially after you begin committing program money prior to actual fee collection.

Program Fee Collection

Ideally, your institution's business office will bill and collect student program payments. If this is the case at your institution, you will need to establish a positive working relationship with key personnel in your financial office. Through your business office, you will need to create an account for your program. Student program fees and program expenses will be funneled in and out of this account. Your financial officers will specify the procedures for collecting and spending the program monies.

If your institution does not have a process for collecting program fees through their financial/business office, you may find yourself in the position of collecting program fees from each student and depositing these fees into an established program account. This is unfortunate, as now you may find yourself in the position of tracking down your student participants regarding their program fees. In some cases this may be after you have purchased airfare and have assumed other course costs. This is not ideal, to say the least, and is something you therefore want to anticipate and avoid.

Paying for Program Expenses

When it comes time for you to pay for the various components of your program, both at home and abroad, there are a number of considerations to keep in mind. As with all other budget-related matters, the sooner you determine how you will be paying, the better for all involved.

Spending at Home

Here again, your institution is likely to have policies to structure how you will pay for everything from airline tickets to third-party provider fees. You may simply need to establish purchase orders (POs) or an institutional credit card linked to your travel account for larger expenditures. It is definitely best to attempt to pay for as many program expenses prior to travel as possible. This will save you from carrying and disbursing large sums of money when you are abroad and will give you more time to focus on your course without having to be distracted by program billing. Overall, it is much easier for you if your business office is able to handle your expenses.

Securing flights, accommodations, or other program expenditures may require deposits (or even full payment). These will often be due prior to when students have paid their complete program fee. Since the needed funds may not be in your trip account when payments are due, you should check on your institution's procedure for covering these costs. Some institutions set up accounts and allow you to be essentially "in the red" for a period of time. Other institutions require that an office or department cover the costs then receive reimbursement.

Spending Abroad

Handling program funds while abroad can be a hassle. If your institution issues ATM or debit/credit cards linked to your program account, you will be able to access money in locations around the world. This will save you from carrying large sums of cash. Check to see if your institution offers travel cards and/or debit/credit cards for your use. But even if you have access to institutional debit/credit cards, you will need to carry some cash. Although cash machines (ATMs) exist in most places these days, there are some exceptions. Cash machines are ubiquitous in European cities, but not so readily available in isolated communities in developing countries. To secure the cash you will need, it is a good idea to apply for a travel advance a few weeks before departure.

Documenting Program Expenditures

It is prudent and in most cases mandatory that you keep detailed documentation of all your program expenditures. This is usually the last thing faculty want to spend time on after they have worked to secure all the program logistics and academic components of their international course. However, you will be dealing with large sums of money that the students and your institution have entrusted you to hold and use. Therefore, you need to keep an expense journal and often all receipts in order to balance accounts upon your program's completion. We suggest developing an organizational system to track each expense and collect each receipt. You might want to carry a special notebook to log your expenses that features a zippered, waterproof pouch for your receipts. If you are bringing a laptop along, you may set up an accounting log to digitally record your costs. At the end of each day, take a few moments to rectify your accounts. Whatever system you institute, this will be your way of accounting for money spent when you return to your home institution.

Developing the Itinerary

Now that you have tackled some of the more tedious aspects of designing an international program, it is time for the fun of drafting the itinerary. While we all want to pack as much into the international experience as possible, keep in mind as you design your journey that travel is both exhilarating as well as exhausting. The students will get tired and you will too—really, really, really tired. When you travel with others, you are lugging along a lot more weight than you might have anticipated.

Let's consider a few examples. It is likely to take longer to get to places as some of your students will inevitably move at a slower pace than others. If your mode of travel is public transportation, it may be more time-consuming and difficult to go from one site to another. At the beginning of your course you might be dealing with jet lag, which will mean the first few days you and your students will move more slowly than normal. You may (and often will) face travel delays as you navigate around your destinations, and you will need to factor in free time for when you and your students simply need a break. Then there is the question of bad weather, which can delay or change your plans at the last minute. It is often easy to forget these travel realities when planning your trip from the comfort of your home office.

When beginning to draft the program itinerary, remember that you will need to balance the tendency to overload the schedule with the realities of your overall program goals and the actuality of living and traveling abroad. Some discretionary time is also important, as it has been found to enhance the experience for students and it allows for some independent exploration (Stanitski & Fuellhart, 2003). Noting that some scheduled free time is important, too much free time can present its own problems as students can feel underwhelmed or unguided. Striking just the right balance is therefore something you'll want to plan for, but also discuss with your students. Let them know from the outset that there will be time along the way that will be intentionally unstructured. You might try asking them why they think this would be important. Chances are, they will have good answers to this question and will then be grateful when some unscheduled time happens.

Wherever your program begins, it is often a smart idea to start with an orientation and a tour of your host city or community, even if your program is a travel course (moving from place to place) rather than a residential course (taking place largely in one location). A tour of their new surroundings allows you and your students to become grounded in and oriented to your selected international setting. In addition to viewing key cultural and physical sites unique to the location, a scheduled tour can also help students find resources particularly important to them, such as ATMs and Internet cafés. After the initial "get acquainted" period in your host location, your itinerary should turn to the activities and excursions that support the goals of your program. It is critical to use academic goals as the focus as you select site activities and travel excursions. Be ready to articulate how each activity or excursion supports student learning.

Along these same lines, the *Standards of Good Practice for Short-term Education Abroad Programs* calls for faculty to carefully consider the number of sites visited and the travel distances between them when designing the itinerary (Forum on Education Abroad, 2009). This recommendation is born of the need to offer students more in-depth experiences rather than a whirlwind tour of numerous sites within a brief time span. Again, while it may be tempting to see it all, revisit your goals and intended course outcomes when selecting your excursions and academic activities. You may also consider allowing your students to be involved in researching and selecting some of the potential excursions. This can result in greater student buy-in and excitement. Taking into account the impact of your program on host-country resources, you will also want to consider the unintended negative consequences of the activities scheduled. It is ultimately up to us as faculty leaders to mitigate negative impacts and hopefully amplify the positive aspects instead.

Some faculty-led international programs, particularly those that are longer than 2 or 3 weeks, schedule a day or two in which students can travel in pairs or small groups within a given area independent of the faculty member. This encourages students to feel confident about their ability to navigate foreign landscapes on their own. But before sending your students off to travel independently, it is of course prudent to clearly agree upon guidelines for safety and conduct, and to establish a return time and place where student explorations can be shared.

As you design your itinerary, you are sure to go through many changes and iterations. Time devoted to developing a well-thought-out schedule will pay off when you are overseas and able to focus your attention on the academic and personal happenings rather than on problematic travel logistics.

Continuing to Set the Stage

The many travel considerations we have offered in this chapter should increase the likelihood of you and your students having a smooth and purposeful journey. But as pointed out in our opening travel tale, even with the best-laid plans, unexpected circumstances may occur that will call upon you to make decisions as quickly and reasonably as possible. As noted in the tale, I am still not sure if I was correct in my decision—if I was being perhaps overly cautious and thereby falling back on a tourist position rather than welcoming what might have been a good chance to interact with local residents. There is no clear-cut answer. And perhaps there's a lesson to be learned in this fact. While it is important to be flexible and open to the possibilities, there are times when being too open is risky for all involved. Our next chapter is designed to help you define the difference between the two as we delve into actual safety issues you may face when you take students abroad.

8

Passports, Liability, and Dealing With the Unexpected

The trouble is, if you don't risk anything, you risk everything.
—Carl Jung

TRAVEL TALE 8: A Trip to Hampi Land

Jo Beth Mullens

We were coming to the end of our Honors course in Peru when we received an early morning phone call informing us that one of our students, Krist, was violently ill and had been taken from his home stay to a local clinic. To make matters worse for Krist, it was his 20th birthday. The doctor at the clinic quickly determined that Krist would need to be moved to a hospital in a small city about an hour away. Although it is not uncommon for students (and occasionally faculty) to become ill while traveling overseas, the situation with Krist was more extreme than most. Within minutes of receiving the call, we determined that

Fostering Global Citizenship Through Faculty-Led International Programs, pages 111–126
Copyright © 2012 by Information Age Publishing
111

I would accompany Krist in the ambulance and Pru would carry on the scheduled day's activities with the rest of our students—what an ill-fated way to bring home the critical importance of having co-leaders.

I soon realized that I had picked the more challenging alternative as the ambulance ride to the hospital gave new meaning to the term "nail-biter." The ambulance careened down the mountain road, swerving around large rocks which had been deposited during a regional strike that had occurred only days earlier. During that seemingly endless hour-long journey, I held Krist, who was curled in a fetal position and in great pain, and thought about the risks involved in participating in these international adventures. They could be rewarding, yes, but they were not without the possibility of heart-pounding danger.

We were finally deposited at a small hospital with the unlikely name Hampi Land, which apparently had catered to foreign travelers before. After signing Krist in and getting him into a room, two doctors who spoke only Spanish began to examine him. We managed to communicate on a basic level. They were concerned that Krist was suffering from appendicitis but were willing to watch him for the day (instead of operating imme-diately, their initial/horrifying idea). At this point, Krist, who had bravely managed the treacherous mountain ride, could contain himself no longer and projectile vomited across the room—all over me.

After a long day and evening in the hospital, Krist began feeling no-ticeably better and the doctors were willing to release him. By around 9 p.m., we had filed the necessary paperwork for the hospital's payment and were ready to check out. Luckily, the insurance Krist had secured for the trip covered all of the hospital's charges. Before we left, the director of the hospital, who was aware that it was Krist's birthday, threw an impromptu party for him, including a present—an Incans vs. Conquistadors wooden chess set. Before we headed off, the director's only request was that we sign the hospital's comment book: *Memories of Hampi Land*. To his credit, Krist graciously complied.

•••••••••••••••••••••

Hope for the Best, Prepare for the Unanticipated

We offer Travel Tale 8 not to alarm you, but to show you how the unex-pected can happen and what you need to consider regarding health and safety before you leave campus. Covering topics ranging from the crossing of international borders, to health, safety, and unexpected situations is best attended to as your international program begins to gel. Particularly since 9/11, international travel has seen a rise in the number of considerations and barriers you will need to both recognize and address. For example, passports and visas can now take a significant amount of time to acquire, and cargo for student/faculty research or work abroad may require a special license or may be totally restricted. And not surprisingly, insurance requirements from your institution or partnering host organizations are likely to be much more comprehensive than they were in decades past.

Travel requirements, even in countries that you have visited as little as a month ago, may have changed significantly. Welcome to life in the 21st, globalized, digital century. As a faculty leader, it will be critical for you to stay apprised of changing entry requirements and fees as well as safety issues and warnings affecting your host country. The good news is that this is easier to accomplish today thanks to a constant stream of online information. However, be sure your sources are current, as information (especially regarding fees) is subject to frequent change. For example, it is common for countries in Central and South America to charge exit fees when flying out of their borders. These fees are typically under $50 but are often subject to change and can be quite different than what is stated online. More than once we have arrived at a South American airport ready to fly home only to find the exit fees have increased and our students have too little money left to cover the charge. Leaving them behind is not an option.

Changes can also occur regarding safety warnings and health concerns for countries around the world. Who knew in the early winter of 2009 that Mexico would become the epicenter for a new and lethal strain of the H1N1 virus by May? And, as students conducted service-learning projects in Haiti during their J-term in 2010, who would have expected a devastating earthquake to strike? While no one wants to dwell on worst-case scenarios, these events highlight the need for faculty and their institutions to develop proactive protocols for dealing with situations such as natural disasters, disease outbreaks, civil unrest, or other dangerous events that can occur while traveling. Despite your careful planning and preparations, you and your institution will still need to secure a level of legal protection against the unforeseen. So after you have formulated initial plans for your short-term study-abroad program, you will next need to turn your attention to topics that ensure healthy, safe, and legally documented travel.

Required Travel Documentation

There are a number of documents that will need to be secured before you and your students depart for the study-abroad destination. Each country establishes its own entry requirements based on the citizenship of the visitor, the length of stay, and the purpose of the visit. In addition, if you are planning on carrying certain materials such as equipment or technology for research, you may need to secure approval for transporting such resources. The length of time to secure these documents, in some cases, can be lengthy. As such, it is important to determine which requirements pertain to your program early in the planning process.

Passports and Visas

Travel to all countries outside of the United States (yes, even Canada) now requires a valid passport. You and your students will need to obtain a passport that will be valid for at least 6 months after the end of your proposed study-abroad program. Some of your students may be applying for their first passports. For you and other students already in possession of a passport, be sure to check the expiration date. The "passport" section of the U.S. Department of State Web site provides information on how and where to apply, the requirements involved, the costs, and the estimated time for processing and receiving a new passport or renewing an existing passport. Because your students will be responsible for securing their own passports before travel, it is best if you impress upon them the need to apply early. No one wants to be denied participation at the last minute because a passport has not arrived.

A visa is permission for you to enter a country for a specific purpose (such as study or work) for a specific period of time. You and your students may not need a visa for a short-term program in which you can enter as a tourist. However, some countries require a visa to enter even for a short stay as a tourist. If your program is longer, you may need either a visa or a residence permit. This is especially true if your program runs for a full semester. The official government Web site for your program's destination will detail the requirements for entry and will also provide information on how to apply for a visa if one is required. A visa application typically involves a fee ranging from less than $30 up to a few hundred dollars. Given this, it is best to check this requirement when you are developing the program budget and defining the costs not covered by student program fees. Some visas are obtained quickly while others may take a few months to receive. Your international education office may need to be involved when obtaining visas for some countries, so plan to check in with them about this early.

We recommend that students make paper photocopies of their valid passports and give two copies to you, the faculty leader. You can then carry a copy of each student's passport (and visa, if required) with you overseas and file the second copy with the staff in your office of international education; in fact your institution may require this. Additionally, make a point to research and document the location of the nearest U.S. Consulate or Embassy in your host country in case a student's passport is lost or stolen. A report will need to be filed with the police in the area where the passport was lost and official papers submitted that document your claim. You will then need to help your student apply for a new passport with the nearest U.S. Embassy or Consulate.

Export Control

Today, faculty leading study-abroad programs involving research or teaching endeavors that call for special equipment or technology (e.g., GPS units, materials such as remote sensed images or software) must check on restrictions for traveling with such items. In the legal arena, this area is called export control. Export control involves the laws and regulations the United States has put into place to regulate technology, services, information, and equipment leaving the country. While we may consider the taking of a piece of equipment, even a laptop, to some countries as a needed resource for our research project or teaching pedagogy abroad, the staff enforcing the Export Administration Regulations (EAR) and the International Traffic in Arms Regulations (ITAR), the regulatory bodies most likely to impact academic institutions export of materials/information, may see things differently.

While a short-term study-abroad program to most countries will not result in an export control problem, if you are planning on carrying or shipping certain technology and materials, it is prudent to check if you will need to obtain a license for your cargo. You can also contact EAR to determine the rules that will apply to the specific needs of your program and to obtain government approval for your course/research materials and equipment.

Health Issues

Students come to your international program with a variety of health needs, both physical and emotional. In her article "Faculty Abroad: What Do *These* Innocents Need to Know," Janet Hulstrand (2008) points out the many health and other student issues faculty will have to deal with during their study-abroad program. These include accompanying students to the hospital, dealing with alcohol overconsumption, and even, in some cases, addressing bouts of serious depression. First-time faculty leaders can be understandably caught offguard when they realize the responsibility of addressing health-related issues that often occur overseas. From intestinal troubles to anxiety issues, you need to be prepared and need to speak with your students about the wide range of health difficulties that may confront them when they are abroad. The reality is that health-related issues *are* likely to occur for some participants during a study-abroad program as your adventures will involve traveling, eating, drinking, and sleeping differently than when at home.

Physical Health

As noted, it is common for some, if not all, participants to experience physical and health-related problems during an intensive study-abroad program. Issues as minor but inconvenient as a sprained ankle, to much more serious (even life-threatening) conditions, such as appendicitis, can occur. Faculty can find themselves having to make judgment calls on whether students who have developed health problems during the program can participate in some planned activities and even whether a student's condition warrants a trip to the hospital. Regarding hospitals and other medical facilities, you should be aware of their availability, especially if you are leading the course without a local provider, host institution, or tour guide.

In the pre-trip meetings long before traveling, you will need to collect information regarding each participant's physical health. On a medical form, usually required by your institution, ask your students to outline all their existing conditions and medications. Do not fail to review this information prior to travel. While existing conditions can create problems for participants, it is often the unanticipated but not uncommon conditions such as travelers' diarrhea that can send a faculty leader hurrying to the local pharmacy and/or having to rearrange travel plans.

Discussing the importance of taking care of their own health is a critical part of pre-travel preparation. Students who have never traveled before do not think about the safety of water running from a tap at home. They also take for granted the ability to access medical supplies and facilities while at school and may not understand that these can be limited or even inaccessible overseas.

With a little foresight, traveling abroad with prescription or over-the-counter (OTC) medication is usually not a problem. All individuals with prescription medications must be sure to carry enough doses for their time away. Remind students that prescription medication(s) should be kept in the original containers to avoid difficulties with airport security and customs. Finally, medications need to be safeguarded to circumvent loss or theft. All participants may want to carry a small amount of commonly used

OTC medications such as those for headache or diarrhea. In addition to the participants' individual stash of medications, one faculty leader should carry a fully equipped medical travel kit. Your institution's student health clinic or international education office may provide you with a medical kit for your course. If supplied by your institution, personally check its contents before traveling. During one short-term course, the medical kit provided to us had colored condoms but no Band-Aids. We needed the Band-Aids.

Again, it is possible that at least one participant (and it could be a faculty leader) will experience physical illness or injury while abroad. While you can't prevent this from happening, you can minimize the toll it will take on your program by having all participants take sensible precautions.

Immunizations

For traveling in a number of countries around the world, certain immunizations will be required or recommended. Country recommendations vary widely; however, common inoculations for travel include Hepatitis A and diphtheria/tetanus shots, a polio booster, and some form of malaria prevention when in rural areas of tropical and subtropical countries. You will need to sort through the requirements and recommendations for your program destination and provide student participants with this information months before the departure date. Students will then need to check with their physicians to be sure they receive all of the immunizations that are required. It is not a bad idea for the students to also have a physical check-up before going abroad.

For information on recommended immunizations, consult the Web sites on travel and health from the U.S. Centers for Disease Control and Prevention and the World Health Organization. Both will provide specific health risk and immunization information. If you have questions regarding country requirements, the host country government Web site should provide further clarification.

Faculty leaders for some international programs have arranged to have students visit the travel clinic in the hospital nearest to their institution (or even the campus health clinic) for the required inoculations. This can help assure that all participating students, while they are at school and away from their primary-care physicians, receive the appropriate vaccinations. It is a good idea to document such visits and to bring the documentation along when you leave the country.

Mental Health

Students may come to the study-abroad program with underlying mental-health issues, either temporary in nature or an ongoing condition that they may or may not have disclosed. These problems can be exacerbated during the international experience when they find themselves in unfamiliar and sometimes uncomfortable settings, quite possibly with a group of strangers. Increased mental health issues can also occur if students are engaging in risky activities such as excessive alcohol consumption. As the faculty leader, you probably will not know all of the mental health concerns of all your students. However, forms regarding health issues that they will complete for your program should solicit as much information on this as possible. Knowing if a student is being treated for specific conditions could help you be aware of and thus better prepared for possible mental health problems before they occur.

Pre-travel meetings with students should also include a discussion of this issue. Students receiving prescription medication for existing conditions can be reminded of the need to take care of themselves in this area as travel interrupts normal routines and may thus interrupt medication schedules. Consideration of your participants' mental health status is just as important as the consideration of their physical health during your program.

Insurance

If a medical emergency occurs for one or more of your students while abroad, their health insurance policy will be invaluable. All program participants must have medical insurance policies that are comprehensive in coverage, and students should provide you with proof of the policy prior to departure. Additionally, some students may want to consider a trip cancellation insurance policy in the event that they face a medical emergency that requires them to withdraw from the program prior to or even during travel.

Medical Insurance

Each participant in your program should produce evidence of medical and accident insurance coverage. Health and accident insurance policies vary widely, so this issue bears consideration by both the faculty leader and the home institution. It is common for many students to be covered by a parent's policy. If your students are older, they may fall under a spouse's or their own independent policy. In pre-travel meetings, you will need to have your participants file a form with your institution that outlines their insurance policies. Their personal policies will need to include the costs for a medical evacuation in addition to more traditional health and accident coverage.

Because it will be difficult for you to fully evaluate the comprehensive nature of the approximately 12–20 individual insurance policies for your participants, your institution may require that students purchase a time-limited policy for the program. If this is the case for your program, include the insurance cost in the student program fee. Also, if using a third-party provider, check to see if they supply you and your students with medical insurance during the program.

As noted in Chapter 6, you may want your students to purchase the *International Student Identification Card* as it will provide them with discounts for various sites abroad. This card also provides limited insurance coverage for basic health problems and accidents. The emphasis here is *basic* coverage, not comprehensive. Your students will still need to have a primary and more comprehensive coverage policy.

Traveler's Insurance

Students may elect to also purchase individual traveler's insurance that covers costs if they have to cancel their participation in a study-abroad program for medical reasons. Not often mandated for faculty-led international programs, this type of insurance, depending on the policy, can cover costs related to flight cancellation, lost baggage, and trip interruption due to medical emergencies. Students interested in obtaining this type of insurance can contact a number of private companies such as STA, who specialize in student travel.

Safety Concerns Abroad

Chances are good that your host destination is not considerably more risky in terms of safety than your home environment. The difference is that the location is full of unknowns. The culture and social protocols will be different. The geographic landscape will be unfamiliar. Then there is the behavior of your program participants while they are away from home, which may further compromise their safety. You do not want your program participants to be unduly worried about their safety, but you do want all to be aware of the real risks and threats they could encounter. With proper precautions, your program can be run with few if any unpleasant safety incidents. Various Web sites for travelers such as the travelers' page from the U.S. State Department can provide you with warnings and safety recommendations for your targeted host country. Sadly, U.S. embassies around the world receive numerous daily reports on crimes, some minor and some major, that U.S. citizens have experienced. Again, it is unlikely that a major event will happen to your program participants, but it is wise to proactively consider and take action to avoid the following situations.

Theft

Given that some portion of a study-abroad program may involve tourist sites, just as in the United States, petty crime happens in such public places. Theft of cameras, money, or other personal items can befall anyone, even those aware of the possibility. You should coach program participants on ways to safeguard their valuables at all times, especially when in crowded situations, on public transportation and when traveling in groups. And, of course, remind them to always lock their rooms. If one of your students is robbed, you, along with the victim, will need to make a decision regarding how you will respond. Depending upon the value (perceived or real) of the stolen items, you may or may not want to file a formal police report.

Violence

Physical assaults can also happen abroad, just as they can here at home. These are more likely to occur when a student participant has elected to strike out on his or her own. For this reason, always have your students travel with others when spending free time away from the group, at least in pairs, if not in threes or fours. If an act of violence against one or more of your participants should occur, it must be reported to the local authorities and to your home institution.

Terrorism

In the past decade, Americans have become hyperconcerned about terrorism at home and when traveling abroad. There is only a very, very remote chance your program will be impacted by a terrorist attack. Having said this, there is (as there always has been) a chance that it could occur in a location where your program is based or at a site you visit. Your best safeguard is to avoid countries and locations within countries that are likely targets for these unpredictable acts of violence. If you are planning on visiting a country where there is a higher risk for terrorist activities, you might want to minimize time spent in key sites and locations that are of higher risk such as unprotected public spaces and controversial religious or cultural sites.

Harassment

While students may work hard to avoid a typical tourist look, the fact that they are traveling in a group that includes a leader or two, carrying cameras, and oftentimes fumbling with the native language quickly stamps them as foreign visitors. Unfortunately, rules of conduct toward visitors vary greatly from one foreign setting to the next (as they do within the U.S.). In some locations, it is not uncommon for female students to receive catcalls. Seemingly innocent to the harasser, this may elicit shock and outrage from the student recipient. To deflect such a scenario, students need to be aware that their dress and behavior can enhance the likelihood of being the target of harassment. Although harassment is indefensible in any situation, students' poor choice of dress for their host setting (think short shorts and scanty halter tops in an isolated, more traditional community) can result in poor treatment by a segment of the population. This also holds true for behavior. If students riding a local bus are being loud and acting silly, it is not hard to imagine why a mother with small children in tow might scoff at the group. To avoid being poor ambassadors for our country, all participants should modify their behavior and dress to accommodate the host community.

Alcohol Use and Abuse

One of the most challenging safety issues when traveling abroad involves the program participants' overconsumption of alcohol. Students who are traveling together will naturally want to seek evening entertainment. This may involve alcohol use. Combine this with the fact that they may be too young to legally obtain alcohol at home but are suddenly considered legal to drink in the host country. While it is not true of all students, many 19-year-olds traveling with friends in a location where they can be served drinks legally will not pass up the opportunity.

It is important to state that alcohol abuse abroad can turn a safe situation for a student into one that is dangerous and possibly even life-threatening. Students are already navigating unfamiliar physical and social landscapes when abroad. When alcohol is overused, their ability to make prudent choices regarding their own safety is greatly impaired—period! As a result, you will want to establish drinking guidelines and clearly communicate and enforce them with all participants.

Illegal Drug Use

No illegal drug use should occur during your program overseas. It may be helpful to tell your students—in great and frightening detail—about what can happen when they are arrested and jailed in your host destination. The least of their worries will be failing your course. This is one of the few times that we would encourage using some gentle-but-valid scare tactics with your group. Before leaving for an international course in a location known for its illegal drug trade, we had a guest speaker familiar with the country's main prison recount what happened to one of his students who spent half a day there. Following his description of the student experience, we did not have any drug-related issues during our program. However you decide to tackle this issue, make it clear that NO illegal drug use should take place on your watch.

Problems Involving Sex

As with alcohol consumption, some program participants may suspend their usual rules of safe sexual behavior when traveling abroad. Although few faculty leaders relish the idea of having a frank discussion with their students about sexual conduct, it is a good idea to do so. Remind them that the normal cautions regarding STDs and pregnancy are not suspended simply because they find themselves in Paris or Lima. Some international locations may be of particular concern if, for instance, they have high HIV rates or they feature social settings that encourage students to lower their defenses. Without intruding on their privacy, it is critical to remind students to be extremely careful.

Communication for Safety

Cells phones have now made it possible (if not always desirable) to more easily communicate while you are leading a course abroad. Depending upon your country, itinerary, home institution's wishes, and personal preference, you may want to carry a cell phone to facilitate your travel plans and/or more easily communicate with your home institutions and even with your students, if they elect to carry a cell phone. While this option was not so readily available a decade ago, today it is much more common for faculty to carry a cell phone during the program.

Dealing With the Unexpected

Crisis management is an area that many faculty who are new to leading study-abroad programs may tend to downplay. This is understandable, as no faculty initiating an international program wants to assume the worst. However, before you fly, it is wise to carefully consider the range of potential health and/or safety crises that could occur. The travel tale at the beginning of this chapter highlights one of the many possible situations that you could face when leading your course abroad, but there are many, many others that could also await you. Situations range from the more minor but inconvenient, such as a delayed flight or minor pickpocket incident to more extreme cases involving potential life-threatening events such as a natural disaster or transportation accident. Although the majority of faculty-led courses are conducted without a major crisis, it is critical that you and your institution consider the types of events that might occur and have a plan in place to deal with emergencies if they arise.

Minor problems are fairly common during faculty-led courses abroad. These include issues such as minor injuries and illnesses; thefts of money or property; delayed or missed flights, buses, or trains; or situations in the host country that require the faculty to change plans. While at the time these difficulties can seem disastrous, with a calm head and quick thinking, they can usually be managed. In fact, Travel Tale 12 highlights the upside of a civil unrest crisis that occurred during our course in Peru. The national strike that shut down all transportation and business in our area actually resulted in one of the most teachable moments and memorable events of our course.

Major or even extreme incidents, while much less common, unfortunately can occur and must be at least considered. These involve issues such as serious illness and hospitalization, student arrest, natural disasters, assault or rape, terrorist attacks, violent civil unrest, and even death. First and foremost, it is vital to have support in your host country and back at your home institution. If you are going it alone in your host country, you will need to assess the available medical facilities and know how to access them. If you are using a third-party provider or even a tour company, find out their protocol for handling a program participant or country crisis.

During any type of crisis, your home institution will need to be informed as quickly as possible. Campus staff should be able to provide you with support such as making arrangements to fly a student home ahead of schedule when a medical or behavioral issue arises or helping you replace lost or stolen legal documents. In response to a potential crisis abroad, most colleges and universities have established policies and procedures. You would be wise to review these procedures prior to departure and travel with a 24-hour emergency phone number for contacting your institution. At the time of a crisis, it will feel as if you are solely responsible for your students, and on-site, you may be. However, from a legal standpoint, your college or university is ultimately the responsible party. Therefore, you need to have a ready line of communication that will allow you to reach your home institution when an emergency occurs. Many institutions require faculty leaders to file a formal incident report when an emergency situation arises during an international study-abroad program. If this is the case at your institution, you will need to either carry an incident report form, or know how to access it online when traveling.

A Special Word About Parents

When co-teaching a course in Central Europe in the summer of 2005, one student with a history of knee injuries strained her knee while walking in the city streets of Prague. The student determined that, while it was slightly painful for her to walk, with a little rest the knee would be fine. However, this did not stop the student from calling home and leaving her mother a cryptic and slightly alarming message. This in turn led her mother to contact both the international education office and the president of our college (on a Sunday morning). When we finally cleared the matter up, all parties felt that the unnecessary alarm could have been avoided. Parents do need to be kept apprised of their grown children's whereabouts, but the manner in which information is disseminated needs to be clear and thoughtful.

Remind your students that when they call home and leave a quick message on an answering machine that states they are in *Brisbane,* their parents may hear, instead, that they are in *prison* (yes, that happened). It is perfectly natural for parents and guardians to be a little anxious when their sons or daughters are traveling abroad. More so if the parent has little international experience and/or this is the first time their child has been overseas. An important form that students will need to complete in the meetings prior to travel will provide you, the faculty-leader (and your home institution) with emergency contact information. You will want to compile this list and carry it with you at all times while abroad.

A parent's need to be informed of travel events, both good and bad, does not necessarily make him or her a "helicopter parent" (those cases are a whole other matter). To keep everyone relatively relaxed, you may want to establish a method that keeps parents from feeling too out of touch. Your international education office may have a system for contacting parents a few times during your program to report that all is well. You could also establish and periodically post trip messages on a group Twitter account or Facebook page. This allows parents, friends, and your campus community to stay abreast of your activities abroad. Whatever method you select, the key is for clear communication to occur as needed between your program and those back at home.

Forms, Forms, and More Forms

During pre-trip meetings, program participants will need to sign a number of forms. These may range from a fee commitment form, which simply makes participants responsible for the program fee, to a standard liability waiver, which ensures that the faculty leader and the home institution will not be sued if the participant is accidentally injured. Your study-abroad or international office should be able to provide you with the required forms. Have your students complete these early (especially the fee commitment form) and make a copy for yourself and your institution.

Although the required forms will vary from institution to institution, the following forms (Table 8.1) are commonly required prior to travel. When possible and age-appropriate, we suggest having your students show all forms to their parents or guardians.

An Ounce of Prevention

As faculty new to leading study-abroad programs (or even those who are used to an old or less structured approach) begin to contemplate practical

TABLE 8.1 Student Forms for a Faculty-Led International Program

Form	Purpose
Course Registration Form	Participants agree to the conditions of the faculty-led short-term study-abroad program.
Fee Commitment Form	Participants legally agree to be responsible for and pay the program fee prior to travel.
Liability Wavers	Releases the institution and faculty leaders from liability in the case of injury, illness, and death during the program.
Medical Report	Participant reports physical and mental conditions, dietary restrictions, and medications.
Insurance Information	Participant provides proof of and information on medical insurance company and policy.
Emergency Contact Information	Participants provide emergency contact phone numbers and e-mail addresses.
Conduct Contract	Participants agree to behavioral requirements meant to ensure safety, health, and academic success for the group during the program.

issues around safety, health, and overseas travel, the list of tasks and things to keep in mind can seem overwhelming. As we have stated many times, advanced planning and preparation can go a long way to calming initial nerves and ensuring that a program will run as smoothly as possible. Most of us can rely on our institutions to help us with some of the tasks discussed in this chapter. In fact, staff in your international education office may be willing to attend your pre-trip meetings to explain and distribute the many forms participants are required to complete, have a frank discussion with them around safety and health issues, or even help participants get the recommended immunizations at a local clinic. While you are ultimately responsible for your program, chances are very good that there are a number of people from your home institution and from support organizations both at home and abroad who are willing to aid you with these many tasks.

9

Filling the Roster

I have found out that there ain't no surer way to find out whether you like people or hate them than to travel with them.

—Mark Twain

TRAVEL TALE 9: My Friends, Your Friends
•••

We were set to embark on our second Honors course to Belize. Our participants for this international program came from different Honors classes. We had five seniors who knew each other extremely well. They had spent the last 3 years living and studying together in a tight cohort group and had studied abroad through the Honors program the year before. Our younger cohort included 10 junior-level students who were less familiar with each other and had not yet participated in an Honors international course. The juniors had historically been more separated from one another in both their campus living arrangements and their classes. In addition to the divisions mentioned, we also had, as one would expect, an interesting array of personal stories

Fostering Global Citizenship Through Faculty-Led International Programs, pages 127–142
Copyright © 2012 by Information Age Publishing
127

within the group. Some students had physical challenges while others had medical issues; some seemed outgoing and confident, while others appeared either shy or simply nervous about what lay ahead. Taken together, we had a range of youthful humanity on our hands, and we were en route to an adventure.

Despite our efforts to have the students become a community of learners during our pre-trip classes, there was a definite "class" division. The juniors arrived and left together. The seniors, for the most part, showed little interest in the younger group. They were nominally polite to each other, but that was as far as it went. Things didn't change when we waited to board the jet to Miami, the first leg of our journey. The seniors, while not necessarily best friends on campus, were relaxed in each other's company. They sat together, joking and chatting about common experiences and their expectations for the journey ahead. The juniors, on the other hand, were loosely gathered in a different section of seats; most were involved in singular activities such as gaming and texting. There was little interaction or even eye contact between the two groups unless we deliberately drew them together.

We were getting increasingly worried. We had plans for continued community-building activities, but some of this work lay in the hands of the students too. Given ample opportunities, would this seemingly unrelated group be able to pull together and create an academic and personal learning community? Or would we be constantly called upon to find ways to connect these individuals?

••••••••••••••••••••

Pulling Together Your Program Participants

After designing your international program, you will then need to start the important business of filling your roster. Unless you have a group of students handed to you, the process will involve recruiting and marketing to a large pool of eligible students, then determining a judicious means for selecting your final participants. How they will eventually interact with each other—the focus of our Travel Tale—is another whole chapter in the course creation and delivery story.

As you begin filling your roster, you will want to highlight not only the appeal of your short-term international program, but also what it can mean to students in the long run—in their academic programs and more importantly, to their careers and lives. There is now research to draw upon regarding how a study-abroad experience has long-lasting positive impact on students. One such study involving over 6,000 students reported that study abroad was the most significant experience of their undergraduate degree (Paige, Fry, Stallman, Josic, & Jon 2009). These students also spoke of the dramatic impact it had on their eventual career paths and their tendency toward enrolling in postgraduate educational programs.

Despite the long list of benefits associated with study abroad, there are also many legitimate reasons students do *not* elect to do so, even on a short-term basis. To recap, these include fear of foreign travel, financial constraints, conflicts between the time needed to study abroad and time needed to complete program requirements (especially for STEM and education majors), social inertia, little information about different opportunities, and lack of understanding regarding the benefits. Without a doubt, a short-term faculty-led program can mitigate some of these barriers. However, as Luethge (2004) argues, the decision to study overseas, even on a short-term basis, is a decision that involves some element of risk for the student, whether hypothetical or real. Such risk might include perceived physical and psychological factors as well as financial and time-related concerns. Relyea, Cocchiara, and Studdard (2008), in examining why certain individuals did or did not embrace opportunities to study abroad, found that students likely to participate were those who showed a high propensity for risk and believed that an international experience would have a direct and positive impact on their careers.

Thus for many students, the decision to participate in your program will be a function of how it is valued and how it is promoted. And when you *do* fill your roster, there are many issues you will need to address to ensure that your program runs as smoothly as possible for all involved. These issues include individual conduct, group dynamics (as presented in Travel Tale 9), and the possibility of participants experiencing culture shock while living and traveling in the host country. While we will discuss all of these topics in more detail, we felt it best to begin with a glimpse at today's potential travelers.

Who Are These People? A Look at the Millennials

Most students in college today continue to fall into what has been referred to as the Millennium Generation. With no definitive beginning or end date, a liberal interpretation includes individuals born from the mid-1970s up to as late as 2000. As such, they have been and will continue to be your students for the next decade. Of course, some "nontraditionally aged" students may travel with you as well, but the Millennials are likely to comprise your core group of participants. So what does this particular group of young people look like? What do we know about them based on the culture they have experienced since birth? In effect, how have they been characterized based on the body of research that has explored their actions and proclivities?

In the oft-cited text *Millennials Rising: The Next Great Generation*, Strauss and Howe (2000) identify seven key traits consistently present within this group of young people. For starters, Millennials have grown up being extra special to their parents, and simultaneously sheltered by parents who are often older and have fewer children than in generations past. Millennials also tend toward optimism and are confident about their futures. Through educational and social experiences, Millennials have become more team oriented, but also motivated by achievement. This may be a result of the fact that Millennials have been raised by parents and in a society that is pressured to produce. Finally, the group is reported to be more family oriented and conventional than some of their earlier counterparts. While Wilson and Gerber (2008) argue that Strauss and Howe fail to adequately deal with race, ethnicity, and class in their text, the traits they identify still offer points of departure for envisioning students today and are therefore, in our opinion, worthy of consideration.

In light of what will be asked of them during a faculty-led international program with their Millennial peers, the traits identified by Strauss and Howe (2000) are largely more encouraging than worrisome. A "strong relationship with parents" would probably fall under the *mixed blessing* category. Being "extra special" may well feature parental support for such a life opportunity, but "being sheltered" might also dissuade parental support because of the risks involved in such an endeavor. On the other hand, being "optimistic, motivated, confident, and both team and achievement oriented" are traits that most faculty members would gladly embrace in a student participant. The "pressure to produce" that Strauss and Howe, among others, view as inherent to current U.S. culture, is also a generally positive trait, so long as the pressure does not take away from students' ability to take the time to be reflective and to think critically about what they are experiencing. The desire to produce (whatever the product may be) should not hurry the process of deep thought and engaged learning that must precede worthwhile end-product delivery. But this of course is one of the many responsibilities of faculty leaders, to see to it that "production" happens in a reasoned and meaningful way. Finally, being "family oriented and conventional" poses a unique opportunity for student growth in the international setting. This, too, calls for deft skills on the part of faculty who need to encourage student growth beyond conventional/ethnocentric thinking into a broader, more global realization of what family, in the human sense, entails. We believe that consideration of Millennium Generation traits, stereotypical or not, can be initially helpful in the process of getting to know who your students may be.

As noted earlier in this text, the students who tend to freely seek out study-abroad opportunities continue to be predominantly White, middle- to upper-class women majoring in a social science or humanities field. In 2004/2005, some 83% of the students who studied abroad were Caucasian, a percentage largely unchanged from the previous decade (Obst, Bhandari, & Witherell, 2007). Unfortunately, data regarding the typical profile of participants in short-term faculty-led programs is less comprehensive as a separate category. It appears, however, that despite generally low participation rates in all study abroad, racial and/or ethnic minorities are more likely to gravitate to a short-term program over longer-term study-abroad opportunities (Dessoff, 2006). This is also true for first-generation college students and students from low-income families who may not have considered the value of a study-abroad experience or believed that they could access such an experience (Martinez, Ranjeet, & Marx, 2009). Understandably, this is often the case for students who must work to support themselves while pursuing a college degree as well.

Salisbury, Umbach, and Paulsen (2009) note that a student's predisposition to study abroad generally "reveals a complex interplay between socioeconomic status, social and cultural capital accumulated before college and other social influences" (p. 137). They continue to assert that even among students with solid financial means, if their pre-college environment does not recognize and/or value the benefits of study abroad, they are less likely to even investigate such an opportunity. In such cases, faculty who are in direct contact with a wide range of students through on-campus courses should begin conversations with the many students who would benefit from, but are unlikely to seek out, an international program.

Given all of these findings, there is obviously a wide range of students who may eventually fill your roster. From seasoned voyagers to travel newbies, the following list offers a glance at those who may populate your course.

- Seasoned travelers who have completed other short-term programs and/or longer study-abroad experiences.
- Students without any prior international travel experience who need to acquire their first passport.
- Nontraditional students who have longer life experience that may or may not have included international travel.
- Minority students, in most cases, having a different racial, religious, or sexual orientation from other members of your group. This group, too, may or may not have had previous travel experience.

- Students with physical, emotional, or other health-related challenges that have historically refrained from travel.
- First-generation college students who are not sure if the value of an international experience is worth the cost and therefore have little, if any, prior experience.
- Students working to put themselves through college who have not traveled abroad before and who may have little discretionary money for such an experience.

For faculty leaders planning a meaningful course and all of the associated logistics, it is easy to see how such a mix would be both a blessing (in terms of representation of many perspectives) and a challenge (for the same reason).

Marketing the Program: The Right Number and the Right Students

Students' perceptions of faculty-led international programs will depend in large part on how these opportunities are presented to them. Determining what you will say and how you will go about getting the word out on campus falls under the heading of marketing your short-term study-abroad course.

As noted in Chapter 6, one of the first questions you must ask yourself is whether or not you can attract enough students to make your program viable. But simply attracting the requisite numbers is not your only concern. Before you develop your marketing campaign, it is important to keep in mind that how you describe your program and to whom you present this information can greatly impact the tone of the final course. To ensure that your roster fills, it may be tempting to play up the fact that participants will receive college credit for completing an international adventure, with emphasis on adventure instead of academics. We caution against this message as it does little to recruit students who are committed to an engaged international learning experience. It also does little to reinforce the value of study abroad among your colleagues and administration.

Prior to putting out a program announcement, decide whom you are attempting to recruit and how many students can participate. In determining this, you will need to factor in learning goals, logistics, the dates and length of the trip, the projects/research involved, and whether you are targeting one major or are open to multiple majors. Additionally, ask yourself if you are looking for more mature students or if your program is suitable for students of any age. Again, consider your curriculum and learning goals when making this call.

After defining the target population, you will need to determine the number of students who can participate. Ideally, the student/faculty ratio should be smaller than it would be for on-campus teaching, for obvious reasons. Perhaps most importantly, keeping numbers small gives you the chance to really get to know your students. It also ensures that your group will have a less negative impact on the host environment. On the flip side of this argument is the very real fact that smaller numbers usually mean a higher program cost per student, especially if student fees are covering faculty travel expenses. Smaller numbers may also be harder to justify to administrators who are likely to focus on the financial impact of a low faculty/student ratio. Ultimately, what you are trying to accomplish academically should govern the number of student participants. If, for example, you are doing field research, you will most likely need to keep the numbers low despite administrative/financial concerns. As you can see, determining the number of participants is a careful (and somewhat political) balancing act.

Once you have determined your target number, it is advisable to start advertising as soon as possible, particularly if your program cost is high. A year in advance is not too early to begin getting the word out to your likely pool of recruits. At the very least, you should begin to advertise a semester or two before travel is to occur. Early marketing, while helpful for all students, is particularly important for students of lower means, as advance notice gives them more time to come up with a plan for financing the journey.

If you are fortunate enough to be in a department that either requires students to complete a study-abroad experience or actively encourages and even rewards students who do so, you may have little to worry about. But in most cases, when a short-term study-abroad course is announced, faculty encounter a range of student responses—from those who are ready to sign on and immediately pay the program fee to those who are interested but may need more convincing or may lack the resources to participate. Typically, the number of students showing initial interest will be large, but when it comes down to commitment of money and time, those numbers will decrease significantly. Filling the roster can also prove challenging when recruiting students majoring in fields that historically lagged in study-abroad participation. For example, education and STEM majors may require a tougher sell when marketing your program because of their competing path-to-graduation requirements. On the other hand, they may jump at the chance to participate, as your program may provide them with the only feasible option for being involved in a study-abroad experience.

While many faculty leaders planning a study-abroad program target the more mature (upperclassmen) participant pool, you may decide otherwise. Research has demonstrated that those who participate in a short-term faculty-led international experience are more likely to participate in another international experience before graduation, whether another short-term course or a longer-term program. Therefore you (and your institution) may target freshman or sophomores in order to encourage students to pursue future study-abroad opportunities. A study conducted on short-term study-abroad programs at the University of Delaware by Chieffo and Griffiths (2009) reported that freshman who freely elected to participate represented a unique population who had traveled before and were likely to travel again. They further found that those who waited until their sophomore year were either previously not ready or not as interested in pursuing a study-abroad experience. If your goal, therefore, is to recruit freshmen, in addition to advertising in venues that are frequented by underclassmen, you may need to highlight your course during traditional first-year gatherings, such as orientation and/or parents' weekend.

If you have determined your course is open to a very large student pool, you will need to come up with a fair selection process. First-come, first-served is always an option. Limiting participation to targeted majors is another way to keep your numbers at a controlled level. Course prerequisites can also be used to select appropriate participants. Still others may ask students to communicate their goals for completing a short-term international program during an interview or through a formal essay. At some institutions, students on academic probation or with low GPAs are automatically taken off the roster. In the final analysis, a combination of considerations may help you limit the number of participants in a purposeful but equitable way.

As noted in Chapter 6, another important decision related to student recruitment is the destination of your course. Some countries, such as Italy, will guarantee a full roster (if costs are contained), but this does not mean you cannot fill a roster to a less glamorous or little-known location. In such a case, you might simply need to include an excursion to a well-known site during the program. For example, a site such as Machu Picchu in Peru may be a large draw, even though your visit there will only take up one day of your 3-week course. Certain cities can also draw student interest. Prague, for instance, may entice potential students even though your home base for a course in the Czech Republic will be Brno, the country's second largest, but less well-known city. We are not recommending false advertising and/or promising a program you cannot deliver. However, if you select a little-known program location, you might need to include (if appropriate) a more well-known excursion site or location in the surrounding area in order to attract students to your program. But again, remember that you are not seeking a roster full of students only interested in seeing tourist sites.

The Course Application

Unless you are offering a program in which the students are already predefined and selected (Honors, Modern Languages, etc.), you will need to develop a course application form. Having all interested students fill out an application for admittance is helpful from a couple of standpoints. First, it gives you the opportunity to select students based on a set of criteria. It also sends a message to potential students that participation in the course is a privilege, not a right. And finally, if you find yourself in the fortunate position of having 30 completed applications for 10 student openings, you can rest assured early in the planning process that your course will get the needed enrollment.

A comprehensive course application can also give you an initial idea of your students' interests and tendencies. Information required on application forms might include major, class standing, GPA, prior coursework related to the focus of your program, and proof of program prerequisites. Many applications require a personal statement or application essay that can help faculty gauge student writing ability and more importantly, preliminary applicant interest and level of commitment to the goals of the program. Some faculty leaders also call for students to give a refundable deposit along with the application. In most cases, this helps to ensure that only students who are extremely interested in your program and likely to follow through with their participation will apply.

After the students have been selected for the program, you will need to officially inform them (and those not selected) and have them sign a commitment form that states they are responsible for paying the complete program fee prior to travel. This is critical as it holds them to their commitment and allows you to begin securing flights, accommodations, and other pre-travel logistics. Despite having a signed commitment form from students, there are instances in which students legitimately need to back out, perhaps due to an illness or a family emergency. You should therefore establish a waiting list for those not selected in case someone must withdraw from the program.

Venues for Program Recruitment

As mentioned earlier, it is good to give yourself up to a year to recruit students. For expensive or longer faculty-led courses, you will want to announce even earlier since participants will need to clear their schedules and save their dollars. Even though you will want to make the advertisements attractive, be sure that you are marketing your program as an academic course, not a tour or vacation. Worse than not filling your roster would be filling your roster with students who think they are simply signing on to a fun student trip. In your advertisement/announcement, include the course description, focus, location, the faculty involved, requirements for participation, estimated cost, pre-travel meeting requirements, dates of travel, maximum enrollment, and student selection criteria.

Effective recruitment venues might include discipline-related classes, study-abroad fairs, department or college Web pages, academic department and residence halls, and campus events and newspapers. If you are hoping to capture nontraditional students, be sure to send course information to the classes and activities in which they participate such as evening classes. If you are targeting students campus-wide, you may want to conduct an informational event to discuss the course and distribute applications. College brochures, catalogs, and posters can be used as well as campus announcement listservs. There is no shortage of recruitment opportunities. Shortage of faculty time for this endeavor is more likely to pose a problem, so be strategic and rely upon campus colleagues, including those in your international education office, to get the word out.

The Packing List

In a pre-trip meeting, you will want to provide your students with a list of items they will need to bring overseas. First on the list are important documents. These will include their passport, a photocopy of their passport, an International Student Identify Card (if required), an insurance card, and emergency contact information. As noted in Chapter 8, copies of important documents should also be given to the appropriate office at the home institution and the faculty leader.

For accessing money abroad, students will want to carry a credit/debit card that can be used in ATMs worldwide. Students will often want guidance regarding the amount of cash they should carry with them. Determining cash needs depends upon the location and length of your program as well as the expenses not covered in the program fee. If your students will be routinely paying for meals or other daily expenses, they will need access to larger amounts of money. It is generally best if students carry limited amounts of cash and plan on accessing ATMs while abroad (unless you will be spending the entire time in a remote location). This reduces their chance of losing their money or having it stolen. Also, ATMs typically give a better exchange rate than host country currency-exchange kiosks or banks. It is wise to have your students check with their home banks to be sure they can use their debit/credit cards abroad. To protect customers, some banks freeze accounts when they start receiving out-of-country charges. To avoid this, tell your students to give their home financial institution notice of their travel destination and dates.

The decision on what clothing and nonessential items to bring should be based on both practical necessity as well as physiological comfort. You will want to give your students a packing list to guide them in the basic gear needed. The specific list of items they should bring will reflect the physical and social realities of your host location and program. If you are traveling through or based in a non-tourist (more traditional) community, you will need to emphasize a somewhat conservative and respectful dress code. In this case, faculty may need to remind themselves that their definition of short and/or conservative may not match their students' definition. It is not uncommon for faculty to stress the need for students to avoid wearing short shorts, only to arrive in the host country and find that their students are, indeed, wearing what the faculty member considers very short shorts. So, too, should weather and travel conditions impact what goes into students' suitcases. If your course involves service-learning, participants will want to include work clothing that they may or may not bring back home (consider Travel Tale 2 and the building of the mud stoves). If students are responsible for sheets and towels while traveling, this will need to be mentioned as well, as students may assume these will be provided in the accommodations.

You may also want to help students determine what they have room for and what they do not. It is only natural for some students (and some faculty) to overpack. However, this is where you will want to remind them that what they pack, they will inevitably have to carry at some point during the program. For some programs, especially those that involve frequent movement, dragging a large and heavy bag across a city or on and off trains will take its toll. Additionally, some airlines have weight limits that you will need to consider. Keeping in mind that all participants should travel as lightly as possible, devise a packing list of necessities and the recommended gear for your students. You may even want to define or show them what a suitably sized suitcase looks like. Since many of your students may be traveling overseas for the first time, remind them (if this is the case) that they will be able to purchase some items in the host country. In other words, they do not need to take enough snacks to last them for a month.

Table 9.1 includes typical items that you may want to consider for your program packing list. This list was designed for a 2-week service-learning course in the Sacred Valley of Peru, but it can be modified for your course needs.

TABLE 9.1   International Program Packing List

 Short-Term Faculty-Led Program Packing List

Note: Fit the following into one medium-sized suitcase or one backpack.

Clothing/Shoes	Medical/First-Aid/Toiletries
Shorts (2 pairs)	Prescription medication
Pants (2–3 pairs)	Headache tablets
T-shirts (both long and short-sleeved)	Band-Aids
1 worn shirt and pants for working	Sunglasses
Casual dress outfit	Sunscreen
Sleepwear	Bug spray
Underwear and socks	Water bottle
Waterproof or resistant jacket	Hand sanitizer
Fleece jacket or warm sweater	Anti-diarrhea medicine
Warm hat and pair of gloves	Soap/shampoo
Sun hat	Toothpaste/brush/floss
Walking/hiking shoes	Deodorant
Work shoes (closed toe)	Towel
Sandals or flip-flops	Glasses/Contacts

Required Documents & Course Materials	Optional Items
Passports (and visa if required)	Personal book
International Student ID card	Bathing suit
Plane tickets	Cards/Games
Credit/Debit card	Binoculars
Small daypack	Alarm clock
Notebook	Snacks
Journal	Laundry detergent
Pens/Pencils	Small mirror
Camera	

Participant Conduct

If a student's behavior during the program causes serious problems, you have the authority and the obligation to send the student home. Having said this, you must clearly articulate your expectations to the students before you leave and reiterate them regularly throughout your time overseas. With the use of good judgment, it is likely you will be able to avoid this unfortunate situation. Behaviors that often provide grounds for program expulsion include illegal drug use, violent behavior, sexual incidents (including harassment), violation of local laws, and repeated violation of program rules and/or requirements. If any of these happen during your program, in addition to sending the offending student home, it is advisable that you file a formal report with your home institution as soon as possible.

The vast majority of conduct problems during faculty-led study-abroad programs do not require sending the participant home. Instead, most conduct problems involve students who are disruptive in more minor ways but whose behaviors still negatively impact the program. Alcohol-related incidents such as excessive drinking, conflicts among students such as roommate disagreements, and students who fail to show up or are routinely late for scheduled activities are the most common issues. Still, if faculty leaders spend time prior to departure and also while abroad addressing these issues, it is doubtful that unmanageable problems will persist.

It is a good idea, if not a necessity, to have students read and sign a *Code of Conduct* contract before traveling. This form should clarify required participant conduct during your study-abroad program as well as the consequences if violated. To make the process fair and open, have the students help create the code for your program, keeping in mind that some issues may be nonnegotiable. In addition, make it clear that serious infractions may necessitate the participant being sent home, with the student covering the expenses related to such an action. Furthermore, let students know that in such a case, the participant will be deregistered and will forfeit all program credit.

Group Dynamics

Following on the heels of participant conduct, you should talk with your group in advance about group dynamics. It is challenging to spend large amounts of time with anyone, not to mention with a group of strangers. Mark Twain's quote at the beginning of this chapter is a funny, but also true, statement of what happens when navigating unfamiliar territory with others on a 24/7 basis. You can make this point to your students; not as a profound or enlightened observation on your part, but rather as a reality that all people traveling together are likely to face. Personality issues and differences *do* come up, and they can create a negative climate for all involved, including the faculty. We suggest setting the tone for positive group dynamics early and often, modeling what it looks like to show respect and interest in one another both prior to and during the international experience.

The bottom line is that safety on a field course is also about emotional safety, and this rests, in many cases, on how your students treat each other. Unless you are extremely lucky or have a very small and tightly knit group, you are likely to have some students who get tired and simply get on each other's nerves. The student who is loud or socially awkward might find him or herself being quietly ridiculed by other participants. You may also have groups form prior to or during your course that exclude other participants, not unlike what we described in the travel tale that opened this chapter.

Even though we had required and encouraged interactions among the two apparent factions prior to our departure, we were worried that they had not become a cohesive group. This became more apparent when we sat together in the airport lounge. But we discovered, as we made our way into the field, that the respect and thoughtful interactions we had discussed with them prior to leaving began to emerge once they were engaged in the service project. Yes, we intentionally paired students who would not have selected each other on their own. We then watched as they worked together and later reflected on their experiences with the rest of the group. This is not to suggest that everyone became the closest of friends. By the end of the course, there were still some students who were closer than others, but a few self-designated leaders stepped forward and quietly worked with us so that no one felt emotionally isolated, and everyone felt valued. Over the course of our time overseas, what had begun as a divided class gradually became a more unified community of learners.

It is not just difficult dynamics among students that can surface during a program. The relationship that develops between faculty and students can also present challenges. When traveling and living together, as is often the case during short-term international programs, faculty will experience less formal boundaries between themselves and their students. They may also find themselves in something of a parental role—taking care of students' various needs and mitigating individual or group problems. Hulstrand (2008), however, cautions faculty about being overly involved with their students' social and personal lives when traveling abroad. She instead recommends that we "keep the boundaries that separate faculty from students well-defined and ever-present in an effort to minimize problems that might ensue" (p. 79). This is not to say that faculty should ignore the issues that students are likely to experience during travel, but rather that it is best to maintain the faculty/leadership role that is expected of them, by their institution, and by their students as well.

Good Ambassadors

In addition to discussing the need for respectful treatment of each other prior to leaving the country, it is equally essential to spend time discussing respectful attitudes and conduct with regard to the host community. By doing this, you are taking a first step in the process of developing student ambassadors—students who will represent both their campuses and their country in a positive manner. Suffice it to say that students, particularly those who have had little prior travel experience, may not be aware of the impression their actions and attitudes will make on the host community. Talking with them about this topic, about developing the ability to look at themselves objectively—as the visitor, the "other" who is standing in someone else's culture—is a critical element of thoughtful trip preparation.

Along with discussion of being good ambassadors, it is also important to consider how *culture shock* may impact even the best of student intentions. Culture shock can be loosely defined as the unsettling experience that individuals may have when sojourning from their familiar environ to one in which they are surrounded by unfamiliarity. Because of the short duration and the fact that students are traveling with others from the home campus during faculty-led programs, culture shock may not occur to the extent originally described by anthropologist Oberg (1960). On the other hand, the phenomena can strike students who are traveling for the first time harder than repeat travelers, especially when the host destination is a less-developed country. In such situations, students may be flooded with unsettling emotions as they attempt to adjust to living in and moving through an environment vastly different from their own.

All things considered, culture shock is likely to occur for all of your participants to some degree and at some point while abroad. It is important to keep in mind that each student's experience will be unique. Common reactions include homesickness, irritability, compulsive eating and/or drinking, and stereotyping host nationals—possibly even showing hostility toward them. Scheduling time before and during travel to reflect upon and problem solve such emotions will benefit all participants, even those who express no overt feelings of culture shock.

While it is common (and advisable) for faculty to spend time prior to and during travel discussing culture shock with students, it is less likely that faculty will think to give equal weight to the *reverse* culture shock that may occur when students return home. When returning from an intensive study-abroad experience, students may have difficulty adjusting back into their home culture. They may feel that they have undergone a significant change while abroad that is not recognized by their family and friends back home. They may have also developed different attitudes regarding their own culture and American society while away. In some cases, these feelings can be even more disconcerting than the culture shock they experienced when overseas. Therefore, when planning the course itinerary for posttravel activities, include time for discussing their expected and actual reentry experiences—what is causing their feelings and how this might be considered (and used) in a positive way and as a marker of growth.

Human Rewards

As one might expect, one of the most complex aspects of leading a short-term faculty-led program revolves around working with the student participants. Each one represents a unique history and way of learning and being. From recruiting them, to preparing them for the experience, to responding to them emotionally, cognitively, and physically along the way, this is where the real work lies. Based on our experiences, we would add that it is where real rewards lie as well.

PART III

The Learning: Realizing the Potential of Faculty-Led International Programs

When we consider completing all of the tasks and making all of the decisions involved in faculty-led program logistics, it is natural and easy to become overwhelmed. It is equally natural to have little energy left for the other critical part of the program work—developing the academic curriculum to accomplish the intended student learning goals. But wait. Isn't it enough to carefully plan a travel experience to the key cultural and physical locations in the host country? Isn't it enough to give students a chance to directly experience a location far from the comforts of home? To provide an opportunity for them to learn and grow through thoughtfully planned travel abroad? In a word, no.

To realize the potential of a faculty-led international program, particularly one of short duration, faculty must design a purposeful curriculum and determine the pedagogy to support the course objectives and desired learning outcomes. While we have argued that faculty-led programs can have significant and long-lasting impacts on students, it is the *curriculum*, along with careful teaching and faculty guidance that is the key to making this happen. Providing faculty-led courses that are little more than modern-day grand tours is simply not enough. Although faculty leading such experiences may enjoy positive student feedback, we contend that a vital learning opportunity has been missed. If, for example, the overall course focus is to

Fostering Global Citizenship Through Faculty-Led International Programs, pages 143–144
143

further global citizenship, can we expect students to develop a truly differ-ent and more expansive mindset and attitude toward this concept without offering the learning structures to do so? In short, curriculum design must be at the heart of faculty-led international courses. It is not something that can be shortchanged because too much time and energy has been spent ironing out program logistics.

So what does a long-lasting and impactful program include? First, it must be driven by learning objectives that faculty deem worthwhile and achievable. In tandem with defining objectives, faculty must select (or de-sign) assessment instruments for measuring how well those objectives have been met. After these critical pieces have been drafted, faculty must turn their attention to the different program phases: pre-departure, in-field, and reentry. It is beneficial to consider what will be occurring over time and to design curriculum in light of each of these phases. Before leaving the home campus, what will students need to learn and think about? During travel, how can faculty take advantage of all that is happening—both planned and unanticipated experiences? Finally, how will students demonstrate what they have gained? And perhaps most important of all, what can be done to help students hold on to what they have learned and extend it into other aspects of their lives?

To respond to these essential questions, the final part of our text is de-voted to the critical issues surrounding design, delivery, and assessment of a high-impact, faculty-led international program.

10

Learning Objectives and Assessment

You Can't Have One Without the Other

When we define what matters in education only by what we can measure,
we are in serious trouble.

—Diane Ravitch

TRAVEL TALE 10: Trials, Errors, and Reconsiderations
•••

Pru Cuper

When we began planning our first faculty-led field course to Peru, I was feeling both overwhelmed and ill-equipped to offer much beyond enthusiasm for what lay ahead. While I had been a successful teacher for over 20 years—first at the middle school level and then as a professor of education—I had never taught an international course before. Jo Beth, on the other hand, was very experienced in this arena. Wanting to hold my own, I offered to take the lead on developing the goals, objectives, and assessments for the course. I had earned a doctoral degree in curriculum and instruction after all. I figured that my background in education

Fostering Global Citizenship Through Faculty-Led International Programs, pages 145–160
Copyright © 2012 by Information Age Publishing
145

would surely apply, at least to some degree, and that transferring that background to an international course curriculum was a reasonable undertaking. In some ways I was right; in other ways, I had things to learn.

Defining the purpose for the course was easy enough. We were engaging our students in international service-learning that would give them firsthand knowledge and appreciation of Peru's people, environment, and culture. Moving from there into selecting specific learning objectives and designing assessments that would measure those objectives did not seem too difficult either. Based on the objectives, there would be readings, an exam, journals, interviews, and a research project that would serve as our culminating assessment.

To launch the research projects, we had our students select topics influenced by their respective fields of study and conduct preliminary inquiry the semester before we left. Interviews and observations would follow in Peru. We discussed how topics might deepen or change somewhat based on the data they would be gathering. We let the students know in advance that we intended to be flexible—within reason. One of our students, a health and nutrition major, planned to compare meals served in her hometown with those served in her Urubamba homestay to determine dietary differences based on culture and availability of food staples. Another student wanted to examine textbooks used in Peruvian schools to see how they compared to U.S. textbooks in terms of historic accuracy. We designed a very specific list of expectations and a rubric for assessing the final research papers. What we did not anticipate was how the research would actually unfold during our travel experience.

From the time we touched down in Lima until we headed back to the United States 17 days later, we were on a nonstop learning adventure packed with incidents and information we never could have anticipated. Unfortunately, none of those learning opportunities had much to do with the neat but somewhat confining research topics our students had selected. Oh, they dutifully did what was asked of them, but the final products (even with many adjustments made along the way) felt somewhat restrictive, forced, and inappropriate to the purpose of the course. Ultimately, we agreed that the projects just did not relate to many of the most valuable lessons learned.

••••••••••••••••••••

Assessment 101

Assessment has gotten something of a bad name of late. This is not so much a product of the central *purpose* of assessment but more about how it has been conducted recently and how assessment results have been used (or not used). Ideally, assessment offers a means for determining the value and effectiveness of an educational endeavor, whether it is a first grader showing his ability to sound out new words or an environmental studies major demonstrating her knowledge of the complex processes driving climate change. Rather than being used as a means for comparing one classroom (or teacher) to the next based on tests scores, or laying an administrative layer of requirements onto an already overtaxed group of faculty, assessment is best understood as a means for measuring intended learning and growth, and for determining future action.

In this chapter, we discuss the basics of assessment in light of both student learning and program evaluation—the two areas faculty will need to consider as they embark on teaching an international program. Although they were not designed to serve the same purpose, student assessments are sometimes used to help determine the value of programs. While they can provide helpful data, they capture the perspective of only one participant group and need to be part of a larger assessment system.

Formative and Summative Assessments

In order to appreciate both the nature and value of assessment, it is important to understand the difference between formative and summative methods. It is equally important to understand how the two work together. Looking at formative assessment as the more organic or fluid of the two methods is a helpful way to begin. Formative assessment is done along the way, as the student is "forming" new knowledge. When we assess, for example, how a student is progressing toward a targeted learning objective, we might use formative strategies such as observation and questioning in order to make in-process adjustments to our instruction. If we see that the student is not learning, why would we continue to use an ineffective teaching strategy? After conducting formative assessments and acting on what we have learned from them, summative assessments can offer a "summary" or final means for determining how well the student accomplished the intended objectives.

The use of formative and summative assessment applies not only to student learning, as in the example offered, but also to program assessment. Palomba and Banta (1999) capture the process of program assessment well when they describe it as "the systematic collection, review, and use of information about educational programs undertaken for the purpose of improving learning and development" (p. 4). Whether focusing on students or programs, formative (along the way) and summative (final) assessments offer data (useful information) that help us realize how well we are accomplishing what we set out to do.

Objectives and Their Assessments

Creating meaningful assessments begins with appreciation of how goals, objectives, and assessments are interconnected. Goals define the overarching purpose of a lesson, course, or program. They are broad-based and are not intended to be measured. An example of a learning goal might be, *Students will explore the impact of U.S. media on Peruvian adolescents.* Learning objectives, on the other hand, are specific subsets of goals that pinpoint intended outcomes. They are best stated in measurable and observable terms and should be defined alongside the formative and summative instruments that will be used to establish how well they have been (or are being) accomplished. A learning objective for the goal regarding the influence of U.S. media might be: *Students enrolled in a short-term faculty-led course to Peru will interview the adolescents in their homestay families in Urubamba (or in neighboring families, as needed) to identify youth perceptions of the impact of U.S. television programming in this particular region.* Observable verbs such as "interview" and "identify" lend themselves to creating both formative and summative assessment instruments.

In this case, faculty would work with students as they designed questions and interviewed the target audience (formative assessments). In this way, they could jointly determine questions to add or delete in order to best meet the intended learning objectives. The summative assessment would require students to submit a clean, edited copy of the interview questions and responses as well as qualitative analysis of the data gathered. To extend the learning, a second summative assessment might require all of the students to discuss their findings and write a summary report or chart showing the perceived impact of U.S. media on Peruvian youth. In this way, student achievement of objectives could be measured both individually and as members of a learning community.

Knowledge, Skills, and Dispositions

Student learning objectives generally focus on growth within three areas: knowledge, skills, and dispositions (or attitudes). These are also oftentimes described as the cognitive, psychomotor, and affective domains. Either way, the objectives are focused on slightly different aspects of learning and growth. Within a given assignment, growth in all three areas or domains may be occurring simultaneously, but objectives are usually written with primary attention to one at a time.

Content knowledge (or cognitive growth) would involve mastery of fact-based information such as latitude and longitude, weather patterns, population shifts, or possibly, leadership and governance of a certain country. Skills (psychomotor growth) might involve learning how to make detailed observations or how to conduct interviews, essentially learning how to perform a certain task correctly and effectively. Growth in knowledge and skills are usually quite easy to assess. Dispositions, however, are more challenging to work with as they are the most subjective of the three domains. Encompassing internal/emotional growth, they are less readily quantifiable and therefore call for unique assessment strategies and instruments. If, for example, a student is developing self-awareness by writing about an emotional response to an intercultural encounter during study abroad, how might that be assessed? And who is the appropriate party to determine growth in self-awareness, the faculty member or the student?

As we explained in Travel Tale 10, even with deep experience in curriculum and instruction, the business of assessing learning during an international course is a somewhat different pursuit than assessing learning in the traditional classroom setting. Both versions require solid planning, preparation, and willingness to appreciate teachable moments that may occur along the way. But in the case of international courses, those teachable moments tend to happen with increased frequency. Moreover, they oftentimes involve emotions and/or unsettled feelings related to being far from the home environment and established expectations.

Designing and Assessing Faculty-Led Field Programs

Reviewing the basic components of assessment demonstrates some of the challenges involved in designing curriculum for short-term faculty-led international courses. Fortunately, while there is not a wealth of research in this area, what is available suggests that unique opportunities for academic and personal growth outweigh the challenges. But to ensure such student growth, faculty may need to adapt their pedagogy somewhat. First, we must widen the lens regarding the *kinds* of growth we hope to see in our students. Along with whatever learning objectives we have selected based on the discipline and nature of the course, we must also factor in more "global" objectives related to intercultural awareness, sensitivity, appreciation, and adaptability. Then we will need to determine how to assess these new objectives along with our more traditional course objectives.

Common International Learning Goals and Objectives

Examining the most common learning goals and objectives for international courses, both long and short term, is a sound way for faculty to decide which objectives might be appropriate for their particular programs. From the University of Georgia's GLOSSARI project to AAC&U's LEAP and Shared Futures initiatives to the Forum on Education Abroad (all of which we have referenced in Parts I and II of our text), there is consistent emphasis on student development across certain areas: knowledge of world geography and cultures, intercultural competence, self-awareness and awareness of "other," critical thinking skills, interpersonal adaptability, and global consciousness, to name the most persistent few. Such a list is necessarily somewhat general as the items were not developed with a specific location, discipline, or course in mind. Depending upon the nature of the program, selecting appropriate goals from such a list and determining how to go about writing course-specific objectives is sure to vary.

Another useful source for faculty who have selected their location but are just starting course design is Fink's (2003) Taxonomy of Significant Learning. Fink's categories are particularly valuable in that they align well with each of the learning domains (knowledge, skills, and dispositions) but also encompass the intercultural goals that cross all three domains. Fink's taxonomy includes:

- *Foundational knowledge* (content area, fact-based)
- *Application* (skills such as observing, interviewing, and decision making)
- *Integration* (making connections across concepts and experiences)
- *Human dimensions* (developing self-awareness and awareness of others)
- *Caring* (understanding emotions and values—one's own and others')
- *Learning how to learn* (developing metacognitive, reflective practices)

As with the list of common learning goals and objectives, faculty can sort through Fink's categories to consider what has worked well for others as they select objectives that will work best for them. After that comes development of both formative and summative assessments to measure growth toward the objectives; and finally, determination of where and when in the program to introduce and use the assessments—pre-departure, while abroad, upon reentry, or in some cases, repeatedly along the way.

Content Area Learning and Growth

While content area objectives will vary from discipline to discipline, they are one of the most consistent forms of learning targeted in international courses. Before students enter a foreign country and encounter a culture that is new to them, they need to acquire content knowledge about the country. On a general scale, this might include the country's history, geography, political climate, and current and past cultural influences. Depending upon the more specific goals of the program, this might also include knowledge of environmental challenges, gender issues, or other possible topics of particular interest to the faculty leading the program.

Defining learning objectives related to content area knowledge may be the easiest and most natural task for faculty, as most of us deal with this facet of instruction regularly. We are both comfortable and competent in a certain subject area, and chances are good that our international coursework will touch upon this interest and expertise. When two or more faculty decide to design and lead an international program together, the combination of their areas of expertise can make the work more enjoyable and more academically beneficial for all involved. Consider, for example, faculty from Women's Studies working with faculty from Political Science to offer a course in Saudi Arabia, a country where women are now allowed to vote but are not allowed to drive themselves to the polls. Interdisciplinary coursework such as this is becoming more and more popular on home campuses, but consider the potential for engaged learning when interdisciplinary courses are taught in the very settings that are under study.

As faculty build their syllabi, a typical course goal related to the content area learning domain might follow this general format: *The course will deepen student understanding and appreciation of* [whatever the subject area] *in the context of* [whatever the international setting]. From there, faculty would determine precise learning objectives and design their accompanying assessments. In the cognitive or content area domain, such assessments might take the form of tests or quizzes administered pre-departure, creation of maps or interview reports with analysis when abroad, or explanation of photographs from the field shared in final projects and presentations after reentry.

Intercultural Awareness and Growth

Intercultural awareness is another topic frequently targeted in international course learning objectives currently. In their recent work in this area, Hovey and Weinberg (2009) argue that study-abroad can involve either culturally low-road or high-road programs. They define low-road programs as those that provide "culturally thin experiences" in which students travel in large groups and are often isolated from the place and culture they are visiting. On the other hand, high-road programs are those designed to ensure depth of cultural learning and exchange. These are the programs that emphasize participation in local communities aided by appropriately compensated local staff. The high-road programs give students (and faculty) the opportunity to have an inside view of a place and local culture from the ground, not a passing glance from a tour bus. Hovey and Weinberg further argue that the difference between the two is not about the program length, location, or cost, but about a curriculum with emphasis on immersing students in the host culture.

For faculty addressing this aspect of student learning within their international program, an overarching course goal might state: *The course will forward student growth in intercultural understanding and maturity.* As with most goals, the target is worthwhile but impossible to measure as stated. Learning objectives and assessments would then need to be designed in order to determine whether or not students have, in fact, attained some degree of intercultural maturity. In this case, using a scale to help gauge student growth could be helpful.

Fortunately, there are numerous such scales to choose from. From Bennett's (1986) original Developmental Model of Intercultural Sensitivity (DMIS) to Deardorff's (2004) Pyramid Model of Intercultural Competence, faculty can decide what measures to use and when to present and discuss them with their students. Using such measures as part of the predeparture readings can raise student awareness of the stages people generally go through in locations and cultures that are new to them. Faculty can then refer back to the readings as needed once they are abroad.

To use the scales (and other readings on intercultural growth) to register student growth, the course curriculum must include objectives and activities that require students to interact directly and in an authentic way with various aspects of the host culture. Homestays offer a good start, but formative assessment of what students are learning from their homestays is critical. This might take the form of targeted journal prompts along with ongoing opportunities for follow-up discussion. An objective for this type of work might be: *Using Bennett's DMIS as a measure, students who are living with a homestay family whose culture is new to them will discuss the progress they are making in moving beyond ethnocentric responses.*

Targeting Global Citizenship

Closely related to course goals and objectives involving intercultural growth are those dedicated to global citizenship. Both targets are hard to measure as they are often marked more by internal growth that only the student can fully appreciate than growth that can be conveniently categorized on a scale or checklist. This is not to say that global citizenship, from understanding what the concept means to attempting to embody it in some way, is not an important goal for a faculty-led international program—it is. The bigger question is how to approach the concept.

In teaching both our initial course to Peru and the following year's course to Belize, we found that our students had little knowledge of the concept of global citizenship beyond hearing it mentioned from time to time as a college-wide goal. For us, engaging the students in defining the term and trying to determine what it might look like for them, both as college students and later in their lives, was a good opening into the topic. From there, we revisited the term periodically while we were abroad and very pointedly when we returned to the home campus. We used prompts such as, "When have you witnessed an act of global citizenship?" or "When have you operated as a global citizen—how, where, and why?" The ensuing discussions offered our students a means for examining the concept in their real-world encounters and actions. A learning objective that would thus target the broader goal of encouraging global citizenship might be: *Through completing a writing prompt and engaging in follow-up discussion, students will analyze various ways in which the concept of global citizenship can be embodied.*

As we explained in Chapter 4 of our text, *awareness* is the first of three steps involved in realizing some measure of global citizenship. The overarching goal and specific learning objective listed above would likely lead to enhanced student awareness of what it takes to act as a global citizen. The second step in the process, developing a sense of *responsibility*, can be encouraged from there. The final step, *taking action* that embodies some of the qualities of global citizenship, may then follow. With this in-process model in mind, we found that helping our students gain greater awareness of what global citizenship might involve and how they might begin to stand in this role was a purposeful and realizable initial objective.

Assessing the Students: Grappling With Grading

During the process of curriculum design, most faculty (except for those rare few who are not required to submit a final grade for the course) will need to consider the numeric value of their various assessments. As we have discussed throughout this chapter, so much of the student learning and growth that occurs during study abroad is internal or dispositional in nature and therefore does not readily lend itself to numeric evaluation. Instead, this type of growth is best considered through the use of self-assessment instruments such as summative self-analyses or semistructured reentry interviews. In order to transfer such self-assessment into a numeric grade, students can be invited to grade themselves, with the understanding that their input will be part of the overall grading system. For faculty who decide to go this route, we would advise holding individual sessions with students wherein they will be asked to explain in specific detail why they have given themselves, for example, a grade of "A" in intercultural maturity. What did they experience? How did they respond? How will they sustain and grow further in this area? When we ask students to respond candidly to such questions, we are offering them a chance to think deeply and critically about their own growth. Such an experience can be far more valuable than having an instructor assess intercultural growth based on what they have observed from the outside.

Whatever grading structure faculty decide to use, determining the relative value of the different assessment categories must be completed in the curriculum design stage and is best shared with the students early in the course. In that way, everyone understands the expectations and guidelines at the outset. Leaving room within the grading structure for the spontaneous learning that is likely to occur can be accomplished by designating at least one rather broad-based category, such as "Field Participation" or "Self-Analysis," in which students understand that what they are able to carefully process and gain along the way is of real importance and will be reflected in their final grade.

A Summative Assessment That Worked

We opened this chapter with the tale of a summative assessment that did not work very well. When we solicited program feedback from our students at the end of the Peru course, they were happy to talk over what might have worked better. They began by discussing the overall impact the course experience had had on them and how they wished there were some way to truly capture that impact. Everyone agreed that the research project was well-intended, but that it simply did not reflect what they had learned in any unique or particularly meaningful way. They pointed to their journal entries and photographs, unstructured as they may have been, as more meaningful artifacts of their course experience. We thought hard about what they were saying and used their observations as the basis for a very different summative assessment that we trialed the following spring in Belize. We called the new version the Digital Travel Tale project.

This rendering of our summative assessment rested on the premise that instead of bringing home their required field journals and a travelogue of photos as separate artifacts, it made sense to ask students to integrate these items along with a narrative and music files. Our students, after all, were what Prensky (2010) fondly described as "digital natives." They could take their voluminous megabytes of digital photos and some purposefully selected journal quotes and put them to good use in a holistic, theme-based, multimedia portrait of what they had gained, both academically and personally, from their international course experience. The students were thereby invited to use their own tools, their own media, their own creativity in telling their digital tales.

The directions we gave to the students at the outset were quite simple. We told them that their digital tales would need to include the following: a creative title, a clear beginning narrative (voice or embedded text), a series of no more than 20 digital photos with explanations regarding why (thematically) they had selected each, music files that would enhance the overall message of the tale, and a closing narrative summarizing the impact of the course experience on them as citizens of both America and the world. We encouraged them to be as creative as they would like within these guidelines. We also reminded them that the greatest source of data for their digital travel tales would probably be their journals. We therefore reminded them to take careful, detailed notes daily; not only what we would periodically ask them to write but also their own/spontaneous responses to what they were seeing, hearing, and feeling.

The project objectives were straightforward as well. We told the students that through the project they would (a) share their knowledge and understanding of Belize and its culture, explaining how that knowledge developed during their study and travels; (b) select one theme related to their academic discipline, discussing its relevance through their travel tale; and (c) capture the impact they believed the course experience had on them as citizens of America and as citizens of the world. Along with the description of the project and a clear explanation of the three learning objectives, we also gave the students the grading rubric we would be using to assess how well their work met those learning objectives.

For faculty new to creating rubrics, we share our Digital Travel Tales rubric in Table 10.1. By way of explanation, standard procedure during rubric creation is to use the column to the far left to list the grading criteria presented in the assignment description. In the case of our project, the

TABLE 10.1   Rubric for Assessing Digital Travel Tale Projects

Assessment Criteria	Good Job	Needs Work
Narrative • Creative title • Clear opening and closing • Smooth story flow • Exploration of theme using multimedia tools • No generalizations; specific/detailed explanations • Personal reflection evident • Reference to prior readings	• Creative title sets the stage for the project. • Opening narrative situates student at the outset of the course—initial questions and concerns presented. • Digital photos and narrative flow smoothly as student shares one (or two) themes of particular interest. • Narrative is marked by specific, detailed observations with possible personal (etic) biases defined. • Connections/references to course readings threaded through narrative appropriately. • Closing narrative offers introspective response to the selected theme and to the overall travel/study experience. • Digital story clearly demonstrates the impact of the travel experience.	• Opening and closing do not serve as clear bookends for the core of the project. • Identification of theme (or themes) is not evident or limited. • Narrative includes few specific observations. • Narrative includes generalizations. • Project shows little creativity and/or introspection. • Narrative makes few if any references to prior readings.
Digital Content • 10–20 original images • Embedded narrative (text or audio) • Appropriate music files with credit given	• Required number of photos are marked by careful selection that contribute to the theme selected. • Narrative is clear and demonstrates self-reflection. • Music files are interwoven to enhance the overall effect of the story.	• Project does not include required number of original images. • Narrative is not embedded (text or audio) consistently, if at all. • Music files not included in a meaningful way, if at all.
Editing/Finishing • Technically correct text • 2 DVDs submitted on time and easily opened!	• No grammatical or spelling errors. • Project arrives on time and can be readily viewed.	• Narrative not edited; errors evident. • Project does not arrive on time and/or cannot be opened.

grading criteria included the narrative, the digital content, and the editing (or finishing) of the project. After listing the criteria, many rubrics are structured to show 3–5 levels of student achievement with descriptors that usually range from "Exceeds Expectations" to "Meets Expectations" to "Needs Improvement." In our case, we kept the descriptors simple, either "Good Job" or "Needs Work." We explained to the students that the rubric was useful in two ways: first, as a guideline for them as they created their digital travel tales, and second, for us as a holistic means for determining what they had learned. We were not assigning points for each of the items in the criterion categories, but rather considering how well the project met the grading criteria overall. Beyond this, we asked the students to self-assess their projects using the rubric. In this way, they were asked to candidly review and evaluate all of the elements of their work.

Students were given 2 months to complete their digital travel tales. In comparison to our first summative assessment, we were delighted with the results of this new project. There was great range in themes, photos, music, and narrative style, but each student captured his or her individual experience and growth in a lasting and meaningful way.

Assessing the Program: What Needs to Change?

As we have said from the outset of our text, there are numerous stakeholders involved in any short-term faculty-led international program. From the student participants and their families (who may have helped pay for the experience), to the faculty who designed and carried out the program, to administration and related staff members who offered support, all of the stakeholders should have a say in assessing how the program went and what might be changed to make it stronger and possibly smoother in the future. But despite realizing the usefulness of such a collective endeavor, it is interesting to note that pulling all stakeholders together for program assessment rarely happens. In fact, beyond collecting traditional student course evaluations and enjoying posttrip student presentations, many short-term programs are never assessed in a systematic way. Instead, there seems to be more excitement about sharing forthcoming international course plans than there is about discovering what was actually gained from the courses that were successfully carried out.

In the absence of systematic program review, faculty should conduct some level of program assessment on their own, principally to improve their design and delivery for the future. By inviting students into this work, faculty can gain a valuable second perspective that extends beyond comments made in traditional course evaluations. In fact, if students are encouraged to make suggestions in an open-discussion format, they are more likely to vent whatever they did not like about the program (even very personal likes and dislikes) in a more appropriate way than they might on an anonymous evaluation checklist.

Hopefully, current program evaluation methods will change and improve over time, with the various stakeholders getting together to discuss what was effective about a certain program as well as what might be done to improve upon it in the future. In this way, constructive suggestions as well as appreciation of the positive outcomes of the experience can be shared by *all* of the people involved in the endeavor.

The Best-Laid Plans

Even the best-laid plans for learning do not always happen the way we anticipated or might have hoped. However, as we have argued throughout this chapter, if faculty design a purposeful but also intentionally flexible curriculum, they can take advantage of the actual learning that occurs. From our own experience, and as portrayed in Travel Tale 10, we had designed a culminating project (the research paper) that simply did not work as we had hoped. The greatest problem with it was not its proposed purpose or learning objectives—they were solid enough. The real problem was the lack of genuine student investment in what they were being asked to generate. They were unquestionably learning a great deal, but it didn't fall within the guidelines of the research project. Instead, their growth was occurring through their own observations and their own processing of the new experiences and sometimes unforeseen events that they were living in the midst of each day.

By moving from the research project to the digital travel tales, the final products were much richer and a much truer measure of how our students had actually grown. It is interesting to note that when students return from an international course, they often describe it as a "transformative" experience without necessarily being able to answer the question, "How so?" Keeping in mind this initial reentry response (something of a "stars in their eyes" effect) and how it plays out over time, having their digital travel tales as a reference may help them sustain the reality of what they were feeling at the time they had the experience. Hopefully, when they revisit their digital projects in the years ahead, the music, narrative, and photographs they took will help them reflect back to the actual feelings they had and possibly reawaken the academic and personal growth they experienced.

A final aspect of curriculum design and assessment that is worth keeping in mind for those new to international teaching is that the intended goals and learning outcomes may not be obtained in a single experience. Students and faculty alike make strides each time they move into a new international setting that nudges them out of their known worldviews and cultural comfort zone. Having said this, perhaps our curricular work should focus more on determining ways to encourage further international study and further growth toward worthy goals such as intercultural maturity or global citizenship. It may be true that, as Santanello and Wolff (2008) argue, our most important work is to find ways to "close the circle after the study abroad programs so that the experience becomes part of the continuum of lifelong learning" (p. 189).

11

Pre-Departure Preparation

Setting the Stage for International Learning

The real voyage of discovery consists not in seeking new landscapes,
but in having new eyes.

—Marcel Proust

TRAVEL TALE 11: Location as Text

••

One of the learning objectives for our Global Engagement course to Peru was to develop our students' ability to make detailed and unbiased observations. Our group consisted of a mix of freshmen and sophomores. Most had never ventured beyond U.S. borders; few, if any, had taken research courses that involved developing observation skills. We knew that we needed to introduce and practice such skills before we left, but we weren't exactly sure how to go about it in a way that would be engaging, useful, and memorable for our students.

Fortunately, we attended a conference just before we taught the course that featured an exercise called City as Text (Braid & Long, 2000), in which

---

Fostering Global Citizenship Through Faculty-Led International Programs, pages 161–177
161

the conference participants were invited to explore the conference city (in this case, Washington DC) using the City as Text observation model. Divided into groups, we were directed to explore a section of the city and to keenly observe the "text" or story that we could read from the way signs were displayed, dwellings were designed, the environment was (or was not) respected, people interacted, and so on. The idea being that a place can and does tell a story—of its culture, its people, its history, its preferences for food, for music, for gender, age, and on and on. The exercise was intriguing, open-ended, and, we quickly agreed, rich with possibilities for our student travelers.

Also, in the semester prior to departure, a team of English professors came to our campus to discuss their book and offer a workshop on fieldwork and observation (Sunstein & Chiseri-Strater, 2007). The authors led us through one of their exercises that invited everyone to "make the ordinary extraordinary" by taking an object worn regularly (a watch, a ring) and writing down then explaining to another person in the workshop the object's history and personal significance. The results were fascinating. Who would have expected such a story behind a commonly overlooked object? Who would have expected to learn so much about the people we regularly interact with in a genial (but evidently cursory) fashion?

Borrowing from these ideas, we developed an exercise for our students that directed them to roam the small city in which our campus is located with "new eyes" and with as little personal overlay as possible. "Just write what you observe around the topic of your choice. Don't analyze or judge. Write down exactly what you see." They were given a notebook and 2 hours and were directed to select some aspect of the city that told a story of its inhabitants—their style, their commitments, their preferences, their way of walking in the world. We offered a few examples, but left the students primarily on their own.

When we reconvened later in the day to share our findings, enthusiasm was running high, and notebooks brimmed with observations. One young woman, a communications major, sat on a bench near a busy street corner and observed how people did (or did not) make eye contact with each other when they passed on the street. She then charted the age and gender of those who made eye contact and with whom they made eye contact versus those who made no eye contact at all. She took into consideration cell phone use (and how this related to age) as well as socioeconomic status, which she based on clothing, hairstyle, and vehicle make and model (if that could be determined). Another student tracked the accommodations made for people with disabilities—the number of parking spaces reserved for this group of citizens, the ramps and entrances to public buildings,

the way people either interacted with or shied away f.
There were 16 students in our class, and each student ca.
unique and rich set of observations of our city—details that we
lyzed together and agreed that, despite having lived there for some
we had never taken into deep consideration before.

....

What They Need to Know, Do, and Be Open to Before They Go

Given that the duration of your time abroad will be limited and that students cannot be expected to have the knowledge about the international location or the skills necessary to fully take advantage of their experience once they arrive, there is much work to do prior to departure. To ensure a sound academic program, it is imperative to hold meetings with student participants prior to travel that include, but also extend beyond, travel logistics. You must also dive into an academic curriculum that will prepare your students to make the most of their international experience. Achieving the defined learning outcomes for the program will be much more likely to happen if students are provided with plenty of background knowledge as well as opportunities to develop and improve skills for engaging productively in the host country. For example, a primary goal of your program may be to give students the opportunity to consider the differences between the cultural history they learn about in various texts and what they may observe and experience in the international setting. Such a productive comparison may not happen automatically for students unless they have been guided in what to look for, think about, or reconsider. These are skills that can be nurtured prior to going abroad. In short, when designing the pre-departure curriculum, consider those elements that will move the students' international exposure beyond a shallow, superficial tour, to a rich academic and personal learning experience.

Fortunately, there are a variety of models for pre-departure learning. Some leaders organize their programs to include an entire course or even a few courses prior to the actual international experience. Others schedule a series of meetings with their student participants in the months leading up to travel. Selecting the best approach for your program will involve negotiations between how much time you would *like* to have to fully prepare your students for the experience and the practical realities of your institutional environment and your student participants' (not to mention your own) competing commitments. Having said this, in the meetings prior to travel, it is critical to devote a significant amount of time to improving your students' content knowledge and skills. In many cases, a seminar format in which students are actively involved in preparing for the journey ahead proves particularly productive.

Designing the pre-departure portion of the program must begin with careful consideration of the readings, exercises, skills, reflections, and discussions that will best prepare your students for the experiential learning ahead. What concepts, ideas, viewpoints, and emotions need to be explored before boarding the plane? What skills need to be practiced and maybe even mastered before embarkation? What dispositions or attitudes are they likely to carry into this experience, and how might these need to be explored before entering the field? Essentially, what will help students gain as much as possible from their short time abroad? And what will help make the experience impactful and long-lasting?

Whether an international program is discipline-specific or interdisciplinary in nature, it is helpful to consider pre-departure curriculum as 3-pronged, aligning directly with the cognitive, psychomotor, and affective learning domains discussed in Chapter 10: the knowledge, skills, and dispositions you want your students to develop. First, it is essential to establish the content (historic, cultural) your students need to have regarding the host country and its people. Next, you should consider the skills they will need in order to be fully engaged in the field experience and realize the course learning outcomes. Finally comes determining what they will need to develop in the way of both self and intercultural awareness in order to interact appropriately and respectfully in the field setting. In this chapter, we offer both discussion and concrete examples of ways to design a pre-departure curriculum that addresses these essential areas.

What Do They Need to Know?

Before individuals venture into an entirely new location, it is natural for them to experience feelings of uncertainty about where they are going and what they can expect to encounter there. A wide range of questions about the place and its people inevitably arise. For faculty designing international field programs, such questions are to be welcomed, as they serve as the basis for engaged, inquiry-based learning. While faculty need to select wide-ranging and reputable resources in advance, inviting students into the process of deciding what they need (and want) to learn from those resources (as well as inviting them to locate other appropriate resources) encourages their full involvement.

Background Knowledge: The Country, Its People, Its Challenges

Depending upon your destination, there are likely to be a variety of print and electronic resources that will offer your students a detailed portrait of your host country—its history, geography, climate, people, culture, traditions, and the challenges it has faced in all of these areas over time. Likely resources may include, but are not limited to, comprehensive textbooks of the host region; location-specific histories of the country's significant cultural sites; biographies and autobiographies of leaders who impacted the country's history; guidebooks and travel guides; documentaries or other video resources focusing on your destination; host country newspapers (preferably representing differing perspectives); and journal articles, written either about the host country or by those who call the country home. As you select resources, consider how critical thinking can be brought into student responses to these materials. Try inviting students to consider the perspectives of the authors of the various texts. What personal biases or "agendas" (political, religious, or cultural) might they bring based, for example, on when they were born and the socioeconomic status of their family? What alternative readings might need to be considered to offer another take on the information presented?

Your students need background knowledge of the host country that represents the views of residents, not just the views of writers who may not have directly experienced what they were writing about. While certain historic facts may be readily available and pretty much unarguable, the beginning and end dates of political regimes, for example, what did the residents of the country think of those regimes and their leaders? Whose perspectives did they represent and whose were overlooked? Who prospered and who did not? Asking students to question the texts and to make connections between course readings and their own reality as U.S. citizens can help them begin to appreciate the complexity of the host country and can encourage the kind of engaged learning and critical awareness that international study can promote.

Another excellent source of background information are guest speakers who have researched, lived, or traveled extensively within the host country. In some cases, this might be another faculty member from your home campus or a resident of the surrounding area. First-person accounts of the host country can offer a very detailed portrait of what it will be like to live there for the in-field duration—the cultural norms students may encounter (from the perspective of the guest speaker), the restaurants and nightlife, behavioral norms in public spaces, the variations in language and dialect from one region of the country to the next. Such presentations, which oftentimes include candid, in-country photographs, tend to get the student travelers very excited about what lies ahead. They can also remind students of the realities of the country's legal system. We recall, for example, our students' wide-eyed responses when a guest speaker told them about Belize's solitary prison and how a single drug offense could land a traveler there.

For every pre-departure resource you offer, we strongly encourage requiring an accompanying response. Such responses do not always need to take the form of formal written essays, although you may want to use this technique from time to time, particularly if you are asking your students to research a course topic prior to departure. Instead, you might ask for a quick-write to open a class discussion on the key points made in a given resource. In this instance, students could be asked to jot down a point they found controversial from the resource or perhaps particularly in line with (or counter to) what they have experienced within the United States. Students can then discuss their responses in small groups before sharing some of the more critical points made with the entire class. Most of all, you want to be sure that your students are not only reading what you have assigned but also processing it, first individually and then with their peers, at a deeper and more critical level. Journal entries too, which we will focus on in the next section of this chapter, can be used as a means for responding to readings and sharing responses with others. With appreciation of constructivist practice in mind, the point is to invite students to create their own meaning from the varied resources by relating what they are learning about to their own life experiences thus building upon and expanding their schema prior to travel.

Finally, the use of exams as a pre-departure summative assessment is certainly an option. While the multiple choice or true/false format generally tends to require recall of facts rather than analysis and synthesis of various perspectives, checking on students' basic knowledge of facts about the host country can be achieved in this way. To enrich this type of assessment, we would suggest including some thought-provoking essay questions within the exam as well as asking students why it is important to have factual knowledge of a country before traveling there. Perhaps sharing current research with them on the lack of geographic knowledge among U.S. students would be an interesting channel within a "why is this important to know" discussion.

Course Expectations

Learning as much as possible about the host country is critical prior to departure. The other knowledge-related information your students will need is the expectations for the course, from personal conduct within the host country (covered in Chapter 9) to the academic assessments that will determine how well course objectives have been met. It is important to have both formative and summative assessments clearly outlined early on and equally important to share this information with your students. We also suggest explaining that the plans, while solid, include room for additions and change based on what may happen along the way. Specific journal prompts, for example, may be added based on what you and your students are experiencing. As noted, it is the unexpected that may present the best opportunities for all participants to respond to and examine unique aspects of the international setting.

What Do They Need to Be Able to Do?

As you are engaging your students in learning about their host country before departure, you will also need to help them hone certain skills that will enable them to make the most of their in-country experiences. While there are many that could prove useful, two that stand out and cross most disciplines are the skills of observing (and recording those observations) and journaling. Beyond these, gaining at least a rudimentary grasp of the language most commonly spoken in the host country is not only a useful skill but also a courtesy.

Observation Skills

We opened this chapter with a tale about learning how to keenly observe an object or a place in order to better understand it. This is a skill that students and faculty need to actively develop and nurture before arriving in the host country. Learning exercises, such as those mentioned, can help students become aware of how observant they are naturally and provide structure for them to begin to tune in to their surroundings and reflect on their own perceptions and cultural influences in an intentional way. Such work is critical to moving students toward a more in-depth examination of the human connections between themselves and others; and eventually beyond the ethnocentrism that is common among those who have had little opportunity to directly experience cultures other than their own.

We have found that the qualitative method of *participant observation* is helpful to explain to your students prior to travel. This method has the observer assume a position that involves simultaneous observation of and direct contact with insiders while continuing to stand (by necessity) in the position of outsider. Living for a given amount of time among insiders, but not intent on becoming a member of the observed community, the participant observer gains a more nuanced understanding of the cultural setting. Such an act of observing-while-living-with encourages the observer to become more empathic toward the host community, an attribute that helps to negate whatever natural biases, whether conscious or not, the observer may bring. Putting your students fully into the role of participant observer may be beyond the scope of your program, but teaching them about it and the observational skills required by this method can help them appreciate the depth and complexity of the host culture. We have also found it to be a good introduction to the power and purpose of ethnographic research as a means for connecting people from differing cultures.

When students finally step into the host country, they will be experiencing the new environs through all of their senses, exactly in line with the multimodal learning we discussed in Chapter 2. While such intake is a natural process, it may not be something they will be fully aware of unless prompted to consider both how their sensory perceptions are engaged and what they are innately learning from the new environment. Having students practice making multimodal observations therefore is an excellent pre-departure exercise that can be easily accomplished using the strategies from our opening travel tale. Without such guidance, faculty cannot necessarily count on students' habitual ways of observing and thinking about their cultural and physical surroundings as attuned or focused enough to lead to productive discoveries in the field. Pre-departure activities that help them hone their observation skills will pay off once they step off the plane into the international setting. Students who have been led to fully experience and thus read the "text" or story of the new and unfamiliar setting can begin to reflect on what they are experiencing more confidently and purposefully than those who have not had the benefit of such training.

Journaling

Journaling is one of the most common requirements of students participating in international programs. It can also be one of the richest ways for students to capture and understand what they are experiencing. Unfortunately, journaling does not always live up to its potential. Without careful instruction and guidance, it can become a meaningless required daily function, largely a rambling travelogue of places seen and meals eaten rather than a rich vehicle for students to explore complex feelings about field issues, experiences, and circumstances as they arise.

Giving clear instructions about the intent of journal writing as well as providing prompted journal exercises and feedback on entries are tasks that need to be undertaken in pre-departure meetings with students. Just as with other assignments, students will do best if they understand what they are supposed to do *with* and learn *from* their journal writing. Depending upon your course objectives, journals can be used to record students' observations, express feelings, raise and attempt to answer questions, collect information, as well as respond to faculty prompts. Additionally, journal entries can involve creative works such as poetry, short stories, and drawings. Whatever parameters you place on the journal assignments, students should be knowledgeable about them before their passports are stamped.

One of the best ways to have students understand and buy into the value (and potential pleasure) of journal writing is to bring them into defining what journaling can afford them in their particular program and therefore what expectations would be most appropriate. Following discussion of journaling purposes and options, exploring means for assessing journal writings—perhaps even building a rubric for evaluating journal entries together—is a powerful way to invite students into assessing their own learning. When possible, showing examples of strong journal entries that align with the expectations and needs of your program can also give students a clear idea of your expectations and the learning potential of journaling.

We used a variety of prompts for our students' journal entries, but also gave them plenty of leeway to write whatever they wanted in terms of their personal reactions to the program—before we left, while in the host country, and at home. We simply let our students know in advance which of the journal entries they would be asked to share with us and with their peers. Sometimes the sharing was simply verbal, as part of a class discussion. In other cases, we let them know that we would be collecting certain entries in order to assess course learning outcomes and levels of participation. Such clear definitions help students know when to process more personal responses and when to keep in mind that their writing would be read by others. For this reason, we advised students to use spiral notebooks that would allow them to remove certain pages without destroying their journals.

Another strategy that we found to be very useful was giving a prompt (such as the question about what Peruvians have both gained and lost from

Machu Picchu), then holding a class discussion based on what the students wrote. In this way, each student came to the discussion prepared to talk. We spent time defining discourse expectations prior to the discussion, such as the need to hear from everyone, the need to respond respectfully to each other's points, and the need to self-monitor levels of participation. Finally, we told students they would write a postdiscussion journal entry that would explore how their initial writings were influenced by the discussion—what was reinforced, expanded upon, or changed altogether. We used the rubric in Table 11.1 to capture the value of this experience. The rubric is general enough to be used as is or adapted as needed for other programs. As with most scoring rubrics, the criteria defined in the initial assignment are listed in the far left column. Descriptors of how these criteria were (or were not) met then follow in the categories of Exceeds Expectations, Meets Expectations, or Needs Improvement.

To assign a grade based on this rubric, we have found holistic scoring more useful than allotting points to the various levels of criterion attainment. The simplest way to assess a student's work is to circle the category that best describes his or her efforts. But sometimes assessment just isn't that simple. For example, taking a highlighter to mark the areas in which student work has both met and exceeded certain expectations gives room for students to fall between specific categories, as they oftentimes will. In order to receive an A, a student might need to Exceed Expectations in all areas. Such final assessment decisions need to be determined by individual faculty depending upon their expectations and the nature of their student participants. The comments section at the bottom of the rubric gives space to further explain scoring.

The nature of pre-departure prompts will, of course, vary according to the focus of your program and the background experience and knowledge of your student participants. Certain prompts, however, are interdisciplinary and applicable to a variety of programs. For example, most programs would benefit from having prompted journal entries that encourage students to critically reflect on their roles as global citizens—perhaps asking them to define the term based on their own experiences before they leave the United States. Another overarching journal topic might ask students to critically reflect upon the contested and contradictory nature of globalization. While this would be a strong prompt for any discipline, it is particularly applicable to programs that have an environmental, social, or economic focus.

Whatever the topic or prompt, we have found that students need guidance in effective journal writing (particularly around the expectations and intent of journals within a given program) if they are to engage fully in this

TABLE 11.1   Sample Rubric for Prompted Journal Writing with Discussion

Criteria	Exceeds Expectations	Meets Expectations	Needs Improvement
Initial Journal Entry	Thoughtful reflection and critical analysis of the prompt topic. Multiple references to prior experience and course readings strengthen the points being made.	Reflection and analysis of the prompt topic. References to prior experience and course readings.	Little reflection and analysis of the prompt topic. Few, if any, references to either experience or course readings.
Participation in Discussion	Shared key points appropriately without dominating discussion. Listened and responded thoughtfully to others.	Shared key points without dominating discussion. Listened and responded to others.	Few points added to the discussion with little attention to points made by others.
Journal Entry Postdiscussion	Clearly demonstrates what was gained from the discussion with peers.	Some demonstration of revised thinking based on peer input.	Little to no reference to points made by peers.
Comments:			

Grade: _____

learning activity. Ultimately, if structured constructively, journals can shift some of the responsibility for learning to the students themselves, thus giving them a means to assume future self-growth and learning.

Language

If your international program is to be based in a non-English speaking location, you will need to consider whether to require your students to study the host country language prior to travel. Clearly, this may not be feasible for many faculty-led international programs largely due to time limitations. However, it is usually feasible to teach students at least a few commonly used and needed words to give them more confidence as they negotiate the host country. It is also important for them to realize that attempting to communicate, even on a very basic level, with host country residents in their own language rather than expecting them to accommodate by speaking English is an act of courtesy and respect.

For foreign language majors visiting a country whose language they have been studying but have not had a chance to use in context, an international program affords a chance to not only become more fluent but also to pick up on nuances of the language—to learn current expressions and idioms, for example, that would be harder to learn in the United States.

What Do They Need to Be Open To?

Some of the richest opportunities that international programs provide to student travelers fall within the affective learning domain. This is not to say that background knowledge and field-related skills are not important—they are. But the pre-travel learning that answers the question, "What do I need to be open to?" is unique in that it pushes students to closely examine their own family histories, cultures, and worldviews in light of the lives of others. Such work is not easy, particularly when done for the first time, and it may involve some emotion. In order for students to fully take advantage of and gain from an international program, they should be prepared to be open to exploring the unfamiliar and at times uncomfortable landscape, culture, and conditions that they will find themselves in when abroad. Considering scenarios that may place participants in unexpected or unclear situations prior to going abroad may help students' tolerance for ambiguity when away from their home ground.

Culture Shock

As discussed in Chapter 9, when traveling abroad, students may encounter to one degree or another what is commonly defined as culture shock. Given this, it is important to begin discussions about and exercises on intercultural adaptations with students prior to departure. The truth is, a number of student participants will have given little thought to the emotional challenges that often occur when navigating a foreign country. Therefore it is important in pre-departure meetings to offer readings, exercises, and journal entries that can help students begin to consider what they may feel when they leave the comforts of home. Additionally, pre-departure activities can help them develop tools and strategies to cope with the emotional discomfort they may experience once in the field.

It is quite natural for individuals to revert to criticism, stereotyping, and cultural dismissal when placed in an unfamiliar or uncomfortable setting. Comments such as, "Why don't those people just do it the way we do?" or "How can they live in this dirty, small hovel?" may come from the lips of your students after a short time abroad. While this can dishearten a faculty leader attempting to promote global citizenship, it also requires stopping and considering that behind such statements is an individual who is feeling anxiety from being in a foreign environment in which familiar conditions and social cues are absent. In reality, the emotional feelings ranging from positive to negative that often mark culture shock are a normal part of adjusting to unfamiliar surroundings. However, if left unexplored or incorrectly dealt with during a faculty-led international program, the challenging aspects of culture shock can bring down student morale and result in unfortunate or inappropriate intercultural interactions.

The discourse about and methods used to address culture shock fall under the general heading of intercultural adjustment or adaptation. A number of organizations and individuals have written about and designed exercises for addressing the emotional difficulties that arise when adjusting to life in an unfamiliar international setting. The methods that you select for your program will need to take into account your student population, whether you have first-time travelers or more experienced participants, and the degree and type of independent cultural engagement the students will likely have.

Although individual models highlight a different number of culture shock phases, most generally distinguish an initial period often called the *honeymoon*, in which individuals enter the international setting and are enchanted with its newness. This is usually followed by *disenchantment*, in which the difficulties of living in and traversing an unfamiliar landscape become frustrating and provoke anxiety. This might next be followed by a period in which the individual makes *surface-level adjustments* as they feel a sense of emotional relief. Unfortunately, this brief lifting of unease can be eventually replaced by a *deeper sense of discomfort and isolation*. However, if the individual persists in the new environment, their emotions will usually resurface as they *adapt* and even *assimilate* into the adopted environment. Discussing the possible phases in pre-travel meetings as well as the various emotional and even physical symptoms of culture shock can help students begin to contemplate ways to cope with the uncomfortable feelings they may have when abroad.

Along with descriptions of the phases involved in culture shock, numerous exercises and activities have been created to orient students to what they may experience when overseas. The staff at your institution's international education office will most likely be able to either provide you with effective exercises and/or be available to run an intercultural training session with your program participants. Additionally, organizations that routinely send individuals abroad have online toolkits, including entire curricula on the topic. Two such organizations with materials on intercultural training to deal with culture shock are the Peace Corps, which offers a Cross-Cultural Workbook; and NAFSA, which offers intercultural adjustment activities such as the Broken Squares exercise, which focuses on helping participants adapt to environments in which they must communicate but lack the necessary language skills to do so (NAFSA, n.d.; Peace Corps, 1997).

While pre-departure meetings may be too soon for students to fully grasp what lies ahead in terms of possible culture shock, it is good to broach the subject with them and let them know that such feelings are quite normal. At this time, it is probably also good to talk with them briefly about what can be gained from working to overcome such feelings, not only in terms of internal/personal growth but also growth toward truly understanding what it takes and what it means to be a global citizen.

Intercultural Interactions and Perspectives

As with culture shock, scales and tools have been designed to define the phases involved in becoming more culturally "competent" and to help students (and other travelers) adopt more culturally encompassing perspectives. We explored a number of these in Chapter 3 and believe they can be useful to introduce to students prior to departure. Certainly, being able to somewhat neatly categorize ("Here is where I'm likely to start and here is where I am heading") offers students, particularly first-time international travelers, an entry into awareness that such an idea as cultural competence even exists. But such scales are only one source for preparing students for what lies ahead. We offer a few others that have worked for us and invite you to adapt them to suit your students and your program.

Sample 1: Recognizing Cultural Encounters

Following the first campus sessions for our Belize course, we realized that very few of our students had experienced meaningful (or even surface) interactions with people from cultures other than their own. It was not that they were intentionally provincial in their thinking, it was just that they had spent the majority of their lives in either small towns or small cities in the New England area. Most were excited about what lay ahead but had no schema in place—no prior knowledge to activate—that could help them make meaning of the readings on global citizenship and cultural competence we were feeding them. Rather than getting frustrated, we decided to devote some time to finding out exactly what knowledge and experience they *did* have with cultures other than their own. We therefore asked them to write 1–2 pages in their journals describing an incident in their lives when they had directly encountered someone (or a group of people) from a culture other than their own. If possible, we asked them to choose an incident that left them feeling uncomfortable and to be ready to explain why they felt this way and what they did, if anything, to make the situation more comfortable. We asked for rich detail (qualitative research's "thick description") of the setting, the other parties involved, and of themselves too—in effect, to write the incident as a story in which they stood in the role of main character.

When some of the students said they had never experienced cultures other than their own, we had to get more specific. Had they ever visited Boston or New York City? Had they interacted with people from a different race or ethnicity? Had they ever come in contact with people whose socioeconomic status was very different from their own—people having either far more or far less? Their initial response was that another culture must equate with another country. But once they broadened the definition, we were able to get into a productive discussion of what it can feel like to be in contact with others whose lives have been vastly different from what we are accustomed to. From there, we could talk about how people may deal with such feelings. They could speak from their own experiences and from the experiences of others they knew (or had read about). By listening to themselves and to each other and reflecting together on their stories, they were able to stretch their own experiences a little farther and begin to make sense of the readings we were giving them in preparation for our journey.

Sample 2: Insider/Outsider Perspectives

Closely related to the prompted discussion on encountering other cultures, we asked our students to find out what they could (in 1–2 pages) about the qualitative research terms—*emic* and *etic* perspectives. We suggested a few good Web sites and asked them to come to the next class session ready to share what they had learned and to explain how the terms applied to what might lay ahead for all of us in Belize. They knew we would be involved in a service-learning project with people living on Caye Caulker. They knew that global citizenship was a focus of our course, as was ecotourism, both the positive and negative aspects of this phenomenon. They knew they would be living in homestays for part of our journey.

The following week, our students offered their researched understandings of the terms and grappled with what it takes to truly appreciate the insider (or emic perspective) of another and if in fact that is ever truly achievable. They also discussed how awareness of the two perspectives is the first step in intercultural appreciation, relating how they had felt like either outsiders and insiders at differing points in their lives and how challenging it can be to make meaningful connections across cultural (or other) human differences. Being able to relate back to this discussion as we made our way into Belize, and again when we returned to the United States, proved extremely beneficial to our students' growing sense of themselves and their life roles extending beyond being U.S. students.

Sample 3: Who Gets to Travel?

Along with discussion prompts, we used a number of readings to challenge our students' growing awareness of their global identities. While there exists a growing body of academic material to choose from on global citizenship, some of the most accessible and productive readings for students may come from sources not directly tied to this academic discourse. For example, to explore students' perceptions of themselves and their realities in comparison to others around the world, we used a text called *The Power of Place* (de Blij, 2009).

In a prominent chapter of this text, de Blij divided the world's people into the globals—those "to whom the world appears comparatively limitless"; the mobals—those with some means to "escape their stultifying social environs"; and the locals—those who "are the poorest, least mobile, and most susceptible to the impress of place" (p. 5). One of his points being that the idea of the world becoming increasingly flat is still not true for everyone. Along with this reading, we gave the following writing prompt: "Do you think the categories (globals, locals, and mobals) offered by author de Blij capture the reality of the world's people today? Why or why not? Please give specific reasons for your views and as always, please avoid the use of sweeping generalizations." The resulting discussion was surprisingly heated but also very fruitful, as some of our students moved from initially identifying themselves as locals into a budding realization that the very privilege implied by our impending departure moved them into being "globals."

Providing pre-departure readings such as this can advance productive contemplation and discussions regarding global citizenship. They are therefore important when attempting to help students begin to formulate questions and opinions regarding this nebulous concept as well as in helping them gain greater awareness of self and others.

Ready to Fly

We hope that the information, examples, and options provided in this chapter prove useful to you as you plan the pre-departure portion of your program. Even the most careful planning does not, of course, guarantee a totally smooth international experience for you and your students. What it does provide, however, is structure and the skills needed by students to absorb and make sense of whatever unforeseen circumstances you may encounter during your field experience. While we have separated the pre-departure categories to make them easier to discuss, it is evident how closely intertwined they are. In fact, the work of designing curriculum for a faculty-led field course is as much about addressing all of the learning categories simultaneously as it is about addressing them individually. Add to this the fact that one of the most important pre-departure considerations involves the need to leave enough space in the curriculum (and the itinerary) for whatever spontaneous learning opportunities might arise.

12

Learning During the Journey

Perhaps travel cannot prevent bigotry, but by demonstrating that all peoples cry,
laugh, eat, worry, and die, it can introduce the idea that if we try
and understand each other, we may even become friends.

—Maya Angelou

TRAVEL TALE 12: Global Engagement on the Ground
• •

On the third day of our field course to Peru, we awoke to the sound of people shouting and gathering in the streets of Urubamba. From our window, we could see men and women beginning to pile rocks and roll boulders onto the main road. At breakfast, we learned that a regional strike had been called for and that it would last the next few days and possibly repeat the following week. We also learned that the strikers were protesting attempts by the government to privatize water within the communities in the area. This meant that local farming communities would be required to pay for a vital resource that had always been free. In protest, shops were to be closed and all transportation, public and private, to be stopped as local citizens were asked to voice their objection by marching in the streets.

From our perspective, this could not have come at a worse time. We had just arrived in Peru with our students to undertake a 17-day field course that involved service-learning in communities surrounding Urubamba. The culmination of the course was a trip to Machu Picchu. The strike, which immobilized all transportation in the area, would create a real problem for us in completing our service projects and could even threaten our promised trip to the famous Incan city. In our pre-trip campus meetings, we had prepared our students for a well-thought-out and detailed itinerary. This itinerary did *not* include a strike. While as co-leaders we vented our frustration together, we also realized we would have to make the best of the situation, regroup, and adjust our plans.

After calming ourselves down, we began to appreciate that a course in global engagement could, in fact, include some true global engagement—of the unplanned variety. We called our students together and told them with seeming enthusiasm that, while our plans to visit Machu Picchu might be interrupted, we were experiencing a possible once-in-a-lifetime opportunity to observe and interview our Peruvian hosts as they engaged in an act of economic and political solidarity. Our students, too, had observed the strike that surrounded us. Some were fearful; others appeared invigorated by the event. With input from the service provider who had helped plan our trip (a mix of Peruvian and American guides), the students took to the streets to interview a wide range of participants. Working in pairs, some would talk with young people, others with women and shopkeepers, still others with city officials. Together, we came up with questions to ask that would lead to productive conversations and register the multiple perspectives on the strike.

When we brought our group back together to share what they had learned, we realized that this unanticipated event may have been the most valuable experiential learning opportunity of the entire course—for the students and for ourselves. The students were truly able to connect with the needs and priorities of people from a culture different from their own. They saw collective action and questioned how a similar situation might have occurred or even been *allowed* to occur in the United States. Our students wondered if our country would countenance an act of civil "disobedience" such as this strike that was crippling transportation across the entire country for days. They began to more fully question the concept of *democracy* in their country and in Peru, and whether, in fact, their country truly supports democratic actions that directly challenge established power structures and institutions.

....

You Have Arrived!

After all the planning and organizing of logistics, all the pre-departure meetings, discussions, and assignments, all the worrying and late night panic attacks, you are finally abroad with students in tow. You have done your preliminary work well; your students are prepared for what they need to know, be able to do, and be open to. Now is it time to capitalize on and enjoy the learning adventure that awaits your group as you travel, work, and study in your host country. You have your curriculum and objectives in hand and are ready to bring them to life in the field.

As we discussed in Chapter 7, it will be important to help students acclimate to their new surroundings by providing a general orientation, city/community tour (a walking tour, if possible), and any other activities that might help them begin to adjust to their host community. Some, if not all, of your students will be wide-eyed as they find themselves in a completely new environment, perhaps for the first time. You will have participants who will appear apprehensive, while others will be ready to strike out alone and explore their new setting. Whether your host community is a small village or a large city, starting out with a group tour will be helpful to all.

After preliminary orientation activities and tours have ended, and participants have had a chance to recover from the journey to the host country, it is time to focus on the reality of the field classroom. While there is much to be learned by simply being there, there is much more to be learned by being there with intentional faculty direction.

Maximizing and Capturing the Learning

Certainly there is great variety within faculty-led programs, but the work of meeting course objectives is common to all. Also common to all is the fact that experiential learning will be taking place—some planned and aligning neatly with course objectives, some unique to the course location. As it is impossible to predict all that your location will have to offer, you will find yourselves as acutely engaged in the experiential learning as your students, needing to respond appropriately to cues from them and simultaneously being mindful of your own responses to the field setting.

If you have broached the topic of culture shock in your pre-departure sessions, addressing the reality of these feelings as soon as possible when you are in the host country is a good idea. Students may be feeling disoriented and/or uncomfortable, but they may be reluctant to admit such feelings, wondering if they signify being insensitive or even politically "incorrect." Having a journal prompt and follow-up discussion session devoted to initial responses within the first day or two is very useful. Along with this, if you make it clear that these responses may not be feelings they understand or are particularly proud of, you can help students strip away some internal filters that may be blocking their ability to be candid with themselves (and with you).

The following questions and prompts can offer a productive means for processing initial feelings of culture shock:

- How are you feeling right now? Can you put this into words?
- What in your surroundings make you feel like you're in another country, and what is similar to home?
- Write about the images, sounds, sights, smells, and human interactions that you are witnessing and experiencing.

By having a session that invites open discussion of culture shock, homesickness, and possible insecurities, you can then move into anticipating the more exciting parts of what lies ahead for all. It is worth the time and effort to reassure students that their feelings are normal and likely to become less intense once they acclimate to the new setting. Students who are not experiencing such feelings, perhaps because of prior travel experience, can be invited to help lead the discussion and serve as mentors to those with less experience. We have found that such in-country community building can go a long way and may bring forward students who might otherwise not serve in a leadership role.

Lecturers and Experts From the Host Country

After orienting your students to the host country, in-field learning can begin in earnest. Some of the most authentic resources for such learning are individuals (professors, community organizers, and other experts) from the host country. These local voices bring an understanding, insight, and perspective to your program that will be invaluable. From talks on the specific academic focus of your program to more general presentations on the history, social, cultural, and physical realities of the host country, you will want to have secured all of your local speakers months prior to travel. That is not to say that spectacular spontaneous presentations cannot be arranged while you are abroad—they can. And they sometimes prove to be the most valuable of all, particularly if they tie into some aspect of your curriculum that has emerged in the field, such as the water-privatization strike that we experienced.

In most cases, you will know the credentials of your guest speakers and their particular slant on the topic they will be discussing in advance.

To maximize the learning potential from these resources, we recommend sharing the presenter's background and presentation topic with students in advance and requiring them to think about questions and issues they would like the guest speaker to address. We also recommend giving journal prompts based on the guest speaker's presentation that call for critical consumption of the points being made rather than blanket agreement. For example, you might ask them to respond to these questions, "What resonated with you from this presentation?" or "What did you find yourself disagreeing with, and why?" Such questions help ensure that students will truly tune in to what the speaker is saying. It also encourages them to take responsibility for the follow-up questions and discussion that will happen. If they disagree with any points the speaker makes, they need to be coached in advance regarding how to engage in respectfully critical dialogue.

Journaling in the Field

With careful guidance, journals can be one of the most effective means for reinforcing the content and cultural learning that occurs during study abroad. Beyond this, they can provide a place for students to document both their personal and academic questions and growth while in the host country. By the time you reach your destination, you probably will have required your students to make journal entries based on assigned prompts. If so, students will have had specific instructions, a grading rubric (perhaps), and a few journaling assignments with feedback provided. With this level of preparation, students will be ready to use their journals to productively process their in-country experiences.

We have found that distinguishing between free and required journal entries can encourage student buy-in and use. Open-ended or free journal writing can (and should) be encouraged from the outset, as it offers students a place to grapple with some of the emotions they may be feeling (including homesickness, possible annoyance with co-travelers, etc.). Prompted entries, on the other hand, can be used to help meet course learning objectives and/or to channel discussions around ongoing events. Such in-country prompts may range from responses to service-learning projects and homestays to sightseeing excursions. Some of these writings can be used as a basis for whole-group discussion; others may be considered private. By letting students know in advance that you will not collect all of their journals—only those that you have asked for specifically—they are likely to feel respected and safe to write in whatever voice or style works best for them. We have found that giving students a chance to regularly share their prompted entries and inviting them to share any others that may be interesting and/or appropriate for the entire group to hear works well.

Expanding the Learning Community: Discussions and Processing

In order for in-field discussions (or any class discussions for that matter) to be truly fruitful, discourse expectations need to be put forth clearly and should include input from the student participants. After all, they are the ones who will be doing the talking. Do they want to engage in a balanced discussion format in which everyone feels safe to put forward what she or he is actually thinking and feeling? Or will they simply let the instructor run the show, calling on people and offering evaluative comments on what various students have to say.

Defining how to be part of a discussion group is good to begin on the home campus, but the dynamic is likely to change somewhat and may call for redefinition in the field setting. For one reason, the topics will be immediate and possibly emotionally charged in some way. Students will be living a new reality and may want to talk about their observations and feelings. Second, the group will probably have let its guard down a little in comparison with their interactions on the home campus. They are now living together 24/7 versus getting together once a week (or so) for an hour or two to talk about readings or guest speakers. They now know each other more fully, and their discussions, while happening under the guidance of their faculty, will also extend into their daily activities, their meals, and their evening outings (where faculty may or may not be present).

With this new dynamic in mind and to make the most of in-field discussions, it is important to deconstruct what makes a discussion format valuable for all participants. Openly talking about how to truly listen, how to respond, how to question respectfully but candidly, how to regulate comments and input so that everyone has a chance to speak are conversations worth having. If handled well, it will lead to much more balanced and meaningful discussions for all student participants and for faculty as well. We too need to remind ourselves of how our roles may change based on the setting and purpose of the learning activity. During in-field discussions, putting a question forward or inviting students to put a question forward, then sitting back and listening to the responses and moderating only when necessary, may be the best form of "instruction" we can offer.

Guided Observation

As discussed in Chapter 11, we have found that a guided observation exercise is invaluable when attempting to have students focus on and develop a familiarity with their host community environment. During the first days in the host setting, it will be natural for them to undergo sensory overload as they are trying to understand their new cultural and environmental surroundings. Therefore, offering students a focused observation assignment where they will be tuning in and documenting specific aspects of host country life, can allow them to gain closer appreciation of this new setting.

We suggest structuring such an exercise carefully, with emphasis on making objective, unbiased observations in the ethnographic research style—in effect, telling them to gather only straightforward data to bring back and discuss with their peers. We directed our students to work very intentionally to remove any subjective interpretation of the phenomenon being observed, reminding them instead that their job was to simply pay attention and record what they see. We practiced a few rounds of observation to give them an idea of what we meant. For example, rather than stating, "The woman running the laundromat looked tired and snapped at one of the customers," we asked them to state only what they saw. The revised observation then read, "The woman running the laundromat sat down and sighed, rubbing her eyes and rolling her neck as a customer arrived within 5 minutes of her closing time. She reminded the customer that the shop would be closing very soon." The first version was a story told by an author; the second version was an observation recorded by an ethnographer.

City, Place, or Home as Text

As introduced in Chapter 11, one guided observation we used prior to departure was the City as Text (Braid & Long, 2000) exercise. In the field, we adapted this to Home as Text in Peru and Caye as Text in Belize. For the Home as Text assignment in Peru, we asked our students to observe and explore the lived reality of their homestay houses. We directed them to consider what that house said about its inhabitants—what was present, what was missing, what was used, what was neglected. In essence, we ask our students to reflect on what that home said about its owners—what they valued and their culture.

On the island of Caye Caulker in Belize, we used a similar exercise. Instead of the home or city, we had them consider the story (or text) told by the Caye and its residents. Here we asked the students to spend an afternoon walking around the 5-mile island, making observations and taking notes that told a particular story of the Caye. We brainstormed a few ideas with them before they began their observations, asking, for example: What does this island say about its people? What do they value? What are their challenges and opportunities? How do children and adults interact? How do humans interact with animals? While some followed our leads, others came up with their own observations that told vivid tales of the Caye. Our architecture major examined the condition and style of various hotels. Our sociology major sat at the water taxi dock and observed the attitudes and interactions between arriving tourists and local residents.

In the evening, we sat down together and shared our notes before coming up with some overarching human themes that connected the various observations. One of the most interesting (and consistent) themes, in our case, was the relaxed attitude of most of the Caye's local residents regarding time, an attitude and approach to living that was literally and figuratively *foreign* to our U.S. students.

Mapping Exercise

Along with city, place, or home as text, another related and potentially useful guided exercise for students is a mapping assignment of their host community. In this exercise, groups of two or three students can be sent out to produce handdrawn maps of a section of their host environment. Depending on the focus of the course or even the type of community involved, student teams can be assigned different neighborhoods and asked to observe and map a variety of spatial features. In his international program held in Cuenca, Ecuador, Jokisch (2009) gave just such an assignment, which involved mapping and classifying urban buildings and land uses. His students were also asked to define the major economic activities in their designated section of Cuenca as well as how those local economic activities might connect to the larger regional, national, and international economic realms. Students reported that this mapping exercise made them more intimately aware of their surroundings and enhanced their further inquiry about their host community.

It is easy to see how this mapping exercise could be applied within various programs. You might have students map house types, transportation networks, or public spaces, to cite a few. For sociology, anthropology, or related majors, you might require mapping features that touch upon social issues such as apparent wealthy sections and those areas in the community that are notably more impoverished. While their maps do not need to be of professional quality (they will probably be hand-drawn), students should include a legend or key, orientation information (north arrow), and some type of scale so others can interpret the mapped data.

Language Lessons

If your host country is a non-English speaking location, giving your students a chance to take language lessons while abroad can be extremely beneficial to their experience. You may have already started (or even required) language lessons in the pre-departure part of your program; however, there is little substitute for the experience of taking language lessons when in-country and surrounded by native speakers.

Although students cannot be expected to pick up a foreign language by taking a limited number of lessons during a short-term faculty-led program, this opportunity does offer them a chance to learn basic words and phrases and show respect for local residents by attempting to speak their language. Such lessons can also provide an opportunity for students to interact with instructors and guest speakers who live in the host community. Beyond this, research suggests that U.S. students may be more committed to learning a second language when returning home after attempting to communicate in a non-English speaking study-abroad setting. Bottom line, if language lessons are appropriate, available, and affordable while abroad, we recommend them as a way in which to more fully engage your students with the people of the host country.

Day-to-Day Events

Beyond the examples mentioned, your in-country learning will include a range of other activities. While we have repeatedly mentioned the spontaneous learning opportunities you will encounter, there will be many that you have planned well in advance. The good news is that most of these afford you some element of control and are likely to align directly with your intended learning outcomes. Host country excursions would fall into this category, (having been planned in advance by necessity), as would individual project work ranging from service-learning to research. All of these activities will also need time for ongoing processing and, in many cases, in-field guidance and direct instruction. For example, learning how to build the mud stoves for our Peruvian project was instruction that had to happen in the host country.

No matter how busy your course may be, once you get to your destination, it can be very helpful to factor in some unstructured time for the students to catch their breath, do some exploring on their own, write in their journals, or possibly just catch up on sleep. The pace is likely to be very busy while you are abroad, but to maximize the learning potential, your students will need time to stop and reflect upon all that is taking place. We suggest explaining the purpose for such a respite from the structured itinerary. Your students need to understand that this, too, is an intentional learning opportunity albeit not in the style they may be most accustomed to. When offering such an opportunity and discussing its purpose with your students, it is important to remind them that unstructured time is not simply for them to isolate themselves with their American peers but rather to take the opportunity to deeply consider the cascade of new information they have encountered since their arrival.

Where Did the Time Go?

As you embark on international teaching, Hulstrand (2008) provides a succinct list of six "Rules of the Road for Faculty Abroad" that can help you create the most effective and pleasant experience for both leading and participating in an education-abroad program.

In summary, Hulstrand suggests that faculty should: (a) plan well in advance of the program to create a thoughtful academic experience; (b) be prepared for the 24/7 commitment required when taking students abroad; (c) be flexible when faced with the unpredicted; (d) call upon students to be responsible problem solvers; (e) maintain a positive attitude and a good sense of humor; and (f) despite all the work and challenges, have fun.

While Hulstrand's points are applicable from pre-departure through reentry, we believe they are most pertinent to the in-country portion of an international program—to the many topics we discussed in this chapter and through our opening travel tale. If you consider the strike we encountered in Urubamba and how it changed but also enriched our learning experience, it is evident how being flexible, encouraging students to be problem solvers, and maintaining a positive attitude can have exceptional results. In fact, although we were tired and ready to return home after spending 17 action-packed days with our students in Peru, we found ourselves asking, with a mixture of satisfaction and wistfulness, "Where did the time go?"

13

Reentry and Beyond

Sustaining and Forwarding What Has Been Gained

> *There will come a time when you believe everything is finished.*
> *That will be the beginning.*
>
> —Louis L'Amour

TRAVEL TALE 13: Exploring the Impact

A t the end of our first Honors program to Peru, we scheduled a 2-day reentry period involving follow-up discussions and writings, time for culminating course project work, and semiformal individual reentry interviews. Upon touching down after an exhilarating but also exhausting time abroad, the last thing we wanted to do was continue meeting and processing the experience with our students. We were more interested in getting much needed sleep and a hot shower—but we were not finished yet. In fact, we had read (and had been told) about the absolute importance of the reentry period—that it can be a critical time not only for student readjustment to the life they left behind, but also for appreciating

Fostering Global Citizenship Through Faculty-Led International Programs, pages 189–200
Copyright © 2012 by Information Age Publishing
189

the initial impact of the international experience. So we shuttled the students back to campus, got one good night's sleep, and then began our follow-up work.

While all of our posttrip activities were worthwhile, the individual interviews proved to be one of the most pleasurable and enlightening of all. To prepare for this experience, we gave our students a series of questions to reflect upon. We asked them to jot down key thoughts and responses in their course journals and told them we would collect the journals after the interviews. We intentionally kept the questions broad enough to allow them to take their thoughts and answers in various directions during the 30-minute videotaped sessions. Most students, although used to being videotaped by their parents over the years and (more recently) by their cell-phone-ready peers, admitted to feeling a little nervous. But once we got started, they loosened up and talked openly and in rich detail. As we listened, we found that their stories offered us an unexpected new lens on the experience—a capture of some of the small but very significant thoughts and memories each of them carried.

One student, when reflecting upon the service-learning experience noted, "We were making a stove for a woman who was very old and sweet. She spoke Quechua and nothing else. She brought us mud, laughed when I hit my head on the ceiling, and then cried when the stove was finished." Another student, when responding to a question about one of the things she felt she gained from the course, stated, "I have been sheltered. I hope to gain inner strength from this experience and be a more aware person in the future, not so dependent on others." Still another student, discussing her homestay mentioned, "It is amazing how much you can learn about your own life when thrown into someone else's." A final student, in remarking on his encounters with other perspectives and ways of being while traveling, noted, "Conversations and shared experiences [with host country citizens] brings the realization that we are millions of individual minds seeing the world in millions of different ways."

Are these responses particularly eloquent or profound? Are they the marked signs of new global citizens? Probably not. What they are, instead, are honest statements from young adults who have had the privilege to travel and study abroad—young adults who have been asked to take the time to think about and share some of what they felt along the way. The fact that their words, facial expressions, and body language were captured on video, thus stilled within the days following their re-entry, transforms them into a living record that the interviewees, the interviewers, and invited others can reference for years to come.

••••••••••••••••••••

And Then There Is More . . .

Upon returning home from an international program, it is easy to see why faculty may feel that the bulk of their work is completed. After planning and preparing for the international program for months, if not years, they have survived the long-awaited travel portion of the undertaking in which they spent, in many cases, 24/7 with a group of students. With the return to campus, they also face the momentous task of catching up with their own lives—both at work and at home. But despite the fact that many would just as soon part ways from their student travelers, at least for a few days or weeks (maybe even months), now is the time to help students begin to pull together the entire experience and for faculty to assess both the students and the program. And if that wasn't enough, now is also the time to complete plans for program follow-up activities, from campus presentations to group reunions and more.

"By the time students reenter the flow of campus life, their distinct memories have faded or they have processed the experience to the point where it is not in the foreground of their lives anymore" (Doyle, 2009, p. 144). If Doyle is correct, then one of the challenges faculty face upon reentry involves keeping the experience alive (and central) for their students—in finding ways to help them continue to productively process in-field events as well as the emotions that are likely to surface as they adjust to returning home. On an academic level, for example, students may need assistance in determining ways to integrate their international study into other coursework and future professional goals. And what if the travel has spurred a newfound interest in civic engagement? How can faculty help their students find likely channels for acting on such important new interests? In a similar vein, reentry also involves consideration of how students will give back to their campus communities. How will they share their international experiences, perhaps spurring others from their home campuses to consider taking part in study abroad? These are just some of the many questions that arise when the travel portion of the international program is finally over. Although some can be put on hold, it is generally true that the sooner faculty begin to address these (and other related matters), the better.

Looking Back, Looking Forward

While it is natural to pause for a sigh of satisfaction and relief upon returning home from an international program, it is best to keep such a pause relatively brief, as the reentry period can be one of the most fruitful times of the entire enterprise. It is, in fact, prime time for student processing, growth, and sharing. It is also prime time for faculty assessment—not only of the course goals and learning objectives but of the overall structure and value of the program as well. There are various ways to accomplish these essential tasks. We have found that reviewing the overall experience through discussions and interviews before getting into more formal means of assessment works well. When students are encouraged to revisit and talk about what they have just undertaken in a somewhat open-ended, nonevaluative (i.e., low-stakes) format, their responses are more likely to be authentic and rich with both positive and not-so-glowing details. And this of course is what we want—the individual and group truth of the experience. More formal means of assessment can come later.

Reentry Interviews

The reentry interviews we discussed in our opening travel tale were designed to give our students a chance to candidly respond to a series of questions regarding what they felt they had individually gained from the overall course experience. As we explained, we used a semistructured format, telling our students in advance the nature of the questions but also letting them know that there would be room to extend their responses beyond the original question topics. It is significant to note that we allowed plenty of interview time for this to happen. By explaining the structure and expectations in this way, our students knew that we were intent on hearing from each of them in as much depth as possible before we met with the entire group, thus acknowledging both the value of each traveler's responses as well as the fact that there would be variation within the cohort. Most of all, we wanted to begin by capturing each person's experience in a way that would not involve any group norming of responses.

As we designed the interview questions, we bore in mind that the students were quite tired. We also took into account the likelihood of reverse culture shock—realizing that they were considering (both consciously and subconsciously) not only what they had experienced but also what it felt like to return to their campus and home lives. We appreciated and wanted to sort through the somewhat confusing feelings students often have upon encountering the apparent stasis of home after spending time in a very different culture. How could the people closest to them not immediately see the difference in them, a difference that they were so clearly feeling? How could they put their observations and emotions into words that would help their families and friends appreciate the impact of their international study experience? Such questions help explain why students who have studied abroad return feeling somewhat disoriented and even distanced from the day-to-day lives they left behind, even after short-term programs.

Keeping both reverse culture shock and weariness in mind, we designed a series of reentry questions that led to some invaluable interview sessions with our students. While some faculty may use such reentry interviews as a means for conducting either student or program assessment, we intentionally opted to separate our interviews from formal assessment procedures. Depending upon the intent and nature of the program, the following questions can be adapted to suit individual circumstances. The opening question is intentionally broad-based, with the subsequent questions providing more focus.

- What do you feel you have gained from this experience?
- How has this experience impacted your sense of yourself as a U.S. citizen?
- How has it impacted your sense of "other"?
- What effect, if any, has this experience had on your values and personal ethics? Please explain.
- What specific memories from this experience do you anticipate carrying with you as you move forward with your life?
- Did your perceptions of yourself as a global citizen change as a result of the experience?
- How will you sustain what you have gained from this experience?

If you decide to use reentry interviews at the end of your program, we suggest giving the questions to your students at least 24 hours before the interviews take place. This allows time to respond thoughtfully during the interview and reduces possible stress around the experience. Once the interviews are underway, simply listening and asking occasional clarifying questions can lead students into remarkable consideration of their own growth.

Wrapping Up Group Discussions

Along with conducting individual reentry interviews, semistructured group discussions offer another way to carefully review the international travel experience with students. While you probably held plenty of predeparture and in-field discussions, now that you are back on home turf, your discussions are likely to have a very different feel. No longer are you projecting what might happen or talking about day-to-day occurrences. You are now revisiting what you have accomplished together—a tightly-knit community of learners who have weathered the ups and downs of a major life episode in each other's company. While there may have been disagreements and tensions along the way, your group has also had a unique opportunity to be part of one another's emotional responses and growth. Students who entered the program knowing no one will now carry with them the memory of a group of co-travelers whose responses, laughter, escapades, and idiosyncrasies enriched the overall journey. Before members of this distinct group go their separate ways, it is crucial to invite them to talk together about what they have learned.

Topics for meaningful group discussions are not necessarily different from reentry interview topics. In fact, there can be quite a bit of overlap. The difference is in the interpersonal dynamic and the effect that each student's words will have on other members of the group—in some cases, drawing their thinking into unanticipated channels, in other cases reinforcing original responses. Open-ended questions can be particularly useful during group discussions as students will be able to consider and build upon other's responses. Along with the reentry interview questions offered above, the following questions are also good group discussion starters.

- How did you grow and change as a result of this experience?
- What did you anticipate before you left?
- What surprised you?
- What will you carry forward and how will you sustain what you have gained?
- How will you, as a group, share this experience with others? Do you think this is important to do? Why or why not?
- How did being in each other's company change the experience for you?
- How do you anticipate your family and/or friends will react to your study abroad stories?

With your entire group, it is also important to talk about reverse culture shock (and the form it may be taking for each member) as a means of supporting this emotional reality. It is wise to let your students know that such feelings may not set in immediately; also that they may come back to revisit them from time to time in the months ahead. Interestingly, some describe reverse culture shock as a form of lost innocence, noting that it takes leaving a place to be able to see it objectively. The following questions can help your students discuss the complex feelings involved in reverse culture shock.

- How does it feel to be back?
- What were some of the first emotions that hit you when the plane touched down in the United States?
- How will you go about telling your family and friends about the reality and depth of your experience?
- Once a person has traveled internationally, do you think it is possible to ever look at the home country in the exact same way again? Please explain your response.

As you spend time interviewing individual students and leading group discussions, it is good to keep in mind that you, too, have just returned from a high-impact learning experience. To this end, we encourage you to schedule time for faculty follow-up discussion sessions, to process your own reentry experiences and to determine next steps for your students and your campus communities. Group meetings after returning home, whether with individual students, student groups, or faculty-only groups, provide a critical opportunity to both understand and reinforce what has been gained and to determine best ways to move these gains forward.

Final Project Work Sessions

Along with interviews and group discussions, if your program involves a summative project or presentation, it is a good idea to spend time reviewing this (or working on it, as the case may be) before the group disperses and gets involved in other life demands. While the culminating project or paper was probably assigned before departure and reviewed during the travel portion of the program, spending time reinforcing the expectations for submitting that work and considering how the original intent of the project may have changed along the way is best done immediately upon reentry.

Pulling It All Together: Assessments

Once the program abroad is completed and all participants have returned home, it is time to get down to the final assessments. This involves individual student assessment as well as overall program assessment. While assessment may seem like straightforward work, this is not always the case. Even the most carefully planned curriculum is likely to involve some adjustments and adaptations based on what actually occurred along the way. Students' emotional and physical responses may have played a role in their ability to complete in-field tasks. Final projects may have been altered based on host country circumstances; take, for example, the Peruvian strike that we encountered (Travel Tale 12). Having clear initial expectations, then being somewhat flexible as final assessments are completed is not a bad way to go. This does not suggest going easy on students in terms of assessment expectations. It does suggest determining ways to assess the actual growth of each student in light of the goals and objectives of the course.

Assessment of Student Learning

In a traditional classroom setting, determining how well a student has met the learning objectives of a course can be relatively clear-cut; however, assessing learning objectives may be a bit more challenging in the international setting. While content area knowledge and skills such as observing and interviewing can be determined in a variety of ways, assessment of how a student has developed in terms of his/her cultural awareness and as a global citizen is not as easy to ascertain. For this reason, using a variety of assessment instruments, from exams to journal writings, creative projects and research studies, can be particularly useful for faculty teaching international field courses. In concert with such instruments, another technique that is well-suited to international programs is the use of self-assessment—inviting students into the conversation around what they have gained and how they have grown from the experience.

Exams

At the end of some international programs, faculty may opt to use final exams to determine certain aspects of student learning and growth. Such exams may be constructed by faculty pre-departure, particularly if they target specific course objectives in the areas of content knowledge and skills. These might range from determining growth in language proficiency to growth in the ability to record detailed and unbiased observations. Unfortunately, harder to measure in an exam format are the more abstract, dispositional learning objectives. To determine student growth in these areas, it is beneficial to include open-ended questions that give students room to record their responses to contextual factors and/or in-field events, particularly those that could not have been predicted in advance. For example, asking students to cite a specific observation regarding the impact of American media on the host country's youth could provide a means for assessing student observational skills as well as their intercultural awareness.

Journal Submissions

Specific journal submissions offer another solid means for assessing student growth and development within targeted learning objectives. The reason we use the qualifier "specific" is that journal entries are oftentimes somewhat personal in nature and therefore should, in our opinion, be collected in their entirety with some degree of caution. Instead, prompted entries and possibly one or two student-generated entries can be used for assessment.

Additionally, faculty may want to have students write one or more culminating entries after returning home, which attempt to capture what they have learned, how they feel they have grown, and what they think they will do next. If students are allowed to turn in journals a few weeks or even a month after the international experience ends, it will give them a chance to be a little more objective and will also give them the opportunity to write about their process of integrating back into their home environment.

As noted earlier in this text, journals can be some of the most richly rewarding captures of the student experience, but also some of the most frustrating and disappointing if students don't delve into anything deeper than surface-level topics (not liking the food, missing home, missing technology, etc.). Given this, using journals as an assessment tool can be challenging. Requiring prompted responses, as we strongly encourage, and a rubric clearly defining the quality of required journal entries, will help in this complex task.

Culminating Projects

Many faculty-led programs involve a postprogram, culminating project that invites students to synthesize some aspect, if not all, of what has been gained. Depending upon the focus and intent of the course, this may involve a formal report or paper on an assigned or student-selected topic, a visual display, or an action plan for service-learning follow-up, to name a few. A culminating project like the Digital Travel Tale presented in Chapter 10 is somewhat unique in that it resists the natural human tendency to look back on life episodes after they have ended then re-vision and re-version what occurred. This is what tends to happen with the passage of time—the accuracy of details either fades or is reassembled a little apart from reality. Instead, the Digital Travel Tale, as a multimedia and multisensory capture, allows students to show and discuss what they have experienced. "This was my travel story: this is what I saw, this is what I felt, this is what I learned about the place and the culture—about myself and about my fellow travelers." Photos and journal entries are real-time representations of what students were taking in.

Assessment of the Program

In addition to the assessment of students, it is now time to have them help you consider the effectiveness of the overall program. In general, international programs generate highly positive evaluations from student participants. These learning experiences are new and exciting to students; they therefore tend to walk away from them with elevated feelings about the program and the faculty leaders too. In fact, it may be difficult to get students to suspend such feelings when helping you consider the value of each element of the overall program—pre-departure, international learning, and reentry. But faculty and administration cannot do program assessments alone. We need student feedback to determine next steps, not only for program improvement but also to garner future program support.

Unfortunately, standard evaluation forms given at the end of each semester/term for on-campus courses are generally not appropriate vehicles to assess an international program. They are typically formulaic and do not encourage the kind of nuanced responses that international learning experiences generate. Instead, we suggest working with others on campus who have a vested interest in international education to develop a custom-made evaluation form that can be truly useful in determining what worked well, along with areas for improvement.

Sharing the Experience

Sharing the international experience with the home institution, and possibly with others beyond the campus, can be a powerful means for evoking longitudinal reflection on what occurred. Such sharing can present an opportunity for both students and faculty to determine how (and how well) they have integrated the study-abroad experience into their lives back home. Engaging and comprehensive presentations can also serve to recruit future students interested in an institution that prepares its students to succeed in a globally connected world. To this end, there are various follow-up activities that have proven useful to those involved in international education. We offer a few in Table 13.1. Some are primarily focused on reconnecting the fellow travelers; others could be used to demonstrate the value of the program.

Student Ambassadors

Another means for sharing the experience involves the use of study-abroad ambassadors, a program that international education offices on campuses across the country have routinely established. These ambassadors are students who have participated in a successful program abroad. Ambassadors share their experiences with other students who are considering participating in a study-abroad program. While this has been used less of-

TABLE 13.1 Follow-up Activities for a Faculty-Led International Program

Activity/Location	Purpose(s)
Presentation of Course Projects • Department • Campus-wide • Outlying community • Professional organizations	• Give students an opportunity to synthesize and share what they have gained. • Encourage interest in study abroad. • Build appreciation between the college and the community. • Encourage students to participate in professional venues.
Reunion • Senior capstone course • Dinner or other social gathering	• Revisit and analyze longer-term impact of the course. • Further cohort connections.
Social Media Communication • Facebook (etc.) • Twitter and blogs	• Share photos and memories. • Keep in touch with traveling cohort. • Use for recruitment purposes (with permission).

Ongoing Group Activities
• Discussion groups on campus
• Action groups
  – On campus
  – In the outlying community
  – In other locations
	• Continue to process the experience.
	• Reconvene cohort to conduct service-learning or research projects related to the course.
	• Raise money for and/or awareness of host country issues.

Long-Lasting Exchanges • Between faculty and host country partners and faculty • Between students and host families	• Develop partnerships. • Demonstrate commitment to what was gained during the course experience.

ten with short-term programs, establishing an ambassador program may be helpful in promoting future faculty-led programs at your institution.

Follow-Up Courses

You or your department may elect to offer a follow-up course or seminar for students who have studied abroad, whether they were involved in a faculty-led program or studied independently. Although the form such a follow-up course may take will vary from one institution to the next, it can offer an invaluable means for determining which aspects of the faculty-led program proved most impactful and lasting for students. At our college, the Honors program's senior seminar requires students to revisit and analyze their own academic and personal development during their college years, with particular emphasis on the impact of the required study-abroad course. Sharing student responses to the experience 1–2 years later has offered us an exceptional opportunity to evaluate the long-term impact of the courses we taught. For example, when we asked our students to look back on the global engagement course and discuss what stayed with them, two replies included

- My experience in Belize made me realize the benefits of living simply... that you don't really need all of the "materials" and "things" that we Americans need and desire.
- It made me realize that we [in America] tend to pine after more money, bigger houses, nicer clothes—paying little mind to what we have now, but always looking to what we could have in the future if we only worked a little harder.

In both of these instances, our students had held on to what they perceived as a difference in what is valued in their experience of U.S. culture compared to what is valued in what they observed in Belize. These responses, along with others from the student group, led us into a richly rewarding follow-up discussion of how they have acted upon this realization (if at all) and how it has impacted their way(s) of walking in the world. The group agreed that, without having experienced some elements of another country's culture, they would have remained pretty much oblivious to some aspects of U.S. life that they do not personally value.

How Did We Do?

It is no wonder that the reentry period is oftentimes the most neglected portion of the international program. But despite the fact that all participants, students and faculty alike, will be reeling from the intensive time abroad, the activities undertaken during the weeks and months that follow are a critical way to ensure long-lasting growth. From discussions to formal assessments and presentations, reentry can be not only a time for evaluating how the program went, but also a time for celebration at having stepped into new teaching and learning territory and having come out stronger and more insightful as a result.

Conclusion

No journey carries one far unless, as it extends into the world around us,
it goes an equal distance into the world within.

—Lillian Smith

CONCLUDING TRAVEL TALE: Our Elixir

W hen the last of our students left campus after our first co-taught international course in Peru, it was time for us, the faculty leaders, to return to our offices and home lives. Back in New Hampshire, there was much awaiting us—a move into a new home, aging parents to attend to, grown children to visit. As our summer break progressed, the program experience began to naturally fade; although from time to time each of us would recount some of the notable features of the Peruvian journey with our family and friends. It made for good conversation, and people were generally quite surprised at what we had undertaken as teachers who already had full and gratifying careers on our home campus. "Why had we opted to take on something extra like this?" they oftentimes asked. "What was to be gained?"

It wasn't until months later and well into another fall semester that the time came to officially reexamine our Peruvian venture. At the start of the new academic year, we were asked to participate in our college's Sixth Biennial World Affairs Symposium, entitled *From Local to Global*. The organizers of the symposium asked us to present our international program

Fostering Global Citizenship Through Faculty-Led International Programs, pages 201–204
Copyright © 2012 by Information Age Publishing
201

and to focus on the growth and discovery that had occurred for us and our students as a result. The emphasis of the symposium was to explore how the *global* impacts the *local*. Faculty members as well as national scholars, educators, artists, and community leaders were enlisted to examine, through their presentations, how global forces impact cultures, environments, economies, and identities at the local level. It was an exciting topic that promised to fit well with what we had experienced with our students 3 months earlier.

Instead of a routine presentation of PowerPoint slides, we elected to create a multimedia movie for the symposium. We wanted to use pictures and video taken in Peru, the reentry interviews conducted with our students, and quotes from their prompted journal writings. And beyond this, we wanted to create video segments (an introduction and conclusion) that would capture our perspective on the experience. As we convened our students and began putting the movie together, we found ourselves reliving those 17 days in Peru, but this time we had the added benefit of the passage of time to reflect on all that had occurred. Working with the various materials and trying to create apt opening and closing video clips, we began to appreciate what we had gained as a result of this unique call to adventure.

Certainly both of us had deep teaching experience prior to the Peru course—in international settings for Jo Beth and in a variety of U.S. settings (elementary through graduate school; low socioeconomic through affluent districts) for Pru. But this course, this chance to briefly live in a very different location and culture with students who had never had such an experience before, was distinct. Watching the reentry videos, hearing the students talking about what they had learned and how they had been challenged to grow and think differently caused us to truly pause and reflect on what they had gained and on what we had gained as well. Looking back into the photos of the Peruvian landscape and people, those who had guided us as well as those who had crossed our paths for only a day or perhaps an hour, brought back the countless memories in a fresh light. The people we had met were surely going on with their lives just as we were going on with ours, but in those June days of 2009, we had all intersected for a little while. Eating and drinking together, attempting to communicate without common language, occasionally feeling a little confused and overwhelmed, observing and beginning to appreciate each other's daily rituals, habits, and needs—we had briefly shared our humanity.

As we looked back on this, we wondered how our lives would be different if we hadn't responded to this particular call to adventure. What had we gained from taking this on together? What were we bringing back to our "ordinary world" and how had we grown as teachers and perhaps as global citizens too? The more we pondered these questions, the more we realized that it wasn't about the amount of time or the number of sites we'd seen or activities we'd completed, it was about taking time to appreciate and reflect on the finer details of the venture. For how does a person grow as a global citizen anyway? How does a person connect the local to the global if not through stepping fully into one such experience at a time?

••••••••••••••••••••

Return to the Hero's Journey: The Elixir

In his mono-myth, *The Hero's Journey*, Campbell (1968) tells of the hero bringing back an elixir to the ordinary world after responding to a call to adventure into an extraordinary world. Ah, the elixir; a remarkable but indeterminate prize varying not only in form but also in purpose from one hero to the next. Whether a sturdy object (a sword, a crucible) or an internal enhancement (hope, wisdom), the elixir holds the universal promise of "bestowing a boon" not only on the hero who bears it home but on all humankind as well. Without it, the hero is called to repeat the adventure until the elixir is secured. This elixir, Campbell notes, also serves to redefine the role the hero will assume as he or she moves forward in the ordinary world.

As we noted in the introduction of this text, we were two professors who were given a call to adventure by our college's new Honors program. In this venture, we journeyed forth to create and carry out an international program that would begin to develop a sense of global citizenship among our students. This initial quest has led to so much more for us, both professionally and personally, and has resulted in our dedication to writing a text to share with others ready to respond to a similar call. We do not pretend to have all of the answers in this arena or to have attained a pinnacle of global or cultural awareness. What we have gained—our elixir—is an appreciation of what bringing students into an international program can do for them (and for their teachers) in terms of eliciting internal growth that can move them forward as global citizens. We have learned through our journeys that such growth can be as uncomfortable as it is ultimately rewarding, and that it may not register to its fullest extent immediately. Instead, with a little age and careful revisiting, it may continue to develop over time. In Campbell's version, the hero who does not secure the elixir is required to repeat the adventure, to continue the quest. We would look at such a continuation of the story as the best circumstance possible, as it might thus draw the hero into other new lands, new cultures, and new growth with each subsequent journey.

What we have shared above is our take on the elixir, but what form might it take for the other participants and stakeholders involved in an international call to adventure? For faculty, beyond what we have found, it may offer a chance to step back from their disciplines and see them from a broader perspective, to appreciate how their own work and their students' futures fit into the global arena. For students, the possible elixirs are as wide-ranging as the students themselves. If they are carefully guided along the way, given plenty of time for reflection and processing, international study can expand their worldviews and encourage growth toward becoming responsible and active global citizens who are both effective and comfortable in this role. For institutions, fully supporting and investing in international programs can move their campuses forward (in an authentic way) toward attaining the goal of internationalization.

And finally, what is the elixir for society? What can we hope to realize as a nation if we step fully into encouraging faculty-led international study as a part of the higher education experience for all students? Most importantly, we may become less myopic. We may begin to put citizens into the world rather than just the country—citizens who are at ease interacting with and respecting others' ways of living and being. Our trip to Peru, our call to adventure, was not a monumental undertaking that changed the world in any way; rather, it was a step in the critical process of realizing that we are part of a larger human family—old and young and from many nationalities and cultures, all inhabiting and impacting the globe and each other during our stay.

References

Chapter 1

Altbach, P. G., & Knight, J. (2007). The internationalization of higher education: Motivations and realities. *Journal of Studies in International Education, 11,* 290–305.

American Council on Education. (2008). *College-bound students' interests in study abroad and other international learning activities.* Washington, DC: American Council on Education.

Association of American Colleges and Universities (AAC&U). (2010). *LEAP and Shared Futures initiatives.* Retrieved March 8, 2012, from http://www.aacu.org/leap/

Chieffo, L., & Griffiths, L. (2009). Here to stay: Increasing acceptance of short-term study abroad programs. In R. Lewin (Ed.), *The handbook of practice and research in study abroad. Higher education and the quest for global citizenship* (pp. 365–380). New York, NY: Routledge, Taylor & Francis.

Commission on the Abraham Lincoln Study Abroad Fellowship Program. (2005). *Global competence and national needs.* Retrieved March 8, 2012, from http://www.nafsa.org/resourcelibrary/default.aspx?id=16035

Dewey, J. (1938). *Experience and education.* New York, NY: Simon & Schuster.

Forum on Education Abroad. (2009). *Standards of good practice for short-term education abroad programs.* Carlisle, PA: Dickinson College.

Gutierrez, R., Averbach J., & Bhandari, R. (2009). Expanding U.S. study abroad capacity: Findings from an IIE-forum survey. *Meeting America's Global Education Challenge, 6,* 14–15.

Hoffa, W. W. (2007). A history of study abroad: Beginnings to 1965. In B. Whalen (Ed.), *Frontiers: The interdisciplinary journal of study abroad* and *The forum on education abroad* [Special publication]. Lancaster, PA: Whitmore.

Fostering Global Citizenship Through Faculty-Led International Programs, pages 205–215
Copyright © 2012 by Information Age Publishing

Hovland, K. (2006). *Shared futures: Global learning and liberal education.* Washington, DC: Association of American Colleges and Universities.

Institute of International Education (IIE). (2011). *Open doors report.* Retrieved March 9, 2012, from http://www.iie.org/en/Research-and-Publications/Open-Doors/Data

Knight, J. (2008). *Higher education in turmoil: The changing world of internationalization.* Rotterdam, The Netherlands: Sense.

Lewin, R. (2009). Introduction: The quest for global citizenship through study abroad. In R. Lewin (Ed.), *The handbook of practice and research in study abroad: Higher education and the quest for global citizenship* (pp. xiii–xxiii). New York, NY: Routledge, Taylor & Francis.

National Survey of Student Engagement. (2007). *Experiences that matter: Enhancing student learning and success.* Retrieved March 9, 2012, from http://nsse.iub.edu/NSSE_2007_Annual_Report/docs/withhold/NSSE_2007_Annual_Report.pdf

Olson, C., & Green, M. (2006). *A handbook for advancing comprehensive internationalization: What institutions can do and what students should learn.* Washington, DC: American Council on Education.

Williamson, W. (2010, July 25). 7 signs of successful study-abroad programs. *Chronicle of Higher Education.* Retrieved March 9, 2012, from http://chronicle.com/article/7-Signs-of-Successful/123657/

Chapter 2

Battistoni, R. (2002). *Civic engagement across the curriculum: A resource book for service-learning faculty in all disciplines.* Providence, RI: Campus Compact.

Bernacki, M., & Bernt, F. (2007). Service-learning as a transformative experience: An analysis of the impact of service-learning on student attitudes and behavior after two years of college. In S. B. Gelmon & S. H. Billig, (Eds.), *From passion to objectivity: International and cross-disciplinary perspectives on service-learning research* (pp. 111–134). Charlotte, NC: Information Age.

Boyer Commission on Educating Undergraduates in the Research University. (1998). *Reinventing undergraduate education: A blueprint for America's research universities.* Stone Brook: State University of New York.

Bringle, R. G., Phillips, M. A., & Hudson, M. (Eds.). (2004). *Critical thinking. In the measure of service-learning: Research scales to assess student experiences* (pp. 201–213). Washington, DC: American Psychological Association.

Che, S. M., Spearman, M., & Manizade, A. (2009). Constructive disequilibrium: Cognitive and emotional development through dissonant experiences in less familiar destinations. In R. Lewin (Ed.), *The handbook of practice and research in study abroad: Higher education and the quest for global citizenship* (pp. 99–116). New York, NY: Routledge, Taylor & Francis.

Dewey, J. (1938). *Experience and education.* New York, NY: Simon & Schuster.

Engle, L., & Engle, J. (2003). Study abroad levels: Toward a classification of program types. *Frontiers: The Interdisciplinary Journal of Study Abroad, 5*(2), 39–59.

Erickson, J. A., & O'Connor, S. E. (2000). Service-learning: Does it promote or reduce prejudice? In C. R. O'Grady, (Ed.), *Integrating service-learning and multi-cultural education in colleges and universities* (pp. 59–70). Mahwah, NJ: Erlbaum.

Friere, P. (1970). *Pedagogy of the oppressed.* New York, NY: Continuum International.

Hovey, R., & Weinberg, A. (2009). Global learning and the making of citizen diplomats. In R. Lewin (Ed.). *The handbook of practice and research in study abroad: Higher education and the quest for global citizenship* (pp. 33–48). New York, NY: Routledge, Taylor & Francis.

Katkin, W. (2003). The Boyer commission report and its impact on undergraduate research. *New Directions for Teaching and Learning, 93,* 19–38.

Kolb, D. (1984). *Experiential learning: Experience as the source of learning and development.* Englewood Cliffs, NJ: Prentice Hall

Kuh, G. D. (2008). *High-impact educational practices: What they are, who has access to them, and why they matter.* Washington, DC: AAC&U.

Lewin, K. (1952). Group decisions and social change. In E. Swanson, T. M. Newcomb, & E. L. Hartley (Eds.), *Readings in social psychology* (pp. 197–211). New York, NY: Henry Holt.

Montrose, L. (2002). International study and experiential learning: The academic context. *Frontiers: The Interdisciplinary Journal of Study Abroad, 8,* 1–15.

Piaget, J. (1975). *The equilibration of cognitive structures.* Chicago, IL: University of Chicago Press.

Plater, W. M., Jones, S. G., Bringle, R. G., & Clayton, P. H. (2009). Educating globally competent citizens through international service-learning. In R. Lewin (Ed.) *The handbook of practice and research in study abroad: Higher education and the quest for global citizenship* (pp. 485–505). New York, NY: Routledge, Taylor & Francis.

Putnam, R. (1995). Bowling alone: America's declining social capital. *Journal of Democracy, 6*(1), 65–78.

Raman, P., & Pashupati, K. (2002). Turning good citizens into even better ones: The impact of program characteristics and motivations on service-learning outcomes. *Journal of Nonprofit & Public Sector Marketing, 10*(2), 187–206.

Steinberg, M. (2002). Involve me and I will understand: Academic quality in experiential programs abroad. *Frontiers: The Interdisciplinary Journal of Study Abroad, 8,* 207–229.

Streitwieser, B., & Sobania, N. (2008). Overseeing study abroad research: Challenges, responsibilities, and the institutional review board. *Frontiers: The Interdisciplinary Journal of Study Abroad, 16,* 1–16.

Wideman, R. E. (2005). Empathy development in undergraduate students through the cross-cultural learning experience. *Dissertation Abstracts International Section A: Humanities and Social Sciences, 66* (2-A), 494.

Zamistil-Vondrova, K. (2005). Good faith or hard data? Justifying short-term programs. *International Educator, 14*(1), 44–49.

━━━━━

Chapter 3

Adler, P. S. (1987). Culture shock and the cross-cultural learning experience. In L. Luce & E. Smith (Eds.), *Toward internationalism* (pp. 24–35). Cambridge, MA: Newbury.

Antal, A. B., & Friedman, V. J. (2008). Learning to negotiate reality: A strategy for teaching intercultural competencies. *Journal of Management Education, 32*(3), 363–386.

Bandura, A. (1986). *Social foundations of thought and action: A social cognitive theory.* Englewood Cliffs, NJ: Prentice Hall.

Banks, J. (2004). Teaching for social justice, diversity, and citizenship in a global world. *Educational Forum, 68*(2), 289–297.

Bennett, M. J. (1986). A developmental approach to training for intercultural sensitivity. *International Journal of Intercultural Relations, 10*(2), 179–195.

Bile, J. J., & Lindley, T. (2009). Globalization, geography, and the liberation of oversea study. *Journal of Geography, 108*(3), 148–154.

Caine, R., & Caine, G. (1997). *Education on the edge of possibility.* Alexandria, VA: Association for Supervision and Curriculum Development.

Chickering, A. W., & Braskamp, L. A. (2009). Developing a global perspective for personal and social responsibility. *Peer Review, 11,* 27–30.

Chickering, A. W., & Reisser, L. (1993). *Education and identity.* San Francisco, CA: Jossey-Bass.

Dewey, J. (1933). *How we think: A restatement of the relation of reflective thinking to the educative process.* New York, NY: D.C. Heath.

Dolby, N. (2004). Encountering an American self: Study abroad and national identity. *Comparative Education Review, 48*(2), 150–173.

Erikson, E. H. (1959). *Identity and the life cycle.* New York, NY: International University Press.

Freire, P. (1974). *Education for critical consciousness.* New York, NY: Sheed & Ward.

Gibson, H. W. (1985). Critical thinking: A communication model. *Dissertation Abstracts International, 46*(11), 3235A.

Kaplan, E. J., & Kies, D. A. (1994). Strategies to increase critical thinking in the undergraduate college classroom. *College Student Journal, 28,* 24–31.

Kolb, D. (1984). *Experiential learning: Experience as the source of learning and development.* Englewood Cliffs, NJ: Prentice Hall.

Kuh, G. D. (2008). *High-impact educational practices: What they are, who has access to them, and why they matter.* Washington, DC: AAC&U.

Lewin, R. (2009). Transforming the study abroad experience into a collective priority. *Peer Review, 11,* 8–11.

Milstein, T. (2005). Transformation abroad: Sojourning and the perceived enhancement of self-efficacy. *International Journal of Intercultural Relations, 29,* 217–238.

Moon, J. A. (1999). *Reflection in learning and professional development: Theory and practice.* London, England: Kogan Page.

Özturgut, O. (2007). Study/teach abroad programs for higher education faculty. *Essays in Education, 22,* 42–49.

Paul, R., & Elder, L. (2008). *The miniature guide to critical thinking concepts and tools.* Dillon Beach, CA: Foundation for Critical Thinking Press.

Petras, J. (2000). Overseas education: Dispelling official myths in Latin America. *Frontiers: The Interdisciplinary Journal of Study Abroad, 6*(1), 78–81.

Raggatt, P. (2002). The landscape of narrative and the dialogical self: Exploring identity with the personality web protocol. *Narrative Inquiry, 12*(2), 291–318.

Spencer, S. T., Murray, K., & Tuma, K. (2005). Short-term programs abroad. In J. Brockington, W. Hoffa, & P. Martin (Eds.), *NAFSA's guide to education abroad for advisers and administrators* (pp. 373–387). Washington, DC: NAFSA: Association of International Educators.

Stone, N. (2006). Conceptualizing intercultural effectiveness for university teaching. *Journal of Studies in International Education, 10*(4), 334–356.

Tsui, L. (1999). Courses and instruction affecting critical thinking. *Research in Higher Education, 40*(2), 185–199.

Williams, R., & Wessel, J. (2004). Reflective journal writing to obtain student feedback about their learning during the study of musculoskeletal conditions. *Journal of Applied Health, 33*(1), 415–423.

Zamastil-Vondrova, K. (2005). Good faith or hard data? Justifying short-term programs. *International Educator, 14*(1), 44–49.

Chapter 4

Appiah, K. A. (2006). *Cosmopolitanism: Ethics in a world of strangers.* New York, NY: Norton.

Arneil, B. (2007). Global citizenship and empire. *Citizenship Studies, 11*(3), 301–328.

Association of American Colleges and Universities (AAC&U). (2002). *Liberal education and global citizenship: The art of democracy.* Washington, DC: AAC&U.

Banks, J. A. (2008). Diversity, group identity and citizenship education in a global age. *Educational Researcher, 37*(3), 129–139.

Biles, J. J., & Lindley, T. (2009). Globalization, geography, and the liberation of overseas study. *Journal of Geography, 108*(3), 148–154.

Carlsson-Paige, N., & Lantieri, L. (2005). A changing vision of education. In N. Noddings (Ed.), *Educating citizens for global awareness* (pp. 107–121). New York, NY: Teachers College Press.

Collins, N. F. (2009). Understanding our new cultural context through the liberal arts. *International Educator, 18*(5), 58–59.

de Blij, H. (2009). *The power of place: Geography, destiny, and globalization's rough landscape.* New York, NY: Oxford University Press.

Deardorff, D. K. (2006). Identification and assessment of intercultural competence as a student outcome of internationalization. *Journal of Studies in Intercultural Education, 10*(3), 241–266.

Deardorff, D. K. (Ed.). (2009). *The Sage handbook of intercultural competence.* London, England: Sage.

Dolby, N. (2004). Encountering an American self: Study abroad and national identity. *Comparative Education Review, 48*(2), 150–173.

Erikson, E. H. (1959). *Identity and the life cycle.* New York, NY: International University Press.

Falk, R. (1994). The making of global citizenship. In B. van Steenbergen (Ed.), *The condition of citizenship* (pp. 127–139). London, England: Sage.

Hendershot, K., & Sperandio, J. (2009). Study abroad and development of global citizen identity and cosmopolitan ideals in undergraduates. *Current Issues in Comparative Education, 12*(1), 45–55.

Hovey, R., & Weinberg, A. (2009). Global learning and the making of citizen diplomats. In R. Lewin (Ed.), *Handbook of practice and research in study abroad: Higher education and the quest for global citizenship* (pp. 33–48). New York, NY: Routledge, Taylor & Francis.

Kuh, G. D. (2008). *High-impact educational practices: What they are, who has access to them, and why they matter.* Washington, DC: AAC&U.

Ladson-Billings, G. (2005). Differing concepts of citizenship: Schools and communities as sites of civic develop. In N. Noddings (Ed.), *Educating citizens for global awareness* (pp. 69–80). New York, NY: Teachers College Press.

Lagos, T. G. (2002). *Global citizenship: Toward a definition.* Retrieved March 9, 2012, from http://depts.washington.edu/gcp/pdf/globalcitizenship.pdf.

Maslow, A. (1954). *Motivation and personality.* New York, NY: Harper.

McIntosh, P. (2005). Gender perspectives on educating for global citizenship. In N. Noddings (Ed.), *Educating citizens for global awareness* (pp. 22–39). New York, NY: Teachers College Press.

McLaughlin, J. S., Tzafaras, N., & McCollough, J. (2008) Designing an interdisciplinary short-term program in China. *International Educator, 17*(2), 65–70.

National Geographic Education Foundation and Roper Public Affairs. (2006). *Geographic literacy report.* Retrieved March 9, 2012, http://www.national-geographic.com/foundation/pdf/NGSRoper2006Report.pdf

National Assessment of Educational Progress (NEAP). (2011). *Nation's report card: Geography 2010.* Washington, DC: National Center for Education Statistics.

Oxfam. (2006). *Education for global citizenship. A guide for schools.* London, England: Oxfam.

Paige, R. M., Fry, G. W., Stallman, E., Josic, J., & Jon, J. E. (2009). *Study abroad for global engagement: Results that inform research and policy agendas.* Presented at the Forum on Education Abroad Conference, Portland, OR.

Schattle, H. (2008). *The practices of global citizenship.* Lanham, MD: Rowman & Littlefield.

Schattle, H. (2009). Global citizenship in theory and practice. In R. Lewin (Ed.), *The handbook of practice and research in study abroad: Higher education and the quest for global citizenship* (pp. 3–20). New York, NY: Routledge, Taylor & Francis.

Sperandio, J., Grudzinski-Hall, M., & Stewart-Gambino, H. (2010). Developing an undergraduate global citizenship program: Challenges of definition and assessment. *International Journal of Teaching and Learning in Higher Education, 22*(1), 12–22.

Stephenson, S. (2006). Globally responsible study abroad. *International Educator, 15*(6), 67–71.

Stromquist, N. P. (2009). Theorizing global citizenship: Discourses, challenges, and implications for education. *Inter-American Journal of Education for Democracy, 2*(1), 6–29.

Sutton, R. C., & Rubin, D. L. (2010). *Documenting the academic impact of study abroad: Final report of the GLOSSARI project.* Retrieved March 9, 2012, from http://glossari.uga.edu/?page_id=42&did=24

Zamastil-Vondrova, K. (2005). Good faith or hard data? Justifying short-term programs. *International Educator, 14*(1), 44–49.

Chapter 5

Bodycott, P., & Walker, A. (2000). Teaching abroad: Lessons learned about inter-cultural understanding for teachers in higher education. *Teaching in Higher Education, 5*(1), 79–94.

Boyer, E. (1990). *Scholarship reconsidered: Priorities of the professoriate.* New York, NY: The Carnegie Foundation for the Advancement of Teaching.

Boyer, E. (1996). The scholarship of engagement. *Journal of Public Outreach, 1*(1), 11–20.

Brustein, W. I. (2007). The global campus: Challenges and opportunities for higher education in North America. *Journal of Studies in International Education, 11*(3–4), 382–391.

Chieffo, L., & Griffiths, L. (2009). Here to stay: Increasing acceptance of short-term study abroad programs. In R. Lewin (Ed.), *The handbook of practice and research of study abroad* (pp. 365–380). New York, NY: Routledge, Talyor & Francis.

Childress, L. K. (2009). Planning for internationalization by investing in faculty. *Journal for International and Global Studies, 1*(1), 30–49.

Dooley, K. E., & Rouse, L. A. (2009). Longitudinal impacts of a faculty abroad program: 1994–2007. *Journal of Agricultural and Extension Education, 16*(3), 47–58.

Finkelstein, M., Walker, E., & Chen, R. (2009). *The internationalization of the American faculty: Where are we? What drives or deters us?* [Research paper]. South Orange, NJ: Seton Hall University.

Havighurst, R. J. (1952). *Human development and education.* New York, NY: Longmans, Green.

Hulstrand, J. (2009). Attracting faculty to education abroad. *International Educator, 18*(5), 48–51.

Kuh, G. D. (2008). *High-impact educational practices: What they are, who has access to them, and why they matter.* Washington, DC: Association of American Colleges and Universities.

Lewis, T., & Niessenbaum, R. A. (2005). Extending the stay: Using community based research and service learning to enhance short-term study abroad. *Journal of Studies in International Education, 9*(3), 251–64.

National Survey on Student Engagement. (2007). *Experiences that matter: Enhancing student learning and success.* Retrieved November 12, 2011, from http://nsse.iub.edu/NSSE_2007_Annual_Report/index.cfm

Noddings, N. (2005). What does it mean to educate the whole child? *Educational Leadership, 8*, 8–13.

O'Hara, S. (2009). Vital and overlooked: The role of faculty in internationalizing U.S. campus. In P. Blumenthal & R. Gutierrez (Eds.), *Meeting America's global education challenge: Expanding study abroad capacity at U.S. colleges and universities* (pp. 38–45). New York, NY: Institute of International Education.

Özturgut, O. (2007). Study/teach abroad programs for higher education faculty. *Essays In Education, 22*, 43–49.

Siaya, L., & Hayward, F. M. (2003). *Mapping internationalization on U.S. campuses.* Washington, DC: American Council on Education.

Chapter 6

Biles, J. J., & Lindley, T. (2009). Globalization, geography, and the liberation of overseas study. *Journal of Geography, 108*(3), 148–154.

Forum on Education Abroad. (2009). *Standards of good practice for short-term education abroad programs.* Carlisle, PA: Dickinson College.

Hulstrand, J. (2008). Faculty abroad: What do these innocents need to know. *International Educator, 17*(3), 76–79.

Laubscher, M. R. (1994). *Encounters with difference: Student perspectives of the role of out-of-class experiences in education abroad.* Westport, CT: Greenwood.

Mullens, J. B., Bristow, R. S., & Cuper, P. (2012). Examining trends in international study: A survey of faculty-led field courses within American departments of geography. *Journal of Geography in Higher Education, 36*(2).

Redden, E. (2007). The middlemen of study abroad. *Inside Higher Ed.* Retrieved March 9, 2011, from http://www.insidehighered.com/news/2007/08/20/abroad

Schroeder, K., Wood, C., Galiardi, S., & Koehn, J. (2009). First, do no harm: Ideas for mitigating negative community impacts of short-term study abroad. *Journal of Geography, 108*(3), 141–147.

Zamastil-Vondrova, K. (2005). Good faith or hard data? Justifying short-term programs. *International Educator, 14*(1), 44–49.

Chapter 7

Forum on Education Abroad. (2009). *Standards of good practice for short-term education abroad programs.* Carlisle, PA: Dickinson College.

Fusch, D. (2010). Affordable, high-impact study abroad. *Academic Impressions, Higher Ed Impact.* Retrieved March 9, 2012, from http://www.academic impressions.com/news/affordable-high-impact-study-abroad

Guerrero, E. (2005). Making the most of short-term immersion. *Education Abroad, 14*(4), 42–45.

Martinez, M. D., Ranjeet, B., & Marx, H. A. (2009). Creating study abroad opportunities for first generation college students. In R. Lewin (Ed.), *The handbook of practice and research in study abroad: Higher education and the quest for global citizenship* (pp. 527–542). New York, NY: Routledge, Taylor & Francis.

Stanitski, D., & Fuellhart, K. (2003). Tools for developing short-term study abroad classes for geography studies. *Journal of Geography, 102*(5), 202–215.

Chapter 8

Hulstrand, J. (2008). Faculty abroad: What do *these* innocents need to know. *International Educator, 17*(3), 76–79.

Chapter 9

Chieffo, L., & Griffiths, L. (2009). Here to stay: Increasing acceptance of short-term study abroad programs. In R. Lewin (Ed.), *The handbook of practice and research in study abroad: Higher education and the quest for global citizenship* (pp. 365–380). New York, NY: Routledge, Taylor & Francis.

Dessoff, A. (2006). Who's not going abroad. *International Educator, 15*(2), 20–27.

Hulstrand, J. (2008). Faculty abroad: What do these innocents need to know. *International Educator, 17*(3), 76–79.

Luethge, D. J. (2004). Perceived risk and risk reduction strategies in study abroad programs. *Journal of Teaching in International Business, 5*(4), 23–45.

Martinez, M. D., Ranjeet, B., & Marx, H. A. (2009). Creating study abroad opportunities for first-generation college students. In R. Lewin (Ed.), *The handbook of practice and research in study abroad: Higher education and the quest for global citizenship* (pp. 527–542). New York, NY: Routledge, Taylor & Francis.

Oberg, K. (1960). Culture shock: Adjustment to new cultural environments. *Practical Anthropology, 7*, 177–182.

Obst, D., Bhandari, R., & Witherell, S. (2007). Current trends in U.S. study abroad and the impact of strategic diversity initiatives. *Institute of International Education White Papers on Meeting America's Global Education Challenge, 1.*

Paige, R. M., Fry, G. W., Stallman, E. M., Josic, J., & Jon, J. (2009). Study abroad for global engagement: The long-term impacts of mobility experiences. *Intercultural Education, 20,*(Suppl S1-2), S29–S44 (EJ870912).

Relyea, C., Cocchiara, F. K., & Studdard, N. L. (2008). The effect of perceived value in the decision to participate in study abroad programs. *Journal of Teaching in International Business, 19*(4), 346–351.

Salisbury, M. H., Umbach, P. D., & Paulsen, M. B. (2009). Going global: Understanding the choice process of the intent to study abroad. *Research in Higher Education, 52*(2), 119–143.

Strauss, W., & Howe N. (2000). *Millennials rising: The next great generation.* New York, NY: Vintage.

Wilson, M., & Gerber, L. (2008). How generational theory can improve teaching: Strategies for working with the "Millennials." *Currents In Teaching and Learning, 1*(1), 29–44.

―――――

Chapter 10

Bennett, M. J. (1986). A developmental approach to training for intercultural sensitivity. *International Journal of Intercultural Relations, 10*(2), 179–195.

Deardorff, D. K. (2004). *The identification and assessment of intercultural competence as a student outcome of international education at institutions of higher education in the United States.* Unpublished dissertation, North Carolina State University, Raleigh.

Fink, L. D. (2003). *Creating significant learning experiences: An integrative approach to designing college courses.* San Francisco, CA: Jossey-Bass.

Hovey, R., & Weinberg, A. (2009). Global learning and the making of the citizen diplomats. In R. Lewin (Ed.), *The handbook of practice and research in study abroad: Higher education and the quest for global citizenship* (pp. 33–48). New York, NY: Routledge, Taylor & Francis.

Palomba, C. A., & Banta, T. (1999). *Assessment essentials: Planning, implementing and improving assessment in higher education.* San Francisco: Jossey-Bass.

Prensky, M. (2010). *Teaching digital natives: Partnering for real learning.* Thousand Oaks, CA: Sage.

Santanello, C., & Wolff, L. (2008). Designing assessment into a study abroad course. *Frontiers: The Interdisciplinary Journal of Study Abroad, 15*, 189–196.

Chapter 11

Braid, B., & Long, A. (Eds.). (2000). *Place as text: Approaches to active learning.* Lincoln, NE: National Collegiate Honors Council Monographs in Honors Education.

de Blij, H. (2009). *The power of place: Geography, destiny, and globalization's rough landscape.* New York, NY: Oxford University Press.

NASFA. (n.d.). *Intercultural activity toolkit.* Retrieved March 9, 2012, from http://am.nafsa.org/knowledge_community_network.sec/iatool_broken

Peace Corps. (1997). *Culture matters: The Peace Corps cross-cultural workbook.* Washington, DC: U.S. Printing Office.

Sunstein, B. S., & Chiseri-Strater, E. (2007). *Fieldworking: Reading and writing research* (3rd ed.). New York, NY: Bedford St. Martins.

Chapter 12

Braid, B., & Long, A. (Eds.). (2000). *Place as text: Approaches to active learning.* Lincoln, NE: National Collegiate Honors Council Monographs in Honors Education.

Hulstrand, J. (2008). Faculty abroad: What do these innocents need to know. *International Educator, 17*(3), 76–79.

Jokisch, B. (2009). Making a traditional study-abroad program geographical: A theoretically informed regional approach. *Journal of Geography, 108*(3), 105–111.

Chapter 13

Doyle, D. (2009). Holistic assessment and the study abroad experience. *Frontiers: The Interdisciplinary Journal of Study Abroad, 18,* 143–155.

Conclusion

Campbell, J. (1968). *The hero with a thousand faces* (2nd ed.). Princeton, NJ: Princeton University Press.

About the Authors

Dr. Jo Beth Mullens is professor of geography at at Keene State College, New Hampshire. Since 1995, she has designed and taught numerous international courses in Central Europe (Czech Republic, Slovak Republic, Hungary, and Poland), and Central and South America (Mexico, Peru, Ecuador, and Belize). In 2002, Dr. Mullens was a Fulbright Senior Scholar in the Czech Republic where she taught in the Department of Environmental Humanities at Masaryk University in Brno. In 2008, she was awarded a Marion and Jasper Whiting Foundation Grant to  travel and study global climate change issues in Australia. Dr. Mullens was also the recipient of the Keene State College Distinguished Teacher Award in 2006. During her academic career, she has presented at numerous national and international conferences on topics including faculty-led international programs, water resources, and environmental geography issues.

Dr. Prudence Cuper is professor of Education at Keene State College. Following 10 years of teaching at the middle school level, Dr. Cuper earned her doctorate in curriculum and instruction from North Carolina State Uni-

Fostering Global Citizenship Through Faculty-Led International Programs, pages 217–218
Copyright © 2012 by Information Age Publishing
217

versity under a Kenan Research Fellowship. Since arriving at Keene State, she has taught within the Elementary Education, Secondary English Education, and Honors programs where she has focused on engaged learning, curriculum development, and the interaction between learning objectives and assessment. Dr. Cuper is co-author of a Corwin Press text on teacher leadership, numerous professional journal articles, and invited chapters on current approaches to curriculum development and assessment.

Recently, Dr. Mullens and Dr. Cuper pioneered one of the first faculty-led field courses for Keene State College's newly established Honors program. Wanting to support faculty who are stepping into the growing field of faculty-led international studies, they decided to combine their areas of experience and expertise to co-author this text. Dr. Mullens brings extensive experience in designing and implementing international field courses for undergraduates. Dr. Cuper brings deep knowledge of curriculum development and assessment. Together they offer a practical and pedagogically sound text that is enhanced and humanized by their own tales of traveling and working with students abroad.

CPSIA information can be obtained at www.ICGtesting.com
Printed in the USA
BVOW11s0813210514

354150BV00004B/162/P

9 781617 358319